Armies of the Dark Ages 600–1066

by Ian Heath

AMENDED SECOND EDITION 2015

ISBN 978-1-326-23332-7

Cover Picture – taken from the 1980 edition.

Published by Wargames Research Group Ltd.

CONTENTS

FOREWORD TO THE 2015 EDITION.. 9

INTRODUCTION TO THE 1980 EDITION 10

ORGANISATION...13

    THE BYZANTINES.. 13
        The Themata.. 14
        The Tagmata.. 18
        Later Changes 20
        Mercenaries and Auxiliaries 21
        The Varangian Guard 22
        Servants... 23
        Medical Staff.. 25
        Artillery 25
        The Navy.. 25
    THE SUB-ROMAN BRITONS 28
    THE IRISH AND EARLY SCOTS... 30
    THE VISIGOTHS.. 33
    THE LOMBARDS 35
    THE FRANKS... 36
        Merovingians... 36
        Carolingians.. 38
        Ottonians 40
    THE VIKINGS 42
    THE RUSSIANS 46
    THE SLAVS.. 48
    THE ASIATIC HORDES 49
        The Avars 50
        The Khazars 50
        The Magyars.. 52
        The Danube Bulgars... 53
        The Volga Bulgars.. 54
        The Pechenegs 55
        The Ghuzz 55
    THE ARABS 56
        Medical Staff.. 61
        Artillery 61
    ANDALUSIA... 61
    CHRISTIAN SPAIN... 63
    THE SAXONS... 64
        The Navy.. 68
    THE NORMANS.. 69

TACTICAL METHODS 71

THE BYZANTINES 71
    General 71
    Against Arabs 73
    Against Slavs 74
    Against Turks 74
    Against Franks and Lombards 75
    Against Normans 75
    Naval Tactics 76
THE SUB-ROMANS 77
THE SCOTS 78
THE IRISH 78
THE VISIGOTHS 79
THE LOMBARDS 79
THE FRANKS 80
THE VIKINGS 81
THE RUSSIANS 84
THE SLAVS 86
ASIATIC HORDES 87
THE ARABS 90
THE SAXONS 93
THE NORMANS 95

MAJOR BATTLES OF THE PERIOD **97**

VIMINACIUM 601 97
HALYS 622 98
NINEVEH 627 98
YARMUK 636 99
QADISIYYA 637 100
NIHAWAND 642 100
TRANSDUCTINE PROMONTORIES 711 101
TOULOUSE 721 101
MARJ ARDABIL 730 101
TOURS 732 102
RONCESVALLES 778 103
PLISKA 811 103
AMORIUM 838 103
FONTENOY 841 104
ASHDOWN 871 105
BULGAROPHYGON 896 105
BRENTA 899 106
AUGSBURG 910 106
MERESBURG (RIADE) 933 106
BRUNANBURH 937 107
LECHFIELD 955 107
SILISTRIA 972 108
COTRONE 982 109

MALDON 991 109
SVOLDR 1000 109
CLONTARF 1014 110
BELASITSA 1014 111
BUG 1018 111
STIKLESTAD 1030 111
MONTE MAGGIORE 1041 112
CIVITATE 1053 112
MORTEMER 1054 113
VARAVILLE 1057 113
NISSA 1062 113
GATE FULFORD 1066 113
STAMFORD BRIDGE 1066 114
HASTINGS 1066 114

DRESS AND EQUIPMENT **116**

1. LAMELLAR ARMOUR 116
2. 7TH–8TH CENTURY BYZANTINE SKUTATOS 116
3 & 4. 9TH–10TH CENTURY BYZANTINE SKUTATOI 117
5. 10TH CENTURY BYZANTINE FRONT-RANK SKUTATOS 119
6. 9TH–10TH CENTURY BYZANTINE INFANTRY OFFICER 119
7. 10TH–11TH CENTURY BYZANTINE PELTASTOS 120
8, 9, 10 & 11. BYZANTINE PSILOI 121
12. BYZANTINE SAILOR 122
13 & 14. 10TH CENTURY BYZANTINE TAGMATIC KATAPHRAKTOI
.... 123
15. 10TH CENTURY BYZANTINE KLIBANOPHOROS 125
16. 7TH–10TH CENTURY BYZANTINE TRAPEZITOS 126
17. BYZANTINE AUXILIARY LIGHT CAVALRYMAN 127
18. 10TH–11TH CENTURY BYZANTINE THEMATIC
KATAPHRAKTOS 127
19. LATE–10TH OR 11TH CENTURY BYZANTINE SKUTATOS 128
20, 21 & 22. 11TH CENTURY BYZANTINE KATAPHRAKTOI 129
23, 24 & 25. VARANGIAN GUARDSMEN 130
26. BYZANTINE EMPEROR IN PARADE ARMOUR 132
27. BYZANTINE STANDARDS 133
28. SUB-ROMAN BRITISH CAVALRYMAN 134
29. SUB-ROMAN BRITISH INFANTRYMAN 135
30. SUB-ROMAN GALLIC INFANTRYMAN 136
31 & 32. PICTISH CAVALRYMEN 136
33. PICTISH CHIEFTAIN 137
34 & 35. PICTISH INFANTRYMEN 137
36. PICTISH CROSSBOWMAN 138
37. IRISH CHIEFTAIN 139
38 & 39. IRISH WARRIORS 140
40. IRISH AXEMAN 141

41. 7TH CENTURY VISIGOTHIC INFANTRYMAN 141
42. 7TH CENTURY VISIGOTHIC CAVALRYMAN 142
43. 7TH–8TH CENTURY LOMBARD CAVALRYMAN 143
44. 7–8TH CENTURY LOMBARD INFANTRYMAN 143
45. 6TH–7TH CENTURY MEROVINGIAN FRANK 144
46 & 47. 8–10TH CENTURY CAROLINGIAN INFANTRYMEN 145
48 & 49. 9TH CENTURY CAROLINGIAN HEAVY INFANTRYMEN 146
50. CAROLINGIAN HEAVY ARCHER.....................................147
51. CAROLINGIAN MUSICIAN 148
52 & 53. 7–8TH CENTURY MEROVINGIAN CAVALRYMEN 148
54. 8–10TH CENTURY CAROLINGIAN MEDIUM CAVALRYMAN 149
55. 9TH CENTURY CAROLINGIAN HEAVY CAVALRYMAN........150
56. CAROLINGIAN GUARDSMAN 151
57. 10TH CENTURY CAROLINGIAN CAVALRYMAN....................152
58. CAROLINGIAN SHIELD PATTERNS....................................153
59 & 60. OTTONIAN HEAVY CAVALRYMEN 153
61. OTTONIAN HEAVY INFANTRYMAN....................................154
62. OTTONIAN MEDIUM INFANTRYMAN 155
63. CAROLINGIAN AND OTTONIAN STANDARDS 155
64. 7TH CENTURY SCANDINAVIAN CHIEFTAIN 156
65. 7TH CENTURY SCANDINAVIAN WARRIOR 156
66. VIKING CHIEFTAIN 157
67. VIKING HIRDMAN OR HUSCARL 158
68. VIKING BONDI 159
69. VIKING ARCHER..160
70. VIKING BERSERKR...160
71. VIKING ULFHEDNAR 161
72. VIKING STANDARDS 161
73. 10TH CENTURY RUS CHIEFTAIN..162
74. RUS WARRIOR..163
75. SLAV WARRIOR...163
76. SLAV ARCHER...164
77. 10TH CENTURY SLAV CHIEFTAIN 164
78 & 79. 11TH CENTURY SLAV INFANTRYMEN............................165
80. 11TH CENTURY SLAV CAVALRYMAN....................................166
81, 82, 83 & 84. ASIATIC LIGHT CAVALRYMEN.............................166
85, 86, 87 & 88. ASIATIC HEAVY CAVALRYMEN.........................169
89. ASIATIC STANDARDS...170
90. ALAN LIGHT CAVALRYMAN 171
91. ARMENIAN CAVALRYMAN 172
92. ARMENIAN INFANTRYMAN 172
93. LATE SASSANID CLIBANARIUS 173
94. LATE SASSANID LEVY INFANTRYMAN 174
95. SOGDIAN HORSE-ARCHER..175
96. ARAB INFANTRYMAN 175
97. ARAB ARCHER 176

98 & 99. ARAB CAVALRYMEN 177
100 & 101. ARAB HEAVY CAVALRYMEN 178
102. ARAB STANDARDS 179
103. SUDANESE TRIBESMAN 180
104. SUDANESE GHULAM 180
105. BERBER TRIBESMAN 181
106. DAYLAMI TRIBESMAN 181
107. KHORASANIAN HORSE-ARCHER 182
108. PERSIAN CAVALRYMAN 182
109. GHAZNAVID INFANTRYMAN 183
110. GHAZNAVID GHULAM 184
111 & 112. 7TH–9TH CENTURY ANGLO-SAXON CHIEFTAINS 184
113 & 114. 7TH–10TH CENTURY ANGLO-SAXON WARRIORS 185
115. ANGLO-SAXON ARCHER 186
116 & 117. SAXON SELECT FYRDMEN 187
118 & 119. LATE SAXON FYRDMEN 188
120. LATE-SAXON OR ANGLO-DANISH HUSCARL 189
121. MOUNTED SAXON WARRIOR 190
122. SAXON STANDARDS 190
123. PEASANT INFANTRYMAN 191
124 & 125. 11TH CENTURY NORMAN, FRENCH OR BRETON
HEAVY CAVALRYMEN 192
126. 11TH CENTURY NORMAN, FRENCH OR BRETON STANDARDS
.... 193
127. 11TH CENTURY NORMAN, FRENCH OR BRETON MEDIUM
CAVALRYMAN 194
128 & 129. NORMAN ARCHERS 194
130. FRENCH CROSSBOWMAN 196
131. 11TH CENTURY FRENCH INFANTRYMAN 196
132 & 133. 11TH CENTURY EUROPEAN HEAVY INFANTRYMEN 197
134. ITALO-NORMAN HEAVY CAVALRYMAN 198
135 & 136. SPANISH HEAVY CAVALRYMEN 198
137. SPANISH HEAVY INFANTRYMAN 199
138. ANDALUSIAN CAVALRYMAN 200
139 & 140. ANDALUSIAN INFANTRYMEN 201
141. KITE-SHIELD PATTERNS 201
142. GREEK FIRE 203
143. BYZANTINE CAVALRY HORSE 205
144. BYZANTINE FULLY ARMOURED HORSE 206
145. ASIATIC HORSE 206
146. 7TH–10TH CENTURY CAVALRY HORSE 207
147. 11TH CENTURY CAVALRY HORSE 208
148. ASIATIC WAGON 209

SELECT BIBLIOGRAPHY 210

FOREWORD TO THE 2015 EDITION

When I wrote the first edition of this book back in 1979 interest in post-Roman and early medieval warfare was itself undergoing something of a Dark Age. It seemed to have become an academic backwater in which enthusiastic laymen such as myself could not hope to do more than paddle in the shallows. There were many books and articles on the *history* of the Dark Age period, but very few were devoted to its military aspects, and those that existed were often not easy to come by. But what a change the past four decades have seen – a mere browse through the updated bibliography of this new edition will reveal the astonishing breadth and depth of modern research and interest in the military history of the Dark Ages. In addition, the existence of the Internet has improved our knowledge of and access to such material immeasurably.

Nevertheless, much of the most important basic information was already available even when the first edition was published, if you knew where to look and who to ask, and I was fortunate in having the resources of Cambridge's University Library close by and the guidance and advice of other enthusiasts, Phil Barker not the least of them. Consequently it was gratifying to find, on reading through the proofs for this latest edition, that such mistakes as I had made 'back in the day' were those of omission rather than fact. This is just as well, since revising the text wholesale for this reprint was not an option, alas; all I have been able to do is completely revise and update the bibliography and correct a few text issues that have irritated me for years.

Ian Heath

August 2015

INTRODUCTION TO THE 1980 EDITION

Following on from, and in places slightly overlapping, Phil Barker's *Armies and Enemies of Imperial Rome*, this book deals with the armies and warriors of an era which saw the steady decline of classical military systems and the evolution of early mediaeval feudalism. Despite a wealth of illustrative and written sources it is a period which, militarily, has been sadly neglected, and is today only just beginning to receive its true share of attention. Admittedly much has been written already on some of the subjects covered here – the Normans, Saxons and Vikings in particular - and a lot of the information here is not new, but to date there has been no single work dealing with the military activities of the Dark Ages as a whole.

The choice of the title *Dark Ages* for this book resulted from the simple need for a term under which all the different periods and peoples could comfortably appear without fear of incongruity. 'Dark Ages' is, after all, the epithet by which this era is known to most people. However, taken literally it is far from accurate. New archaeological and literary finds as well as recent reappraisals of older material are steadily pushing back the shadows of this period and shedding light on much useful information hitherto neglected or overlooked. In fact so much material came to light during the preparation of this book that much has had to be omitted or generalised sometimes to the point of over-simplification, and there is much more research that could yet be done; however, compiling the material for the first edition of this book took over two years, and though a considerable amount of new material (and several revised opinions) will be apparent to those who have read the original, there are nevertheless dark corners that remain substantially unexplored.

For those who wish to delve further, many sagas and chronicles are available in print. It would take too much space to list them all, but suffice to say that Oxford Mediaeval Texts, Penguin Classics and the Everyman Library cover a fair selection, from Guy of Amiens, Gregory of Tours, Bede and Notker the Stammerer to the semi-legendary 'Njal's Saga' and the 'Heimskringla' of Snorri Sturlusson. Liudprand of Cremona, Paul the Deacon, 'The Russian Primary Chronicle', 'The War of the Gaedhil with the Gaill' and innumerable other chronicles are also available in older 19th and early-20th century editions now out of print but sometimes available in large libraries or through the Inter-Library Loan system. 'The Anglo-Saxon Chronicle' is around in a number of editions, the best of which is that edited by Dorothy Whitelock, while a full reproduction of 'old faithful' – the

Bayeux Tapestry – was published in its most recent form by Phaidon. 'Gododdin', 'Taliesin', Psellus, al-Masudi, Einhard, Constantine Porphyrogenitus, Anna Comnena, Asser – the list of translations is practically endless. Many of these and others are often quoted in the works of modern authors, and unfortunately unless you are fluent in Greek, Arabic, Russian, Hungarian, Polish or sometimes German, it is largely only in quotes that many of the Byzantine, Arab, Persian and other Eastern sources are to be found. For modern works see my select bibliography at the end of this book.

The choice of 1066 as the close of the Dark Ages was arbitrary. The Viking threat is taken by many to have ended in that year, while William of Normandy's conquest of England marked the beginning of a new era for the British Isles at least. Two other dates might have been chosen with a certain amount of justification – 1071, the year of the Battle of Manzikert and the end of Byzantine military greatness, and 1096, the commencement of the First Crusade. However both these dates are best dealt with in the light of their results rather than in the events of the years themselves so are covered in a separate volume, *Armies and Enemies of the Crusades 1096–1291*, also published by the Wargames Research Group.

Ian Heath April 1979

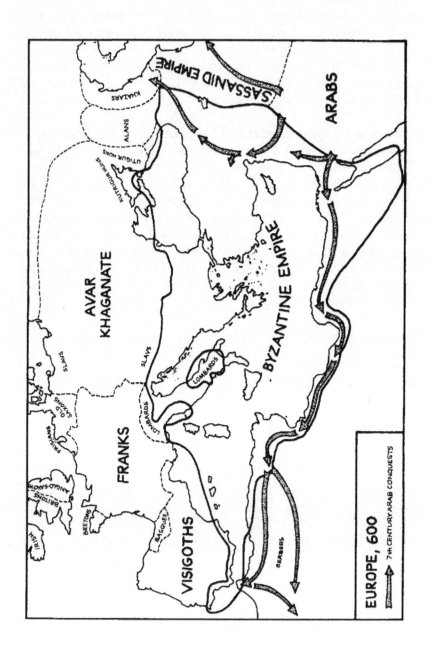

EUROPE, 600

7th CENTURY ARAB CONQUESTS

ORGANISATION

THE BYZANTINES[1]

At the beginning of this period the Byzantine army consisted of 7 Exerciti or Stratoi, these being field armies each commanded by a magister militum or strategos with an ypostrategos as second-in-command. These 7 Exerciti were the Exercitus Orientalis in Syria, Palestine, Cilicia and Mesopotamia; Exerciti Ilyricam and Thracianus in the western and eastern Balkans respectively; Exerciti Africam, Italiae and Armeniam in Africa, Italy and Armenia respectively; and the Obsequium, formed from the troops formerly attached to the Magistri Militum Praesentales, stationed in north-west Asia Minor and usually under the Emperor himself. Each of these Exerciti or Stratoi consisted of 3 dhoungoi or merai, each dhoungos or meros of 3 moirai, and each moira (commanded by a moirarchos or dux) of 6-8 or sometimes 10 arithmoi or banda, described below. The numbers were apparently deliberately kept vague to mislead enemy intelligence. The Strategicon, a military manual probably written by the Emperor Maurice in the late-6th century but edited and finished by Heraclius (610–641), gives moira strength as 2–3,000 men and meros strength as 6–7,000.

Besides these regular units there were also the Bukellarii, the private mercenary regiments of the generals, whose loyalty was to their employers rather than the Emperor. Their name derived from the word 'bukellum', a military biscuit, and could be translated 'hard-tack eaters'. The Bukellarii regiments were impermanent and varied in size, the largest known being that of Belisarius (mid-6th century) which allegedly numbered 7,000 horsemen, largely Huns. On the whole the Bukellarii appear to have been comprised of Isaurians from the Taurus mountains.

According to the Strategicon the basic unit was the arithmos, alternatively called a bandon or tagma, a straight translation into Greek of the Latin 'numerus'. This was commanded by a komes or count, also at this early date still sometimes called a tribounos or tribune. The

---

[1] I would personally prefer to call the Byzantines by their own name of Rhomaioi or Romans, the Byzantine Empire being descended in a direct and uninterrupted line from the Eastern Roman Empire, which, unlike its Western half (which collapsed in 476) did not fall until as late as 1453. However, the erroneous convention that they should be called Byzantines (despite the fact that none of their contemporaries called them that) is now far too well-established to be rectified.

term 'bandon' was derived from the German word for a banner, Germanic mercenaries predominating in the Byzantine army at the time that the Strategicon was written.

The infantry arithmos consisted of 16 lochaghiai, each of 16 men, commanded by a lochaghos (file leader) assisted by a dekarchos (leader of 10), pentarchos (leader of 5), tetrarchos (leader of 4) and ouraghos (file closer). The total strength of the arithmos was therefore 256 men, of whom one-quarter (not one-third as normally stated) were archers and three-quarters spearmen, though some units consisted entirely of light infantry.

The basic cavalry unit was subdivided into 3 hekatontarchia, each commanded by a hekatontarchos of whom the senior acted as second-in-command and was called an illarches. Each hekatontarchion comprised 10 dekarchia, each commanded by a dekarchos, with pentarchos, tetrarchos, ouraghos and 6 men, giving the total strength of the cavalry bandon as 300. However, both infantry and cavalry banda could vary between 200 and 400 strong.

3 elite 'Epilekta' regiments are recorded – the Optimati, the Bukellarii (now a regular cavalry unit), and the Foederati, a leftover of the earlier barbarian mercenaries, now forming a guard unit.

The Themata

During the 7th century the Themata were created, possibly by Heraclius but more probably under Constans c. 650 as the old Exerciti crumbled under external pressure. The Theme system was basically the settlement of soldiers on small agricultural plots subject to the obligation of mounted military service, hereditable from father to eldest son.

In addition these Thematic troops were paid; Ibn Khordadbah, an Arab source of c. 845, says they were paid once every 3 years, or in some cases, every 4, 5 or 6 years, while Constantine Porphyrogenitus in the mid-10th century says that the 'old practice' had been to divide Thematic troops into 4 groups and pay each of them once every 4 years (though he does not, alas, tell us what the 'new practice' was). Probably one-third to one-sixth of the available troops served in rotation once every 3–6 years. However even with this payment plus rations and special bounties some Thematic farmers remained so poor that at one point a system had to be introduced whereby poor men clubbed together to equip one of their number, and later some even had to be equipped by their wealthier neighbours. On the other hand some Thematic landholders were wealthy enough to have their own servants, some even owning slaves.

The early Themata were regions in which a particular regiment had been placed for its defence, such as the Optimaton Thema (the Optimati), Opsikion Thema (from Obsequium), the Anatolikon, Armeniakon and Thrakesion Themata (respectively the troops of the Exerciti Orientalis, Armeniam and Thracianus), and the Bukellarion Thema (the Bukellarii). Later Themata were instead named geographically.

By the 9th century at the very latest most Themata were commanded by a strategos, exceptions being the Opsikion (commanded by a komes) and the Optimaton, which by the 9th century had no military status and was under a domestikos. The strategos of the Anatolikon Thema was the most senior military officer until the 10th century. Each strategos was accompanied by his own full-time military retinue organised in units of 100 men called kentarchia (comparable to hekatontarchia) and commanded by officers called kentarchai spathariorum, the men being called spatharioi. Their numbers probably varied according to the size of the Thema, but the retinue of the Thrakesion strategos is probably fairly typical in comprising 6 kentarchiai.

As perfected Thematic organisation saw each of the Themata divided into 2 or 3 turmai or merai. Each of these, under a turmarchos or merarchos, was further divided into 3 moirai or dhoungoi each commanded by a moirarchos or dhoungarius (or dhoungarokomes). A varying number of banda (probably between 2 and 5 in practice, each commanded by a komes) went to make each moira. Ibn Khordadbah gives a somewhat different account of the organisation of one of the larger Themata as follows. It comprised 10,000 men under a strategos, divided into 2 turmai each of which contained 5 'banda' of 1,000 men (presumably moirai are meant since these 'banda' are commanded by dhoungarii). The 'bandon' consisted of 5 pentarchiai of 200 men commanded by kometes, which indicates that these 'pentarchiai' are the real banda. The pentarchia contained 5 units of 40 men commanded by officers that Ibn Khordadbah calls kòntarhin, presumably kentarchai or pentekontarchai in which case the units represent understrength hekatontarchia or allaghia.

Certainly the considerable variations in province sizes must have resulted in comparable variations in the size of units. Without a shadow of a doubt the moira and meros strengths quoted in the Strategicon were no longer possible in Themata which could have as few as 4,000 horsemen to spread over 2 or 3 turmai, and in 838 one source actually refers to turmai of 'not more than 2,000 men'.

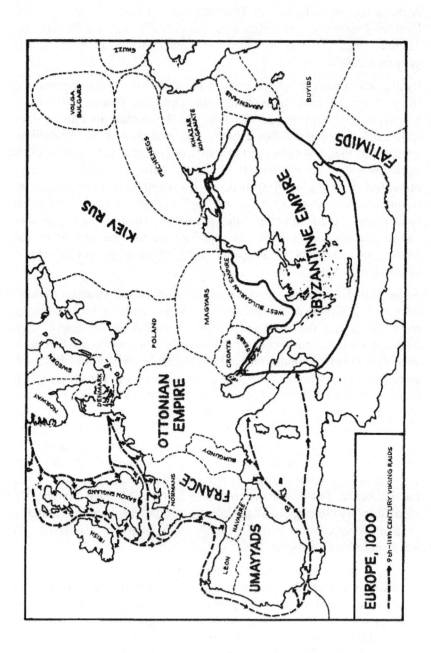

EUROPE, 1000

- - - ► 9th–11th CENTURY VIKING RAIDS

The Thematic cavalry were either first-class or second-class, the former being raised from the richer landholders (whose income guaranteed better equipment), while the latter were often given non-military duties or held as a reserve. If more cavalry were needed within a Thema it seems to have been preferable to summon first-class troops from another Thema rather than one's own second-class troops. In 778 we are told that each Thema could muster 3,000 first-class cavalry, while Leo VI's Tactica of c. 900 states that the maximum number of first-class cavalry in a Thema was 4,000 (who he says are to be kataphraktoi, implying armoured or half-armoured horses), and that without drawing more than 4,000 men from each Thema the Eastern Themata could muster 30,000 such first-class cavalry. He also seems to indicate that a single Thema could muster 24,000 infantry, perhaps a gross exaggeration although troops numbering up to 30,000 are recorded on occasion in single Themata. Infantry probably did not receive land grants like the cavalry anyway, being instead recruited by conscription. They were fairly certainly divided into first and second-class troops like the cavalry.

Ibn al-Fakih, an Arab who wrote c. 902, records the following strengths for the Eastern Themata:

Anatolikon 15,000	Paphlagonia 5,000
Thrakesion 10,000	Seleukeia 5,000
Chaldia 10,000	Macedonia 5,000
Armeniakon 9,000	Thrace 5,000
Bukellarion 8,000	Kappadocia 4,000
Opsikion 6,000	Charsianon 4,000

The strength of Seleukeia, omitted by al-Fakih, is inserted from an alternative list by another Arab, Kodama, who wrote 30 years later. Kodama's list differs slightly from al-Fakih's in one or two other respects, giving Thrakesion only 6,000 men and Chaldia only 4,000. Both lists give 4,000 for the non-military Optimaton Thema, though al-Fakih states quite specifically that these 'are not men of war'. One other Thema, called Talaya, Talaka or Tafla, is also listed, but no strength is given and the word appears to be no more than a corruption of Tagmata (see below). Both al-Fakih and Kodama omit the Thema of Koloneia altogether (probably about 6,000 men) as they do Mesopotamia (probably 4,000). All these figures refer to cavalry.

New Themata were created on the expansion of the frontier by the subdivision of old ones or the detachment of units from other Themata to form the nucleus of the new one. Second and younger sons of Thematic landholders were given plots of land on the new frontiers to help strengthen them. Other new Themata could grow from frontier districts called kleisourai, literally meaning 'mountain passes'. These were independent of the Themata and each commanded by a kleisourarchos or an akritas, a border noble whose usual tasks were to reconnoitre, harrass and raid enemy territory with the men of his estates. There were 4 kleisourai on the Eastern frontier when the Arab lists given above were drawn up, these being Seleukeia (which had obviously become a Thema by Kodama's time), Sebasteia, Lykandos and Leontokomis, which could probably raise another few thousand men between them.

After their establishment the Themata tended to be reduced in size by subdivision – thus the Optimaton Thema was originally part of the Bukellarion Thema, itself originally part of the Opsikion Thema. In this way the number of Themata increased from 10 at the beginning of the 9th century to 25 or more by 899. These were divided into 2 groups, the East and West. According to a schedule of officers' salaries drawn up by Leo VI the Eastern group, always the senior, consisted of Anatolikon, Armeniakon, Thrakesion, Opsikion, Bukellarion, Kappadocia, Charsianon, Mesopotamia, Koloneia, Paphlagonia, Chaldia, Thrace and Macedonia; while the Western group consisted of Peloponnesos, Nikopolis, Kibyrrhaiots, Hellas, Sicily, Langobardia, Strymon, Kephalonia, Thessalonika, Dyrrachium, Samos, Aegean Pelaghos, Dalmatia and Cherson. The number of Themata increased to 30 under Romanus Lecapenus (919–944) and stood at 38 by the mid-eleventh century.

The Tagmata

By the 9th century the regular regiments based in Constantinople formed the nucleus of the army. These now consisted of the Scholae, the Excubiti, the Arithmos (which may have been the same as the Vigla), the Hetaereia and the Numeri.

Of these the cavalry units (the Scholae, Excubiti, Arithmos, and also the Ikanatoi, added by Nikephoros I) formed the Tagmata proper. Each was commanded by a domestikos except for the Vigla, which was under a dhoungarius, and at first the Excubiti, commanded by a komes until the 8th century. Each in addition had an officer called a topoteretes as its second-in-command, who often commanded provincial detachments. Kodama lists the Tagmata regiments as Scholae, Excubiti, Vigla and Fidaratiyin (undoubtedly the Foederati). The name Foederati was still in use until the 9th century but later apparently changed to Hetaereia, recorded as a bodyguard unit probably including both cavalry and infantry and largely comprised of foreign mercenaries. It was divided into 2 parts – the Great Hetaereia and the Middle Hetaereia. Other guard units which seem to have been associated with the Hetaereia were the Khazars, the Pharganoi, and the Maghlavitae, possibly Western Arab mercenaries. All were cavalry. The Pharganoi were Turks from Ferghana introduced under Basil I (867–886), up until whose reign there had also been a Little Hetaereia. A detachment of the Hetaereia accompanied the Emperor at all times whenever he left Constantinople.

According to Kodama, who took his information from a source of c. 838–845, the 4 Tagmata regiments were each 4,000 strong, though Ibn Khordadbah seems to suggest either 6,000 men per regiment or an overall total of 6,000, which would mean approximately 1,500 men per Tagma. The Anonymous Vari of c. 980 gives the Scholae 30 banda, which would mean 9,000 men at 300 per bandon; this fact lends some support to Nikephoros II's statement that banda of his day were only 50-strong (see below), and the resultant figure of 1,500 for the 30 banda also tallies with the second figure we arrive at from Ibn Khordadbah. Interestingly, however, if we take Leo's minimum bandon strength of 200 men the 30 banda come to 6,000 men, which tallies with the alternative interpretation of Ibn Khordadbah. Of the other Tagmata we know only that the Excubiti comprised at least 18 banda by 773.

A final clue to Tagmata strength is also provided by the Anonymous Vari, which records that on campaign the Emperor should be accompanied by a minimum of 8,200 men including 1,000 Hetaereia guard cavalry, the remaining 7,200 probably being intended as the Tagmata (and probably not all of them at that). 10,000 Turks and Khazars mentioned by Ibn Rusta c. 903 as accompanying the Emperor on parade are probably equatable to the Khazars and Pharganoi.

The Numeri, an infantry regiment, are also said to have been 4,000 strong (this does appear to have been Kodama's favourite figure), and were commanded by a domestikos and topoteretes like the cavalry regiments. Numeri banda were commanded by tribouni or tribunes. Another unit, probably likewise of infantry, seems to have had the duty of guarding the Long Wall of Anastasius and its gates under an officer called the Count of the Walls. In addition in the late-9th century a naval guard unit about 1,000 strong was established by Leo VI; these crewed the Emperor's 2 galleys and the Empress' barges as well as performing palace guard duties, and were apparently considered part of the Tagmata.

By the mid-9th century the Scholae domestikos had become senior to all but the Anatolikon strategos, becoming the senior military officer in the absence of the Emperor during the course of the 10th century. After the conquest of Bulgaria in 1018 the office was split into a Domestic of the West and a Domestic of the East.

Later Changes

At the beginning of the 10th century basic regimental organisation as recorded in Leo VI's Tactica varied little from that of the Strategicon except that both infantry and cavalry units were always called by the name banda and commanded by kometes (counts).

The infantry bandon consisted of 4 allaghia, each commanded by an illarches, though the allaghia were normally paired off. The allaghion, which can be literally translated as 'winglet', contained 4 lochaghiai of 16 men so that bandon strength remained 256 as earlier. In the standard heavy infantry unit of mixed spearmen and archers three-quarters were still spearmen and a quarter archers; it is not known how the archers were organised, either as a unit of 4 men under the tetrarchos within each lochaghia, as a separate lochaghia within each allaghion, or even as a separate allaghion. Light infantry and guard lochaghiai consisted of only one troop-type and those of the former may have consisted of only 8 men.

Each cavalry bandon consisted of 6 allaghia, again paired off with a hekatontarchos or kentarchos in command of each pair, the hekatontarchion of the Strategicon therefore being the same as the double allaghion of Leo, the division into 2 allaghia probably resulting from the need for greater flexibility. Each allaghion was commanded by an illarches (possibly sometimes called a pentekontarchos) and contained 5 dekarchia organised as described in the Strategicon. Total cavalry bandon strength therefore remained 300, but again infantry and cavalry banda strengths varied between 200 and 400 men, though those in excess of official strength were normally not taken into action. It seems more likely anyway that units were generally under rather than over strength so we should perhaps take the figures of 200–250 as representing the most likely strength of a bandon.

This organisation remained practically unchanged until well beyond the end of this era, though one of Nikephoros II's works of the mid-10th century (he reigned 963–969) seems to indicate that cavalry banda could be no more than 50-strong; however, I personally think that this is a misprint for allaghion. At the same time 'bandon' could conceivably have changed its meaning since the days of Leo's Tactica. Certainly other sources imply that the smallest infantry unit had shrunk to 10 men by the late-10th century, with a ratio of 7 spearmen to 3 archers, though Psellus' 11th century Chronographia still refers to 16-man lochaghiai.

Nikephoros II abandoned the process by which Thematic troops had been expected to support themselves from their agricultural plots and limited pay. He instead put some of them on a full-time basis like the regular regiments and he and his successors ran down and disbanded many others, their effectiveness having been reduced anyway by the gradual takeover of Thematic smallholdings by the greater landowners, who had thereby converted the Thematic units into sort of private armies, effectively reducing the Thema's fighting strength. A parallel increase took place in the strength of mercenary units and the Tagmata, detachments of which were now distributed throughout the Empire, the latter under officers called dukes. In 982 another Arab source, the Hudud al-Alam, recorded that the strength of the Eastern Themata was now only 3–6,000 cavalry per Thema, a Byzantine source of much the same date stating that each Thema could raise at the most only 3,000 cavalry. At about this time a new Thematic office was introduced; this was the katepan, senior to the strategos, first recorded in Langobardia in 975.

The general reduction of the size of the army by Constantine X (1059–1067), both for economy and because of distrust, followed in the footsteps of his predecessors and was a prelude to the Byzantines' disastrous defeat at the Battle of Manzikert in 1071, as a result of which the Empire lost half its Themata to the Seljuk Turks.

Mercenaries and Auxiliaries

In the mid-10th century Constantine Porphyrogenitus records the possibility of avoiding military service by paying an exemption tax (adaeratio), a process which led to a continuing decrease in the size of the Thematic army and a parallel increase in the number of mercenaries employed, so that from the reign of Nikephoros II, under whom exemption payments started to become widespread, light cavalry consisted entirely of auxiliary horse-archers.

The large-scale employment of mercenaries and foreign auxiliaries was in fact one of the most outstanding features of Byzantine armies. A few figures will give some idea of the scale on which they were employed throughout this period:

60,000 Avars against the Slavs in 574

40,000 Khazars against the Sassanids in 627

30,000 Khurrami Persians at Amorium in 838

40,000 Saracens at Cotrone in 982

15,000 Patzinaks (Pechenegs) against the Seljuks in 1049

40,000 Cumans against the Patzinaks at Levunium in 1091

The 80,000-strong rebel Byzantine army of Thomas the Slav recorded in 821 as including Saracens, Persians, Georgians, Armenians, Alans, Zichians (Circassians), Colchians, Slavs, Crimean Goths and 'Huns' (Avars or Onogurs) is typical of the diversity of their forces.

By the end of this period mercenaries were principally Seljuks, Uzes (Torks), Patzinaks, Saracens, Varangians, Russians and 'Franks' (mainly Normans but also Germans and Frenchmen). From about the mid-10th century many were being employed in place of native troops by the provincial strategoi, a Thematic muster of 1067 being recorded to have included Macedonians (Slavs), Bulgars, Kappadocians (probably Armenians), Uzes, Franks, Varangians and 'other mercenaries who happened to be about'. Anna Comnena refers to mercenaries in her father Alexius I's time as 'horsemen and footmen coming out of all lands'. All foreign mercenaries were brigaded by nationality and commanded by their own officers, some being supplied in self-contained units by the Empire's own satellite states and vassals.

Another source of auxiliary troops were prisoners-of-war, principally Slavs and Turks, resettled with their families on Thematic frontier land (far removed from their homelands) in exchange for military service. Many Pechenegs or Patzinaks were settled in this way in 1048, as were a large number of Uzes in 1065. Such troops served under their own officers and were brigaded separately from native Byzantines. Obviously, however, their loyalties were suspect (as were those of many mercenary contingents); desertions of mammoth proportions are recorded, and revolts were all too frequent.

The Varangian Guard

The Varangian Guard was an elite mercenary unit recruited initially, via Russia, from amongst Scandinavian freelances, whom both Russians and Byzantines called Varangians. 700 Varangian mercenaries fought for the Byzantines as auxiliaries at least as early as 911. An earlier treaty with the Rus after their attack on Constantinople in 860 stipulating that the Byzantines should thereafter receive a military levy from Russia appears not to have been regularly honoured, though an expedition to Italy in 935 included 7 Rus ships crewed by 415 men in total. However, similar agreements of 945 and 971 may have been: 629 Rus in 6 ships certainly took part in the attack on Crete in 949, Rus auxiliaries fought in a campaign against the Arabs in 955 and took part in an expedition to Sicily in 966, and in 988 Vladimir of Kiev sent 6,000 Rus to the assistance of Basil II. This last group remained in Basil's service, where they became his bodyguard (the Emperor distrusting his 'Roman' guards), and their strength is still described as 6,000 in 999.

They may have initially been included as part of the Hetaereia, Psellus specifically stating that Basil had 'combined with them another mercenary force'. The first mention of them in Constantinople as the Varangian Guard (Palatio Varangoi) dates to 1034, though they are mentioned in a less specific context in the De Re Militari of Nikephoros Ouranos dating to c. 990–1000. Thereafter they remained the principal bodyguard unit to the close of this period and beyond, except for a brief interval from 1041 to 1042 when Michael V replaced them by Pecheneg eunuch slave-soldiers in Arab fashion. Byzantine sources refer to the Varangians most often quite simply as 'axe-bearing barbarians' or 'the axe-bearing Guard', in reference to their principal weapon the Scandinavian axe. Their commander was similarly entitled either 'The Leader of the Axe-Bearing Guard' or quite often simply the Akolouthos or Acolyte, 'Follower', no doubt because of his constant attendance on the Emperor. A Byzantine official, the Pansebastos, appears to have been responsible for them on the administrative side. The Akolouthos and most if not all of their other officers were Scandinavians, accompanied where necessary by Byzantine interpreters. The famous Norwegian king Harald Hardrada was himself a Varangian officer c.1035–1044.

After the 10th century the full strength of the Varangian Guard is not recorded. Harald Hardrada commanded approximately 500 in 1041, while after leaving a garrison of 300 Varangians in Kastoria in 1081 Alexius I was still able to form a large part of his battle array at Durazzo (Dyrrachium) from the remainder. At the Battle of Eski Zagra in 1122 the Emperor John II was accompanied by only 540. However, on the evidence of the total of 5–6,000 casualties at Durazzo in 1081 – where the Guard was all but wiped out – and a request made to the Scandinavian kings in 1195 for 1,200 men, the Guard was probably about 3,000 strong from the mid-11th century to the close of the 12th.

For the later history of the Varangian Guard see *Armies and Enemies of the Crusades*.

Servants

Each guardsman had a groom, as did each 2.5 elite cavalry or 7, later 4, line cavalry. These looked after the pack animals. The grooms of the Tagmata regiments were supplied from the non-military Optimaton Thema. Each 16 infantry also had a servant who drove a light mule cart containing among other things a bill-hook, hand-mill, saw, mallet, large wicker basket, scythe, 2 spades and 2 pick-axes. These tools were

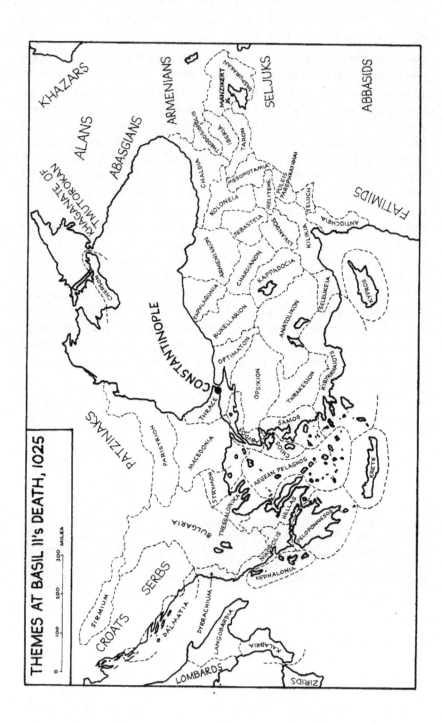

THEMES AT BASIL II's DEATH, 1025

used to entrench the camp at night. If there were not enough servants the worst soldiers had to perform their chores.

All the servants marched together and were armed with slings. Collectively they were known as the Tuldum.

Medical Staff

These included physicians, surgeons and skriboni. The latter were riders whose horses were fitted with special side-saddles with foot-rests for carrying wounded men. They were paid one nomisma, a gold coin, for each man rescued. There were 6–8 skriboni per bandon.

Artillery

The only 'regular' artillery appears to have been those engines maintained on the walls of cities. Field artillery, paid for by a special Thematic tax, was normally supplied by the authorities as and when needed, apparently being made especially.

The engines themselves went under various names, mainly petrobolon, manganon, lithobolon, organon, mechanon, petropompon and spendone. Of these manganon, also called manganika, was the name usually applied to torsion engines similar to the earlier onager; they were generally classified as either heavy, under the name tetrarea or petrarea (the mediaeval petrary), or light ones called alakation.

The spendone, literally 'sling', was in use by the mid-10th century at the latest; this was clearly a trebuchet machine operated by men pulling on ropes. Trebuchets were in use at least as early as the mid-7th century by the Arabs – probably based on Byzantine or Sassanid engines – the normally accepted 12th century date of introduction being completely mistaken. The other engines were all stone-throwers, though whether torsion or trebuchet is unclear.

In addition there were engines called labdereai and toxoballistra apparently specifically for shipboard use. The toxoballistra was a bolt-thrower, probably little different from the Roman ballista, and with a crew of only 3 was the smallest engine used by the Byzantines, a far cry from a spendone recorded in 1071 which was hauled by 100 teams of oxen, fired stones of up to 2.5 cwt and was operated by 1,200 men pulling the ropes!

The Navy

One of the first Themata to be established in the mid-7th century was the naval Thema of the Karabisiani. Like all other Themata it was commanded by a strategos, and in addition was divided into 2 regions each under a dhoungarius. In the 8th century Leo III abolished the Karabisiani Thema, leaving only its 2 component parts which became the Kibyrrhaiots and Aegean Pelaghos Themata.

Not until the reigns of Michael III (842–867) and Basil I (867–886) was interest in the navy revived. A third naval Thema, Samos, was added, and the Themata of Hellas, Peloponnessos and Kephalonia as well as the Italian Themata were supplied with naval establishments. In addition to the Thematic fleets a standing fleet was now based in Constantinople under an officer called the Megas Dhoungarius.

However, as early as 992 Basil II made arrangements with the Venetians for them to perform official naval duties, and the increasing use of mercenary Venetian fleets, which served largely in exchange for trading concessions, led to such a decline in the Byzantine fleet that to face a Russian attack on Constantinople in 1042 a fleet could only be knocked together from hastily repaired old hulks and Imperial transport ships pressed into service, with a mere handful of dromons for a nucleus. This decline was only checked, albeit temporarily, by Alexius I in the late-11th century. He unified the remnants of the Thematic fleets with the Constantinople fleet under a Megas Dux, the Megas Dhoungarius now becoming its second-in-command.

By the end of the 12th century the fleet was again well into decline. Niketas even records that Michael Struphnos, the Megas Dux, had put every large ship out of service in 1204 by selling their masts, anchors, rigging, sails and everything else that could be converted to ready cash!

The standard ship was the dromon, with two banks of oars with 3 men on each top row oar, 1 on the lower and an average crew of 200 oarsmen and 70 marines. A swifter, lighter type called a pamphylos also existed with only 2 men on each upper oar; the crews of these vessels were 130–160 men. It was a pamphylos that usually served as flagship. The ousiakos was smaller still with 1 man to each oar. Single-decked ships called ghalaiai were used for small expeditions and reconnaissance work, eventually becoming larger. By the early-12th century it had begun to replace the pamphylos and dromon, becoming in time the characteristic galley of the Mediterranean. By the end of the 12th century the average ghalaia was of the same size as the pamphylos described above. There were also onerariai, a special type of transport for carrying horses, and siphonophores, ships equipped with siphons for projecting Greek Fire; this became fairly standard equipment for Imperial Fleet ships, though the Thematic ships were only equipped with stone-throwers at least up to the 8th century.

Leo records that in action a fleet should be divided into units of 3 or 5 ships, each unit under a komes.

Each ship's equipment included pots of Greek Fire and pots of powdered quicklime plus incendiary caltrops, all for throwing aboard enemy vessels. Constantine Porphyrogenitus records the equipment carried in a dromon of the Imperial Fleet in 949 as 70 mail corselets, 12 light corselets (probably lamellar) for the siphon operators, 10 other corselets, 50 thick or padded surcoats (probably bambakia or epilorikia), 10 visored helmets, 8 pairs of vambraces, 30 'Lydian' shields, 70 sewn-leather shields, 80 boat-hooks, 20 long-handled scythes to cut enemy rigging, 100 spears, 100 javelins, 20 toxoballistrae and spare parts, 10,000 arrows, 200 bolts (called 'stingers') for the toxoballistrae, 10,000 caltrops, and 4 grapnels.

A few figures are given here as an indication of fleet strengths at different times during the 10th century –

911: a fleet which sailed against Crete contained 60 dromons and 40 pamphyla of the Imperial Fleet, 15, 10 and 10 dromons and 16, 12 and 7 pamphyla respectively from the Thematic fleets of Kibyrrhaiots, Samos and Aegean Pelaghos, and 10 dromons from Hellas. The total crews numbered 47,127 men (34,000 sailors, 7,340 soldiers, 700 Rus mercenaries and 5,087 Mardaites). The Thematic contingents of Kibyrrhaiots, Samos and Aegean Pelaghos were 6,760, 5,690 and 3,100 men respectively.

929: the naval establishments of the Kalabrian Thema could muster a fleet of 7 ships.

949: a third attack launched against Crete. The Imperial Fleet totaled 20 dromons, 8 pamphyla, 33 chelandria ousiaka, and 77 ousiai (which appear to have been fast fleet-tenders rather than warships). Of these 7 pamphyla, 40 ousiai and all 20 dromons and 33 chelandria ousiaka sailed against Crete, together with the Thematic fleets. The complements of the latter's ships were 220 men per dromon, 120 or 150 for a pamphylos (compared to 130 or 160 in Leo VI's attack on Crete c.906) and 108–110 for an ousiakos. Troops included 629 Rus mercenaries.

960: yet another, and this time successful, attack launched on Crete. This is said to have been carried out by 2,000 siphonophores, 1,000 troopships (probably pressed merchant vessels) and 308 supply ships!

968: a fleet sent against Italy consisted of 24 siphonophores, 2 Rus ships, and 2 Galatian ships.

THE SUB-ROMAN BRITONS

By the early-5th century the few remaining Roman troops in Britain had been joined by large numbers of British warriors, who came to be known as the Combrogi or Cymry, meaning 'fellow-countrymen'. The regional armies were at that time commanded by duces, who by 570 had founded a large number of independent Roman successor kingdoms of which the major powers were Dyfed, Powys, Gwynedd, Dumnonia, Brycheiniog, Elmet, Rheged, Gododdin and Strathclyde; of these only the Welsh kingdoms survived – Rheged fell following the Battle of Degastan in 603, Elmet fell to the Deirans c. 620, Gododdin to the Bernicians c. 638, while Dumnonia finally fell to the West Saxons between 815 and 838. Strathclyde lasted as an independent state down to 945, when it was absorbed by Scotland.

The duces, who are usually described in contemporary sources as tyranni, 'usurpers' or 'despots', had bands of personal military retainers, the commanipulares, as the nuclei of their armies. A number of old hill-forts refortified and used as permanent bases during this period were probably garrisoned by these commanipulares. Some more central authority may also have continued to exist, of which Arthur is representative, his title of Dux Bellorum or Tywyssawc Llu, 'Leader of Battles' or 'Leader of the Army', suggesting a primacy over the other duces.

For the armies themselves a few figures are recorded. The Anglo-Saxon Chronicle records 4,000 casualties at the Battle of Creacanford in 456, 5,000 casualties in an unnamed battle of 508, and 2,045–2,065 casualties at the Battle of Beandun in 614. The army which fought at Catraeth in 598 was perhaps as small as 300–363 men though this may only represent chieftains, while at Mons Badonicus (probably c. 503) there were enough Britons to kill 960 Saxons in one attack.

The largest unit to appear in contemporary sources is the Teulu, 'Family', the picked bodyguard of a chief. This varied in size though it was frequently of 300 men, while a poem of c. 650 mentions a certain Cynddylan maintaining as many as 700 warriors at his court. In the 430's one northern British chieftain apparently commanded as many as 900 cavalry, probably a Teulu consisting of 3 units of 300. The Teulu often contained men from other kingdoms, though the majority were relatives of the chief, the 10th century Laws of Hywel recording that the commander of the bodyguard should be a son or nephew of the king. The Teulu still existed in the 12th century, when it is recorded as consisting of 14–21 year old sons of freemen. These bodyguard units were outside regular army organisation and are comparable to the Saxon Hearth-troop. It was they who provided the all-important cavalry, while the bulk of the army consisted of spear-armed infantry, called pedyt from the Latin 'pedites'.

One version of the Anglo-Saxon Chronicle describes the 4,000 casualties at Creacanford as 4 troops, suggesting that a unit of 1,000 existed, which seems more than probable since a smaller unit, the cant, consisted of 100 men, and the smallest unit appears to have been 10 men.

Additional troops were supplied by mercenaries. Although there had been units of 'Saxons' (a loose term at that time for Saxons, Angles, Frisians, Jutes, Franks, Danes and others) posted in Britain under the late Romans it was their employment as mercenaries by the Britons which prompted their immigration in such great numbers during the reign of Vortigern. The first British-employed Saxon contingent, comprising 3 'keels', arrived in 428 under the command of Hengest, a Dane. Assuming a 'keel' to be similar to the Nydam ships this force could not have numbered much more than 150 men. The second contingent, which arrived c. 437, was considerably larger, numbering 19 'keels'. On the subject of ships it should be noted that the Sub-Roman Britons had a few warships of their own; Arthur is recorded to have had at least 2 large vessels, 'Grim Smiler' (sunk c. 512) and 'Fairform'.

In addition Irishmen were employed as late as the end of the 6th century, a Visigothic fleet and troops were employed in the early-6th century, and a 9th century source suggests that Frankish mercenaries were used. In the 10th century Welsh princes sometimes employed Vikings.

In late Roman fashion the army was maintained by annona, fixed quantities of supplies levied from church and nobility which were collected by an officer called a cais. The levy took the form of food, cattle and billeting, and was rather unpopular – particularly with the Church.

Later in this period administration, and therefore probably military organisation, was based on groupings of households similar to those of the Dal Riata Scots described below. The households, or trefs, were grouped into cantrefs, each of a hundred households, or the newer cymwyds, 'neighbourhoods', of presumably 25, 33 or 50 households since 2–4 cymwyds generally constituted a cantref. This can probably be taken as an indication that decimal organisation persisted.

THE IRISH AND EARLY SCOTS

Ireland consisted of a large number of tribal kingdoms, probably never less than 150 at any time in this period, within a number of provinces known as Coiceds, 'Fifths'. These were traditionally Ulaid (Ulster), Laigin (Leinster), Connachta (Connaught), Muma (Munster) and Mide (the Middle), though there were later 6 or even 7 Fifths!

Each kingdom was based on the tuath, a 'tribal' unit consisting of several family groups. These were either doer-chele, 'unfree clients', or soer-chele, 'free clients'. The soer-chele were the nobility, of whom the highest ranking was the aire toise or toisech (who also occurs in northern Scotland), leader of a warband in wartime.

In this period there were 3 grades of king; the Ri Tuaithe, king of one tuath; the Rui Ri, king of a tuath but also overlord of a number of minor tuaths; and the Ri Ruirech or Ri Coiced, king of overkings or king of a Fifth. The additional title Ard Ri, 'High King', appeared some time after the 7th century but its meaning was often imprecise and it was applied somewhat indiscriminately. The loyalty of the lesser kings to the Rui Ri or Ri Ruirech was ensured by the taking of hostages, usually kings' sons, by the overking; the High King Brian Boru's son Murchadh is recorded as having a warrior band of 140 kings' sons at Clontarf in 1014.

Each king was expected to lead the forces of his tuath to his overlord's assistance in wartime. None of them had standing armies and there was no warrior band comparable to the Frankish or Visigothic fideles, Lombard gasindii or Saxon Hearth-troop except in wartime, when it consisted of the soer-chele. These as well as the doer-chele were called upon to perform military service, and it seems that even their women could be expected to fight as late as the 7th or even the 8th century. By the latter date the average Irish tuath could field 700 men, the Rui Ri being recorded in an 8th century law as commander of 2 or 3 buiden, 'bands', of 700 men each.

The only permanent troops used by the Irish consisted of mercenaries. An 8th century law states that a king was accompanied by 4, one each to guard front, back, left and right in battle; judging from later sources these were not single men but more probably commanders of companies of mercenaries. An early piece of poetry suggests Frankish mercenaries while Scots feature quite often in the Irish annals, Dal Riatans being employed by an Ui Neill king at least as early as 733, while from the mid-9th century Norse auxiliaries were often to be found in Irish armies. As an indication of numbers, a minimum of 5–900 Vikings appeared in a Bregian army in 869, over 1,200 in a Munster army of 978, and 10 ships of Manx Vikings, probably about

750 men, were present in Brian Boru's army at Clontarf in 1014. It was a search for mercenary aid by a deposed Irish king that led to the Norman invasion of Ireland in 1167.

Organisation was based on the cet of 100 men. As in later times each town or enclosed farmstead probably supplied one cet, commanded by a tuisech. The Annals of Clonmacnoise record that as early as the mid-3rd century Cormac had established a standing army of paid troops, called the Fiana, whose principal unit was the tricha cet, the 'Thirty hundred'. 3 such units had been maintained in peacetime, 7 in wartime, under a commander-in-chief called the Ri Feinnidh. The smallest unit at that time appears to have been 9 men, the tenth perhaps being an officer, these units being grouped by fives or tens, the latter constituting a cet.

Later organisation remained much the same, the tricha cet remaining the standard large formation and becoming in time a territorial division. Another unit, the cat or cat mor, usually translated as battalion or 'great battalion', frequently occurs in various sources but is so imprecise as to defy definition; it may have been a gathering of any number of cets, recorded strengths varying between a few hundred and 2,000 plus. The mediaeval term 'battal' is often substituted.

Length of service probably varied from tuath to tuath. An instance is recorded in the 8th century where a subgroup were obliged to perform military service to their overlord for 3 fortnights once every 3 years; this service could not be demanded during Spring or Autumn when seeding and harvesting had to take place. If this is typical it explains the increasing use of mercenaries over the next few centuries.

During the Viking era the Irish were not above allying themselves with the invaders, either in wars between Norwegians and Danes or between rival Scandinavian settlements. In this way the Leinstermen were almost permanently allied with the Dublin or Limerick Vikings, one of the earliest Irish-Viking alliances being against the Gall-Gaedhil in 858. These Gall-Gaedhil, or Gall-Gael, who gave their name to Galloway in south-west Scotland, were mixed bands of Galwegians, Norse, renegades, individuals of mixed blood and Gaelic-speaking Vikings from the Isles, the name meaning 'Foreign Gaels'. Irish chroniclers say 'they were usually called Northmen, for they had (adopted) the customs of the Northmen and had been fostered by them'. They plundered both Irish and Scandinavians indiscriminately, apparently earning by their savagery the popular epithet 'The Sons of Death'. The High King Maelsechnaill introduced them into Ireland in 856 under Caithill Finn (Ketil the White), hiring their aid as mercenaries against the Dublin Vikings. Although defeated in Ireland in 857 and 858, after which Irish sources do not mention them again, they continued to rule the Isles undisturbed. There were Gall-Gaels at Clontarf in 1014.

Ultimately the Irish came to accept the presence of the Scandinavians in Ireland. They did so to such a degree that in the early-11th century Brian Boru equipped a combined fleet of Irishmen and Dublin and Waterford Vikings to raid the coasts of England and Wales! The organisation of Irish fleets is unknown. However, the ships they used were built specifically for warfare and raiding. They were large wooden vessels with a helm rather than the traditional curraghs, though they cannot have been overlarge if the total figure of 820 ships is to be believed for 2 of Brian Boru's fleets operating simultaneously. At other times Irish kings employed Scots or Scandinavian fleets from the Isles and western seaboard of Scotland.

In Scotland, the Irish immigrants in Dal Riata eventually founded a unified kingdom with the Picts in 846 under Kenneth MacAlpin. The British kingdom of Strathclyde then became a dependency of Scotland (called at this time Alba) and was absorbed in 945, though it still had its own king into the early-11th century, while the northern part of Northumbria, known generally as Lothian, was annexed in the late-10th century. Scandinavian political influence was very strong, however, and only finally ended with the Battle of Largs in 1263.

The organisation of the Dal Riata Scots was based on households, which were grouped in multiples of 5, the commonest figures being 10, 20 and 30. Larger groupings of 60 or 100 households probably correspond to the later baile. On average 2 households were expected to supply 3 men for a land army, while a mid-8th century source records that for a sea-muster each 20 households had to supply 14 benches, i.e. 28 men.

The total strength of the districts of Dal Riata in the 8th century was 1,500–2,100 men for the land army, or 1,000 benches for the sea-muster. Although these figures seem low they may represent a selective levy only and probably do not include those Picts now subject to the Scots. The land army was organised in units of 300 or 700 men, the latter comparable to the Irish buiden. Later organisation seems to have remained decimal, and until the close of this period at least continued to have a number of affinities with Irish organisation.

However, Scots forces would have been heterogenous to say the least, with lowland spearmen and Strathclyde Welsh little different from the Saxon Fyrd, highlanders and Scots spearmen and javelinmen little different from the Picts, Gall-Gael of very Irish appearance, and well-armoured Viking types probably riding to and from battle. Percentages are impossible to establish, though clearly the latter would have provided the nucleus of the army and lowland spearmen probably the greatest proportion.

THE VISIGOTHS

The Visigothic kingdom in Spain (and, earlier, southern France) lasted down to the Arab invasion of 711. In many ways it can be described as a Roman successor state, strong Byzantine influence persisting from 554 – when the Empire recovered about a third of the peninsula – right through to 631 when they lost their last foothold. The kingdom was divided into 6 provinces – Tarraconensis, Carthaginiensis, Lusitania, Baetica, Gallaecia and Gallia – each under a Dux Provinciae (not to be confused with the Dux Exercitus who usually commanded the provincial levy in wartime).

The main units of the levy were the thiufae, each commanded by a thiufadus. Smaller units were quingentenae, the centenae, and the decania, respectively 500, 100 and 10 men, of which only the centenae and decania, under centenarius and decanus respectively, ever appear in practice. Another official called a millenarius, logically a commander of 1,000 men, seems to have been non-military; his military duties appear to have passed to the thiufadus, and at least one contemporary source substitutes the word mil, 'thousand', for thiufa. This decimal organisation seems to have replaced the traditional tribal organisation during the 6th century. Probably each city was responsible for raising one thiufa; certainly the count of the city, the comes civitatis, was senior to the thiufadus though he had no military authority except the responsibility of ensuring the thiufa was raised when required.

The commanding officer of an assembled army was called the Praepositus Hostis or Comes or Dux Exercitus. The commander-in-chief was a noble called the Dux Exercitus Hispaniae.

In addition to the general levy, the king was always accompanied by his noble bodyguard, the fideles. These were possibly commanded by a noble called the Comes Spathariorum. The king was also accompanied in wartime by freed royal slaves. These served him personally rather than the general levy, and this obligation was hereditable by their descendants.

The nobles too were accompanied by bodyguards. These were the bucellarii, who received land, booty and what is comparable to the

Saxon heriot, and the saiones, who were given weapons and equipment to keep but could retain no captured booty for themselves.

These bodyguards fought as cavalry as did the gardingi, who appear to have been lesser nobility who were in part, at least, responsible for leading bands of trained soldiers in exchange for grants of land. It is not known whether gardingi, saiones or bucellarii served as part of the provincial thiufae or independently. However, some thiufae at least were clearly cavalry and these may have been supplied by such troops.

As early as the reign of Euric (466–484) the obligation of military service was imposed upon the old Roman population of Spain, and perhaps even on slaves. This law was confirmed by Wamba in 673 and extended to include the clergy. Roman troops served under their own officers and could even be found amongst the king's fideles. By the late-7th century if not earlier Visigothic armies consisted predominantly of conscripted slaves, whom all freemen (Visigothic or Roman) and royal slaves, who could own their own land and slaves, were obliged to supply. Each had to bring one-tenth of his slaves, or even as many as half up to a maximum of 50 men, to the levy. Those who did not present themselves with their obligatory quota had those slaves they left behind confiscated by the state. Service was expected only of slaves 20–50 years of age, which is probably also true of those few freemen serving. They mostly served as infantry though some at least were cavalrymen.

Other duties included work on bridges, roads and fortifications. Desertion or failure to serve could be punished in a number of ways varying from exile to death, though the favourites were flogging, fines or enslavement.

Visigothic armies consisted of both cavalry and infantry, though reliance was always principally on the heavy cavalry, supplied by the bodyguard troops of the king and nobles. However, although these were important they were outnumbered by javelin-armed light/medium horsemen probably supplied by saiones, gardingi and richer townsmen serving in the levy. The largest part of the army was always infantry, though many of these rode to battle like the Franks and Saxons; in addition cavalry troops were prepared to dismount and fight on foot when necessary. Few figures exist for actual army strengths; in the early-6th century an Ostrogothic nobleman in Spain maintained a personal warband of 2,000, while in 589 300 Visigoths under a dux (probably a Dux Exercitus) defeated allegedly 60,000 Franks, killing 5,000 and capturing 2,000. Only one reliable figure exists for the 7th and 8th centuries, where in 673, a picked force of 10,000 under another dux was sent forward to relieve Nimes. The figures of up to 100,000 for the army which the Arabs defeated in 711 seem unlikely, but the evidence indicates that it was well over 10,000 men.

In addition after the reign of Sisebuto (612–620) the Visigoths maintained a reasonable fleet. In one engagement in the reign of Wamba (673–680) as many as 270 Arab ships are claimed to have been destroyed.

THE LOMBARDS

Driven from the Danube basin by the pressure of the Avars, the Lombards invaded Italy in 568, some having served there as mercenaries with the Byzantine general Narses in 552. At the time of the invasion they included the remnants of many other Central European nations, including Sarmatians, Gepids, Bavarians and 20,000 Saxons. Within a few years they were joined by many Bulgars, who had been defeated by the Avars.

Their kingdom was eventually annexed by the Franks in 774. A revival of Lombard power took place in the late-9th and 10 centuries, but ended in a decisive defeat by the Byzantines at Cannae in 1018, which cleared the way for Norman expansion in southern Italy. (There were Normans in the Lombard army at Cannae; of the 250 involved only 10 survived).

Every freeman was obliged to perform military service, a freeman being called exercitalis or arimannus, meaning literally 'army-man'. Since the Lombards themselves were a minority many slaves and subject peoples were often created freemen so as to swell the number of available troops, probably providing the bulk of the third category mentioned below; in their early period, however, half-free men and even slaves had sometimes fought in emergencies. (Unlike the Romans in Visigothic Spain, however, the Romans in Italy were largely treated as servile or at best half-free and did not serve in the army.) Aistulf's laws of 750 and 755 required that from each holding of 7 mansi of land one man was to serve with shield, corselet, lance and 'horses' (i.e. more than one), while each man holding 40 jugera (an unknown land measure) up to 7 mansi was also to field a mounted man with at least a lance and shield. A third category comprised those men with less than 40 jugera; the laws state that such men 'who do not have an animal to ride and cannot afford one should at least have a shield and quiver, or that 'if they can afford it, they should have a shield as well as a quiver and bow and arrows.'

The laws also state that all Lombards who could afford a mail corselet should possess one. Such service was required of both freemen and merchants, and heaven help draft-dodgers – Rothair's Edict of 643 states bluntly that deserters 'shall be killed'. Swords and helmets are not mentioned, curiously, but men who possessed them doubtless wore them.

Assuming these laws to be a confirmation in writing of earlier practice, the figures of 2,500 warriors and 3,000 retainers, all cavalry, allied to the Byzantines in 552 is perhaps indicative of the proportion of first-class to second-class cavalry in a picked warband, though the proportion of the latter would have been far greater in a general levy.

When called up each man followed his local lord; these nobility consisted of comes, gastaldi and centenarii, the latter indicative of decimal organisation. The levy of a whole province was led by its dux (there were 34 duces as early as 574). Within the levy the Lombards were organised in faras, clans or related family groups.

In addition the king and nobility had personal bands of warriors known as gasindii, who pledged their allegiance by oaths. Those of the nobility became particularly powerful in the early-8th century. Amongst the gasindii the officers were the Marpahis (equivalent to the Frankish Count of the Stable), the Scilpor, the Shield-bearer or Armour-bearer and the Standard-bearer.

Avars were on occasion used as mercenaries, and on at least one occasion (603) they supplied Slav auxiliaries for use against the Byzantines. In the 10th century Magyars sometimes served as mercenaries, as in the 11th century did Normans and Germans. Alliances were also occasionally made with Saracens, and it was as auxiliaries of the city of Naples that Arabs had first set foot on the Italian mainland in 837.

The Carolingian kings, whose dynasty ended in Italy in 888, continued to utilise the traditional Lombard levy.

THE FRANKS

Merovingians

The king had a personal retinue or bodyguard of warriors (called variously pueri, amici, socii, armati, fideles, sodales, satellites or antrustiones) bound to his service by oaths of loyalty. Of these the chief officers were the Mayor of the Palace, Counts of the Palace and Marshal. As well as those antrustiones actually remaining at the king's side others were posted in various provincial bases called centenae (obviously units of 100 men) under the command of centenarii. The royal antrustiones numbered in thousands, on average 5–10,000. In addition the nobility had antrustiones of their own, a practice which lasted into early Carolingian times. In the 6th and early-7th centuries all antrustiones were supplemented by the descendants of Roman soldiers, the laeti or milites (see figure 30 in the dress and equipment section).

The general levy of able-bodied freemen did not appear until the second half of the 6th century, and initially was only utilised in the cities of Austrasia and Neustria. This levy, the Heerbann, was led by the local comes or count and freemen were obliged to perform such military service up to the age of 60. Generally these obligations also included maintenance and defence of fortresses, roads, and bridges, and guard duties. At first it did not involve the service of all freemen, the poor being generally exempt. Later the levy was reduced to only one man from each family. Failure to serve could be punishable by death but usually resulted in a heavy fine based on the defaulter's social standing. A fine of 60 solidi occurs in the early-9th century, at which time 40 solidi would have supplied a man with complete arms and armour and a war-horse! However, this was the highest fine, payable by those who owned 5 pounds' worth of chattels; those with 3 pounds paid 30 solidi, with 2 pounds 10 solidi, and with one pound 5 solidi. The period of service was unspecified but was limited in practice by seeding and harvesting, and probably lasted a maximum of about 6 months. It began with the Marchfield, the annual assembly in arms to commence the season's campaigning, so-called because it officially took place on March 1st.

Within the levy organisation was probably on a decimal system based, as in Saxon England, on the hundred of land. The Heerbanns of several provinces could sometimes be gathered into a larger army commanded by a herzog or dux.

Service was usually as infantry, though as early as 626 decisive use of cavalry had been made in battle against the Old Saxons, and city levies are sometimes recorded as mounted in the 6th century. Frankish cavalry units had even appeared in the late Roman army and are recorded in the Notitia Dignitatum. From c. 755 the Marchfield was even postponed until May 1st so that adequate forage was available to feed the horses used on campaign, and in 758 King Pepin changed the tribute paid by the Old Saxons from cattle to horses, which is indicative of the growing importance of the horse in Frankish warfare. Probably not many of these were yet used for cavalry, since during the Tours campaign of 732 the majority of the Franks clearly fought as infantry, though they pursued the Arabs on horseback. The 'Mayfield', as it was now called, did not always fall on the given date and by the mid-9th century rarely did.

Carolingians

Because of their expansion beyond the confines of their original kingdoms, Frankish armies were usually multi-racial; for the late-8th century campaign against the Avars the 4 divisions of the army included Ripuranian and Salian Franks, Old Saxons, Thuringians, Frisians, Alemanni, Bavarians and Lombards. Likewise in the civil war of 840–841 the armies included Neustrian and Austrasian Franks, Burgundians, Aquitanians, Old Saxons and Bavarians. The commanders of such units were, however, usually Frankish comes.

Although at the beginning of Charlemagne's reign (768) the majority of the army was still serving as infantry there was a steady increase in the use of cavalry throughout the Carolingian period. This was undoubtedly largely the result of constant campaigning on far borders against fast-moving raiders – Avars, Arabs, Vikings, Lombards and Magyars. For the campaign against the Avars in 795 the chroniclers make special mention of the many thousands of horses which Charlemagne had gathered.

In 864 Charles the Bald ordered that all free Franks who owned or could obtain a horse should attend the Heerbann with it, and in 891 a chronicler states that the Franks did not even know how to fight on foot – an exaggeration, but indicative of the turn things were taking.

The earliest Carolingian capitularies record military service being due from the royal land-holders or vassals (originally from the Latin 'vassus', meaning a servant or slave), though from 807–808 at the latest service was due from every freeman who held 4 mansi of land, either his own or as a benefice, a grant of land from his lord. (Military service thus owed from vassals had replaced the earlier agricultural or personal services in the mid-8th century). The royal vassals, serving as cavalrymen, were known by the term caballarii.

Men who held less than 4 mansi had to combine with other land-holders to supply one man to the Heerbann. The possible combinations were 2 men with 2 mansi each, one with 3 mansi and one with one, and 4 men with one mansus each. The man chosen to serve from these had a large percentage of his equipment and rations supplied by those who remained at home. He probably served on horse. This service of a man from each 4 mansi is clearly comparable to the Saxon Select Fyrd.

A variation of this system recorded in 807 expects one man to serve from a holding of 2 mansi, from 3 men of one mansus each, from 2 men of one mansus each and a third man with only a little land, from 6 men of half a mansus each, and from 6 men having only goods of a certain value. In the last case the 5 men who stayed at home contributed 1 solidus each. In a further variation Saxons are expected to field one man in 6 against the Arabs or Avars, one man in 3 against the Bohemians, or every man against the Wends and Sorbs across the Elbe, while Frisians are expected to field one man in every 7 in addition to service as caballarii from their nobility.

The levies were commanded by the local lords, if they attended the Heerbann, otherwise by the comes. Organisation was still decimal but the period of service was now 3 months. However, service could be demanded more than once a year, but by the time of Louis the Pious (814–840) 40 days had to elapse between each period of service.

In most cases the greater landed vassals were probably accompanied by their tenants, serving as light cavalry or infantry, though the capitularies usually make no mention of them. In addition there were full-time picked or special light units used for raids, complex manoeuvres, frontier guard and other such duties. These elite units first appeared in the early-7th century and were called scarae, scariti homines or excarricati; they seem to have been largely royal vassals. The royal or imperial bodyguard troops were probably scarae.

Each man had to carry enough rations to last 3 months from the 'frontier' (which varied according to how far the troops had to come to commence the campaign), while arms and clothing had to be adequate to last 6 months. Discipline soon collapsed when these self-supplied rations were exhausted, often resulting in the pillaging of their own countryside. For this reason the army was almost always restricted to a single column on the march to keep looting to a minimum. Fodder for the horses was another problem, and there are recorded instances of Frankish armies withdrawing because they had run out of food for them.

Their commissariat was never one of the Franks' strong points, though supply trains are recorded. Ox-drawn covered wagons with a capacity of 12 bushels of corn or 12 small barrels of wine could accompany the army, and amongst the supplies and equipment they carried was flour, wine, port, corn-mills and other rations, plus adzes, augers, axes and fundibuli (staff-slings) with skilled operators. Stones for the fundibuli were carried by packhorses. Other equipment included spades, planes, boards, and iron-shod stakes, evidently to fortify the marching camp, and also spear, shield, bow and quiver of arrows for the wagon driver. The baggage escort were equipped likewise. The leather covers of the wagons could apparently be laced together and stuffed to act as pontoons.

To defend against foreign incursions, border provinces known as marcae (marches) were established, reminiscent of (and probably based on) the Byzantine Themata. Their frontiers consisted of fortresses joined by roads, which as well as ensuring the safety of the hinterland also provided bases for offensive campaigns. Each March was commanded by a markgraf, who granted newly conquered lands as benefices in exchange for military service, thus strengthening the frontier further. Those living in such regions had an additional military duty of maintaining a watch against raids or enemy incursions. Because of the constant threat of Viking raids service in coastal areas could be demanded on shipboard.

In addition, under Charles the Bald fortified bridges were built to obstruct up-river raids by Vikings, such as at Charenton-le-Pont on the River Marne, Auvers on the Oise, and Pistres, Pontoise, Paris and Trilbardou on the Seine. With the exception of Paris, however, these had only limited success because of the difficulties of maintaining permanent garrisons. Others were attacked and destroyed while still under construction.

Vikings were sometimes even given grants of land to protect them against other Viking raiders – such as the granting of Frisian lands to Harald Klak by Louis the Pious in 826, to Rorik by Lothair in the mid-9th century, and to Godfred by Charles the Fat in 882. More importantly, and with considerable consequences to subsequent history, in 911 Charles the Simple granted Normandy to a band of Vikings under Hrolf Gange, more commonly known as Rollo.

Vikings were also employed as mercenaries, though they tended to be unreliable in Frankish service taking advantage of what was, after Charlemagne, a basically weak monarchy.

The 847 capitulary of Charles the Bald ordering that all subjects must become vassals either of himself or his nobles brings us to the threshold of truly 'feudal' organisation, which continued with only slight modification under the Capetian dynasty and throughout the Middle Ages. For full details see 'Armies of Feudal Europe'.

Ottonians

After the death of Charlemagne's son Louis the Pious the Empire passed to his 3 grandsons, each of whom squabbled with the other until the Empire disintegrated. Its 3 principal divisions were the West Frankish Kingdom (France), the Middle Kingdom or Lotharingia, with which went the title of Emperor, and the East Frankish Kingdom (Germany). The Ottonian dynasty succeeded to the eastern kingdom in 936 and lasted to 1125, adopting the title Emperor from 961.

As in France, the nucleus of the army consisted of the feudal vassals of the king and nobility, supported either by benefices of land, money, or even food and equipment, or by tribute money paid by conquered or client Slavic tribes. Ecclesiastical lands maintained feudal troops by the same means. These warbands of vassals are usually referred to in contemporary sources as miles armati, manus militum, milites, satellites, or even by the older name of comitatus. They were all noblemen of lesser or greater standing, often from the estates of their lord but frequently including impoverished nobles from other regions.

The organisation of the milites was decimal, the largest unit being the legio. The legio was also sometimes called a milia, and the chronicler Widukind specifically states that the Bohemian legio at Lechfield was 1,000 men, so the strength of the legio was probably officially 1,000 though in practice its numbers varied; it may be more accurate to compare it to the later mediaeval bataille or 'battle' which varied in strength according to the number of troops available and number of divisions required. Related auxiliary cavalry or less well-armed retainers do not appear to have been included in the legio, probably constituting separate units. The standard unit appears to have been 100 men.

Sometimes permanent warbands were used for the defence of the Marches and frontier regions. One such recorded force which may be typical was the 10th century Legio Mesaburiorum, which was non-feudal and non-noble and consisted of outlaws and bandits who had received pardons in exchange for military service. They probably also included a large number of adventurers, and undoubtedly behaved little better than the raiders they fought.

In addition to the warbands there was the usual general levy of free and half-free peasants, also organised on a decimal basis; amongst the Old Saxons all men over the age of 13 appear to have served during the 10th century, but this was unusual. Their duties were much the same as those recorded for the earlier Merovingians and Carolingians, though they were now summoned less frequently and even when they were they sometimes served in a non-military capacity, as servants or labourers; cash payments in lieu of service are also recorded, the money going to the milites to help them maintain their equipment or employ mercenaries.

The building of fortresses was one of the duties of the levy, particularly in the Marches. Henry the Fowler (919–936, founder of the dynasty), introduced a system where every ninth man lived in a fortified town, helping to build and maintain it, while the other 8 continued their agricultural chores and stored one third of their produce within the town, taking refuge there themselves during Slav or Magyar raids. These men were lower-class vassals, sometimes referred to as agrarii milites, who were in many ways the forerunners of the mediaeval German ministeriales, unfree knights.

It was Conrad II (1024–1039) who actually introduced ministeriales on a large scale. A ministerialis is best described as an unfree man in possession of a benefice and performing the same military service as a free, feudal tenant would. They appear to have originally evolved as a result of church lands being obliged to supply feudal troops in the same way as the nobility had to; so as not to incur a loss of income by granting the land to free vassals to fulfil these obligations, unfree men were granted such lands instead and were obliged to supply the requisite military duties while at the same time, being unfree, not being permitted any of the benefits or income of a free vassal. This practice became widespread in Germany.

Auxiliaries were also employed, Magyars, Poles, Wends and other Slavs all being recorded in the 10th and 11th centuries. Even Danish auxiliaries are sometimes mentioned, by the mid-11th century apparently sometimes serving as cavalry.

As an indication of the numbers of troops available, 32 legiones were mustered for an attack on the Capetian Hugh the Great in 946, though these included Carolingian French and Flemish units, while at Lechfield in 955 there were 8 legiones, probably a more usual size for an army. Otto II, campaigning in Italy in 982, requested reinforcements of 2,080 feudal cavalry from Lotharingia, Bavaria, Franconia and Swabia, 1,482 of whom were supplied by ecclesiastical vassals; this may very well have been after his defeat by the Arabs at Cotrone, where he is recorded to have lost 4,000 men killed plus many more captured. In the mid-11th century Henry II had adequate troops to promise a Milanese rebel the loan of 4,000 knights (probably ministeriales).

THE VIKINGS

The nucleus of a Scandinavian army was the Hird. Its members, the Hirdmen or Thingmen, were paid retainers who had sworn their allegiance to a king or jarl (earl) and were maintained by him as a permanent military force. Most were his subjects, but many were also foreigners.

As early as 885 Harald Fairhair, first king to unify most of Norway, may have decreed that each jarl should maintain 60 men, and that beneath him a minimum of 4 hersir, local military commanders, should maintain 20 each. At this time the Scandinavians were still pagan and their Hirds contained large numbers of Berserkir, warriors who were thought to be the chosen ones of Odin, the father of the gods (see figure 70 in the dress and equipment section).

Olaf II of Norway (St. Olaf, 1016–1030) had a Hird of 120 men resident at court, consisting of 60 Hirdmen (the elite of the Hird), plus 30 huscarls and 30 gestrs (see below), as did Harald Hardrada; this was doubled to 240 by Olaf III (1068–1093). In addition there were others posted elsewhere in the kingdom. The Gestr, a lower echelon of Hird retainers, had been established by the early-11th century, or possibly a little later. These were often used for such duties as tax-collecting. They received only half the pay of a Hirdman and likewise only half the rewards handed out after a campaign.

Probably the retainers were divided into 4 units, each of which was further subdivided into a number of smaller troops, probably on a decimal basis, though in Scandinavian sources it should be noted that 100 usually means 120, the so-called 'long hundred'. Each company was responsible for its own disciplinary courts. The senior Hird officers were the Stallari (Marshal) and the Merkismadr (the Marksman, who was the standard-bearer).

The Hirdmen provided, with mercenaries and pirates (often one and the same thing), the bulk of Viking raiders. The pirates ('tried in the taking of booty, and ready for all things') fought principally for loot, and it was for their maintenance that Danegeld was exacted, Danegeld being a tribute of money levied from the Vikings' victims – an unreliable sort of protection racket. The Saxons were particularly subject to this, the last special Danegeld gathered in England being in 1018 for Cnut to pay off most of his invasion army.

It was probably for the accommodation of Swein and Cnut's 'Tinglith' and other professionals that the great Danish fortified camps of Trelleborg, Aggersborg, Fyrkat and Nonnebakken were built in the early-11th century. Between them these could house a standing army of approximately 5,500 men. The semi-legendary Jomsvikings were probably similarly organised; they were a select military brotherhood of men of 18–50 years of age, with strict codes of conduct. Saga records that the harbour of their encampment at Jomsborg on the Baltic coast could hold up to 300 ships, undoubtedly a gross exaggeration (the oldest version of the story says 3 ships; a compromise of 30 seems reasonable). The later Anglo-Danish Huscarls were based on the Jomsvikings.

The main part of a national, as opposed to a raiding, army was supplied by the freemen, both peasants and bondi (landowning farmers), whose military obligations also included assistance in building fortifications.

Those who failed to fulfil their duties were heavily fined. In times of crisis, such as invasion, even the thralls (slaves) could be called up.

Organisation was based on the Leidang, a levy of ships, men and provisions which evolved in Denmark perhaps as early as the 6th century but only became regularised in the 10th century. The coastal areas were divided up into shipredes responsible for supplying ships of a predetermined size and number, and each shiprede was divided into a number of manngerds or lides, a farm or group of farms, of which each was obliged to supply one man over 18 years old, together with food and equipment, for the Leidang. Single men were called up first, then farmers who had labourers to carry on while they were away, and last of all farmers who had no labourers. Once summoned they had to appear on shipboard within 5 days, the ship crew constituting the smallest distinct army unit; deserters were outlawed. Judging from later sources it was not necessarily the same man who served each year.

The Leidang could be called out locally or nationally. Frequently a half national levy (Half-leidang) was summoned, usually if an attack was planned against an enemy, the calling out of the whole levy (Full-leidang) being generally reserved for facing foreign invasion or large-scale attack. It was often summoned by beacons along the coast, otherwise by a war-arrow being passed from district to district by messengers. The period of service was possibly 4 months annually as in the 12th and 13th centuries, though from the 10th century Gulathinglaw it appears that it may have been only 2 months.

Large fleets could be obtained through the Leidang: King Horik of Denmark had a fleet of 600 ships in 845, Harald Bluetooth a Full-leidang of 720 ships in 975, Cnut 850 in the early-11th century, Svein Ulfsson 720 in 1050, and Harald Hardrada a Half-leidang of 240–300, or possibly even 500, in 1066. In 1026 Sweden and Norway each raised 350 ships for a campaign against Cnut, and he is supposed to have responded by levying a fleet of 1,200 ships from Denmark and England. Although Denmark, with a population probably equal to those of Norway and Sweden put together, could always muster larger forces than her neighbours this last claim does seem a little optimistic, despite the fact that Danish ships were apparently smaller.

The Gulathinglaw gives us a break-down of Norway's Leidang in the mid-10th century thus, listing the men of each region and the number of ships owed:

Vik-dwellers   60 x 20-benchers + 1 other ship (no size given)
Agder   16 x 25-benchers
Hordaland   24 x 25-benchers

Firthmen	20 x 25-benchers
Raumdale	10 x 20-benchers
Trondelag	8 x 20-benchers
Halogaland	1 x 30-bencher, 13 x 20-benchers
Rogaland	24 x 25-benchers
Sogning	16 x 25-benchers
More	16 x 25-benchers
North More	20 x 20-benchers
Naumdale	9 x 20-benchers

This gives a total of 1 x 30-bencher (i.e. a 60-oared ship), 116 x 25-benchers (50-oared ships), and 120 x 20-benchers, plus the one vessel of indeterminate size, or 238 ships in all. A modern estimate of the number of men necessary to man this fleet is over 27,000, i.e. 100 men on a 20-bencher, 125 on a 25-bencher, and 150 on the 30-bencher (which would have been the flagship).

Raiding fleets were usually small but could vary in size, from the 3 ships of the first recorded raid in 789 to the alleged force of 700 ships and 40,000 men which besieged Paris from 885 to 886 and suffered 19,000 casualties at the hands of the Carolingian relief force. The latter figures, however, smack of chroniclers' licence and most raiding fleets probably numbered no more than 10–35 ships; Orvar Odd's Saga mentions a raiding force of 15 ships crewed by 120 men each as 'very great'.

The average Viking ship carried 65–85 or even 100 men, the smallest ship permitted in any recorded Leidang being 26 oars while 32, 40 and 50 oars were the standard, there being 2 men per oar in Scandinavian vessels. In battle, however, ships' complements could more than double so that the largest had crews well in excess of 200. Olaf Tryggvasson's famous ship the 'Long Serpent' had 68 oars (34 a side) and at Svoldr in 1000 it was crewed by 8 men per half room plus 30 extras, a total of 574 men! Other ships of similar size are recorded in the sagas (Hardrada's 70-oared 'Great Dragon' for instance), but they were uncommon and most of them probably only saw home-water service since their size might have made them unsuitable for ocean-going raids. Ships of this size only began to appear at the close of the 10th century.

The bondi levies were not regarded as altogether reliable and were frequently disbanded after only limited service if battle did not seem imminent, only Hirdmen and chieftains being retained. These alone could provide a large force – Hardrada's 150 ships at the Battle of Nissa were such.

Viking armies were commanded by kings and jarls – for instance, one Viking army recorded in Scotland was commanded by 8 kings and 20 jarls, each jarl allegedly commanding about 1,000 men. 'Kings' were either national, regional, sons of royal lines, or self-styled. The jarls were upper-rank chieftains or sons of royal lines on the mother's side.

THE RUSSIANS

Russian armies consisted largely of mercenaries and subject levies of Slavs, the original Scandinavian Rus being a minority and eventually being absorbed by the Slav population. In the 10th and early-11th centuries Varangian (Scandinavian, largely Swedish) mercenaries were a principal source of troops though they were expensive and sometimes difficult to control. By the early-11th century employment of Varangians had dropped off considerably; in an army of 1015 in which specific mention is made of the importing of Scandinavian mercenaries they appear as a corps of only 1,000 in an army of 40,000. If, on the other hand, the Chronicle of Novgorod is correct then the army consisted of only 4,000 men, in which case the 1,000 Varangians still constituted one-quarter of it. The last record of Varangians in Russian service dates to 1043.

It was the Varangians who provided the earliest Russian princes with their military escorts, the Druzhina, that of the Tmutorokan Khagan being recorded in the 10th century as 400 men. Later the Varangians were replaced by Russianised nobles, taking the Turkish title boyar, who served on a quasi-feudal basis whereby they swore an oath to the prince in exchange for food, lodging, horses and weapons, or for land. In addition Torks and Kasogians (Turkish tribes, the latter not implausibly identified with the Khazars by some authorities) were to be found in the Druzhina, as were Magyars, Ossetians (Alans) and Slavs.

The Druzhina was organised in 2 parts, the junior of which was known as the Grid, or from the late-12th century the Dvorianin. These acted as servants to the Druzhina officers, who in the 11th century included Koniushi (Marshal), Ognishchanin (Bailiff), Tiun (Steward) and Podiezdnoi (Adjutant). Each of the greater boyars had a Druzhina of his own.

The bulk of the army consisted of a general levy, the Polk, every able-bodied man being required to serve if called upon. By the 11th century the militia of the various cities was called out in preference to the peasants and farmers of the rural areas. Only on rare occasions did the latter actually serve, and then usually only in a non-military capacity, the normal system being for the towns to supply the men and the surrounding districts to supply the horses, provisions and equipment.

The militia could either serve mounted or on foot, though they tended to make poor cavalrymen and their numbers were in general considerably lower when they served as such. Either way they were not particularly high quality and tended to be impetuous and over-enthusiastic in attack and uncontrollable in retreat (or more often rout). Their main drawback as a military force, however, was that they could only be called up by the Veche, the city council, and could likewise be disbanded by it, without any consultation with the prince or commanders; this often occurred in the middle of campaigns with which the Veche disagreed.

Organisation was on a decimal basis derived from that of their Slav subjects. Officers called tisiatskii, 'thousand-man', sotskii, 'hundred-man', and desiatnikii, 'ten-man', are recorded, though later these were elected administrative officials rather than military commanders. Later, during the 12th century, each of the major cities seems to have been capable of raising 15–20,000 men for the Polk, though in 1093 it is recorded that Sviatopolk could raise only 800 men from the Kiev district at short notice. An elite thousand (tisiach) may have served as the nucleus of the city levy, and Sviatopolk's 800 may represent this in understrength form.

In addition to the Varangians other mercenaries used during this period included Pechenegs (from the mid-10th century), Khazars (sometimes possibly indicated by the name Kasogians), Poles and Hungarians (mainly in the 11th and 12th centuries, though Magyars had been employed from the 10th century), and Torks, Berendei and Koui, all Turkish tribes. The Pechenegs were employed en masse and many were even permanently settled in South Russia as allies and frontier guards from c. 1036. All mercenaries were paid for by special taxes. They were sometimes employed in such vast numbers that they constituted an entire army.

Mixed Slav and Rus fleets of 200–500, or even up to 1,000 or 1,200 ships are recorded and may have been maintained by a similar levy system to the Scandinavian Leidang. Their boats were smaller than the Viking vessels, being river rather than sea-going craft, and were often painted red. They carried between 40 and 60 men or at the very most 100.

For river-raiding the Slav monoxyla were often used, Psellus recording that the attack on Constantinople in 1043 was carried out by monoxyla. These vessels were not, as is so often assumed, dugouts as their name (which means literally a single piece of wood) suggests; 'monoxyla' is merely a reference to the fact that they had one-piece keels. Otherwise their construction was probably similar to that of Scandinavian vessels, except that they were considerably smaller.

THE SLAVS

Prior to this period the Slavs are barely recorded. The Veneti of 1st and 2nd century Greek and Roman sources may have been Slavs; the 6th century Byzantine sources certainly divide the Veneti into Sclavini and Antes, the forbears of West and East Slavs respectively.

The Antes were the ruling element in a confederation of tribes, 100,000 of whom invaded the Balkans in 581, and were possibly Slavicised Sarmatians (Alans). Though their name still occurs in the 10th century, the Antes themselves were defeated in 602 by the Avars; some were then confused with the Avars for some time, though the majority, together with many other East Slav tribes, came under Khazar control by the 9th century.

The western Slav tribes consisted principally of Poles, Pomeranians, Polabians (or Wends, of whom the chief group were the Obodrites), Bohemians and Moravians. The Pomeranians were a Baltic maritime people related to the Poles, while several tribes of Polabians, notably the Rani of the island of Rugen, were also seafarers, famed for their raids at least as early as the 11th century. Rani, Pomeranians and Polabians were all subject to strong Scandinavian influences, using Viking-style ships (in which they often carried horses on their raids) and with a veneer of Viking military aristocracy. The Rani indeed finally came under Danish control from 1168. The Bohemians became 'Germanised' early, while the Moravians, who established an organised state c. 830, fell to the Magyars in the late-9th century, becoming part of the state of Hungary.

Other major Slavic tribes included Serbs, Croats, Mazovians and Silesians. Like the Antes the Serbs and Croats (Khorvatians) were probably Slavicised Sarmatians. Many other tribes were subjects of the Avars, Khazars, Bulgars and other Asiatic peoples.

The armies of the Slavs, even in the organised confederacies, were principally on a basis of clan and tribe. Tribal chieftains were the voivodes, with the clan chieftains, the zupans, subordinate to them. These chieftains maintained Druzhinas, military retinues recruited from amongst their territories, usually cavalry such as the Pomeranian or Polabian Vitiezi (a word derived from 'Viking', indicative of their original composition). The retinue of Mieszko I of Poland recorded c. 965 as 3,000 men is typical, these being supplied by him with clothes, weapons and horses. Organisation was decimal.

The Druzhina members, called Druzynnik, were stationed in various military encampments which were the centres of local administration, fortified with earthworks and wooden stockades and each under a chieftain. Later the more powerful members of the Druzhina recruited retinues of their own from the lower classes of their administrative districts.

The cavalry of the Druzhinas supplied the nuclei of Slavic armies, backed up in times of need by a levy of peasants, organised on a decimal basis and serving as infantry, the basic unit being of 100 men.

Auxiliary cavalry are sometimes recorded as being employed, chiefly Magyars or Pechenegs but also Germans. The Germans likewise employed auxiliary troops from the Slavs, usually infantry from the pagan Wilczi or Lutitians (a Polabian tribe) for use against their Christianised Polish neighbours. Bohemian and Moravian troops were also utilised. At a somewhat earlier date the Old Saxons had been frequently allied with the Wilczi, while the Carolingians used Obodrite auxiliaries on their eastern front. Danish and other Viking auxiliaries are also recorded on occasion.

THE ASIATIC HORDES

Generally these can be spoken of as 'Turks', though racially this title is not altogether accurate. The Byzantines reserved the term 'Turk' for only 5 specific nations in their whole history, these being the original Turks, plus Magyars, Khazars, Seljuks and Osmanlis (Ottomans).

Organisation was tribal and decimal, each horde and tribe being a distinct 'military' element under the command of its chieftain, with units of 10, 100, 1,000 and 10,000 men. The largest, the tuman of 10,000, was commanded by an officer called a tarkhan.

They were normally 100 per cent cavalry but sometimes contained a small proportion of native infantry or a larger proportion of Slav subject infantry. The latter is particularly true of 6th and 7th century Avar armies, as well as Bulgar, Khazar and later Magyar armies. In addition most armies included a number of heavy cavalry, usually the nobility and their guards, armed principally with a long lance but generally carrying bow as well. In later Mongol armies up to 40 per cent might be heavy cavalry, though this high a proportion would be more than exceptional for Asiatic armies of this period. They were undoubtedly usually a minority, the bulk of the army consisting of light horse-archers.

Youths or poorly mounted men were usually left to guard the baggage and women during battle; they could constitute a fair-sized reserve, as many as one man for every 8–10 of the fighting force.

Siege equipment was employed by some Asiatic peoples, notably the Khazars and Bulgars. As with those of the Arabs, the engines were dismantled and transported on pack camels or in wagons. The Magyars also had siege engines by the mid-10th century, probably as a result of Western influence.

Troops were summoned in wartime by the passing of a war-arrow from tribe to tribe.

The Avars

The Avars were descended from a tribe called the Jwen Jwen who had been overthrown and driven west by the Turks in the 6th century, absorbing in the process the remnants of the Huns. Their very name may be a Turkish word meaning 'exiles'. They were all but destroyed by the Franks, Slavs and Bulgars in a war from 791 to 805 and are last recorded in 826.

They lived in fortified earthworks, called 'rings' by the Franks and 'camps' (felds) by the Lombards. These are described in a contemporary source as consisting of 2 banks, each of 2 rows of 20 foot high oak, beech or pine stakes, the rows set up 20 feet apart with the space between them filled up with stones and loam and covered with sods of grass. On the summit of each bank trees were planted and trained so that with their branches cut they stood like upright chevaux-de-frise. There seem to have been 9 such rings. Their armies consisted mainly of subject levies with the Avars themselves a minority group. From the 6th century Sabiri, Utigurs, Kutrigurs, Onogurs (Bulgars), Antes, Croats, Gepids and Dulebians were subjects, the Slavic elements providing the bulk of the troops. Most of these fought in self-contained units, often under Avar officers.

After the failure of their siege of Constantinople in 626, where their army is recorded as 30–80,000 strong, many of their subjects cast off allegiance to the Avars, though Slavs and Onogurs continued to form the largest part of their forces.

The Khazars

The Khazars first appeared in the Caucasus c. 586, apparently as the vanguard of the westward drive of the 10 West Turk hordes. They are usually treated as Turkic but were possibly Hunnic in origin; the Turks called them Sabir and some sources indeed call them Huns. They became fully independent after the defeat of the Turks by the Chinese and Uigurs (a Ghuzz horde), 652–659. Thereafter the Khazar Khaganate remained a major power until 965 when its chief cities of Itil and Samandar were sacked by the Rus. Khazaria, the surviving remnant of the Khaganate, was subdued in 1016 by combined Russo-Byzantine attacks but lasted for a few years more, at least until c. 1030. The last reliable mention of Khazars dates to 1083, by which time their territory consisted of a small region neighbouring Russian Tmutorokan.

After the 7th century the command, supply and training of the Khazar army was the responsibility of the Khagan's deputy, the Beg (also called Aysha, Absad or Malik in various sources) who wielded the real power. The Beg had a deputy called the Kende, beneath whom came the various tarkhans.

The Royal army consisted almost entirely of mercenaries; they received only low pay at irregular intervals, but this was supplemented by booty distributed by the Beg. These mercenaries were chiefly Arsiyah, Khwarizmian horsemen probably employed from some time in the early-8th century and constituting the only regular army of this region. Being Moslems they served only on the understanding that they should not have to fight the Khazars' Arab enemies, their co-religionists; in 965 they even refused to fight the Rus unless the Khazars agreed to become Moslems! The Arsiyah were principally horse-archers, though some served as lancers.

The strength of this standing army is recorded by various 10th century Moslem writers; Ibn Rusta c. 903 and Ibn Fozlan c. 925 say 10,000, al-Istakri c. 932 says 12,000, and al-Masudi c. 940 says 7,000. In a 3-day battle against the Rus c. 912 as many as 15,000 Arsiyah are recorded, though these included part of the population of Itil (both Moslems and Christians) serving as infantry.

Ibn Rusta's figure of 10,000 includes a levy of cavalry from the rich, these supplying their own armour and equipment as well as a number of men depending on the wealth of the individual. Al-Istakri records that the Moslems, the merchants and the villages had their own troops; the Moslems are probably Arsiyah, while the merchants are equatable to the levy from the rich. Al-Istakri also records a bodyguard of 4,000 infantry for the Khagan – these, like the Khagan, were probably Jews.

Studs of horses were maintained by the state for the Royal Army and smallish camels were also used on campaign, probably by infantry.

A second source of troops were the contingents of the Khazars' subject nations. At its greatest extent the Khaganate incorporated 25–28 such tributary peoples, the latter figure comprised of 15 to the south and 13 to the west, in addition to which there were 9 on the Volga (probably Constantine Porphyrogenitus' 'Nine Climates' – the original Khazar hordes?). Turkic auxiliaries were being supplied by c. 625 and probably earlier, while East Slavs, Alans (As) and Magyars provided troops from the early-8th century at the very latest, as probably did the Volga Bulgars. Tarkhans of Antes and Turks are recorded in later sources, and also a Tarkhan of Ras, probably Rukhs-As (the Roxolani or Light As, militarily the most important of the Alan troops, also known in 7th century sources as Rus or Ros – not to be confused with the Scandinavian Rus). Al-Masudi says the 4 hordes of the Alans could muster 30,000 first-class cavalry; he also mentions Rus and as-Saqaliba (Slav) troops, while Ibn Rusta and Gardezi record that 10,000 cavalry were levied from the Burtas. Ghuzz and Georgian auxiliaries also served on occasion.

In the early-8th century, when the Khazar Khaganate was at its greatest extent and still included the tribes of the Magyars and Volga Bulgars, contemporary sources record armies of 10–40,000 and even up to 100,000; on one occasion, in 730, an army of 300,000 is even recorded, and this probably represents their total theoretical military strength with every able-bodied man in arms.

Despite al-Masudi's statement that the Khagan 'does not possess ships nor are his men experienced in handling them', other sources, as well as other references in al-Masudi, would seem to indicate that the Khazars maintained a small fleet on the Caspian Sea (Sea of the Khazars), probably crewed by Slavs and Rus.

The Magyars

These were in origin a Finnish tribe which had begun moving west onto the steppes in the 5th century, eventually becoming subjects of the Khazars. They became independent of the Khazars in the early-9th century, the Beg's deputy, the Kende, becoming their king. They are sometimes referred to in the chronicles as Hongrois, Ungri or Ugars.

They consisted of 7 hordes, though there may once have been 10. An eighth horde, rebel Turkic mercenaries of the Khazars called Kavars, joined them in their move west into modern Hungary and held the pre-eminent position. Each horde, led by a voivode, consisted of a number of clans. The bodyguard of the Kende was unrelated to these clans and probably consisted of the Kavars; early-10th century sources record this escort as 10–20,000 men.

Military command was in the hands of the Kende's deputy, the Gylas, with an officer called the Karchas (or Horka) as his second-in-command. 3 other officers – the Kourt, Tarianos and Genach – gave their names to 3 of the hordes. The office of Gylas lasted until 1003.

The greatest recorded army of Magyars was that of 100,000 at the Battle of Lechfield in 955. Although the figure seems an exaggeration, the chronicler qualifies it by saying that the Magyars had mustered every able-bodied man. Their leader, Bulcsu, was the Karchas. One contemporary source quotes an even larger (though improbable) figure for the Magyars, claiming that at the time of their westward drive their 7 hordes totalled 216,000 men divided into 108 equal-sized clans of 2,000.

After their conquest of Hungary Slav and German auxiliaries are also recorded, and Pechenegs were employed from 1051; there were quite probably many Slavs in the army at Lechfield, which would help to explain its size. Another auxiliary force was supplied by the Szekely or Siculi (apparently meaning 'guardians'), a remnant of the Huns or Avars who still resided in Hungary at the time of the Magyar conquest. As ferocious as their new overlords, and fighting in like fashion, they were entrusted with the defence of the eastern frontiers of the Magyar state.

The Danube Bulgars

The Onogurs appeared after the disintegration of the Hunnic Empire, the collapse of Hun power resulting from their decisive defeat at the hands of their Germanic subject peoples at the Battle of Nedao in 454. The Onogur tribes, together with the Kutrigur and Utigur Huns, then became subjects of the Avars in the mid-6th century and remained so until, taking advantage of the decline of Avar power after 626, they seceded in 638. Once independent they generally adopted the name Bulgar, which first appeared as early as 482. In c. 650 many of these Bulgar tribes became subject to the Khazars, though some escaped to the Danube region where they remained independent.

These Danube Bulgars were largely Slavicised by the end of the 7th century. As early as 705, when Khan Tervel sent a large army to assist Justinian II, Slavic elements constituted a considerable proportion of the army, undoubtedly serving as infantry to supplement the 15,000 Bulgar cavalry (which represented the total Bulgar strength available to Tervel, probably meaning his own retinue – see below). Danube Bulgar armies were always largely Slav, though veneered with a Bulgar military aristocracy. Slavs were often officered by Bulgars.

Military command was in the hands of an officer called the Kavkhan, second only to the Khan himself, though by the 11th century the office may have been split between 2 men. Beneath him came the tarkhans, whose functions were comparable to those of Byzantine strategoi, then kalutarkhans and buliastarkhans. The greater and lesser nobility, boyars and bagaturs, often commanded field armies (as many as 12,000 men were commanded by a boyar in 773).

There were 10 tarkhans in the mid-9th century, giving a total strength of 100,000 men. However, these were not permanent troops, the Khan's retinue or Threptoi Anthropoi, 'Kept Men', together with the retinues of the nobility constituting the only standing army, these being maintained and payed even in peacetime. The general levy summoned in wartime was unpaid except for any plunder which might be taken and divided amongst them.

Armies probably did not generally exceed the 20–30,000 mark; Krum, for instance, had 30,000 men in 813, certainly all armoured and probably all cavalry, including Slavs and Avars or Onogurs, while 32,000 men faced a Rus attack in 967. The 20,000 casualties recorded in a victory over the Magyars in 896 is an exception and may include the casualties of their Pecheneg allies.

One other feature of Bulgar organisation was the Great Fence, an earthwork defence line along the Byzantine-Bulgarian border probably erected in the early-9th century. It was sometimes garrisoned but apparently not often.

The Volga Bulgars

The Onogurs who fled to the Volga in an attempt to escape the Khazars were also usually referred to as Bulgars, often as Silver or White Bulgars, though some tribes appear to have retained the name Onogur. A further group remaining in the Kuban region – the old Great Bulgaria – were known as Black Bulgars. They were probably gradually absorbed by successive waves of Khazars, Magyars, Pechenegs and Cumans.

Although these Volga Bulgars had a degree of autonomy from the mid-8th century, they probably only became fully independent of the Khazars after 965.

They consisted of 3 principal hordes, the Barzula, Ishkil and Balkar, each under a Malik, with at least 2 large sub-groups, the Suwar and al-Barandjar. Despite being initially subject to the Khazars they had their own ruler, the Yiltuwar (later given the title of Amir under Moslem influence), and an independent army of some 20–50,000 cavalry. Some non-Bulgar peoples, such as the Burta, Yura, Wisu and many other Finnish and Slavic tribes, became subject to them at different times. These subject peoples included the Baskirs, a savage 'Turkic' people related to the Magyars, who in the 10th century Idrisi records as some 2,000 strong.

The Volga Bulgars lasted until 1237 when they were conquered by the Mongols.

The Pechenegs

The Pechenegs, the Patzinaks of Byzantine sources, are first recorded in the early-9th century and were probably originally a Ghuzz tribe. They consisted of 8 hordes and 40 clans. Of the 8 main hordes, 3, the Iabdiertim, Kouartzitzur and Chabouxingula (or Charoboi), were the senior and were titled Kangar, possibly meaning 'noble'; the other 5 hordes were the Kato Gyla, Syroukalpei, Borotalmat, Giazichopon and Boulatzopon. Later 13 hordes are recorded.

They were finally defeated by the Byzantines in 1122, the survivors either being forcibly settled as military colonists or sold into slavery. Though unreliable they had regularly served as mercenaries with the Byzantines before, and were also employed by the Magyars from 1051. Those in Magyar service are last recorded in 1146, by which time they were probably being absorbed by the native population.

A 13th century source refers to the Pechenegs as a Cuman horde, though these were probably only a remnant. Others became absorbed by the Karakalpak or 'Black Cap' federation of tribes, first recorded in 1146. The Pechenegs last appear as an independent people in 1152.

Armies of 20–50,000 frequently appear in Byzantine sources, and during negotiations in 1087 the Pechenegs promised to supply 30,000 men to the Byzantine army, representing only a tithe of their strength. Cedrenus records their fighting strength as 800,000 in 1048, though he is notorious for his exaggerations.

The Ghuzz

These originated in the 7th century as a federation of 9 hordes called the Tokuz Oghuz who revolted against the West Turks. Elements of this federation began moving west in the 9th century and are thereafter referred to as Ghuzz (the Arabic form of the Turkic Oghuz or Byzantine Ouzoi). From the late-10th century the name Turcoman was also applied to some parts of this nation; the variant names Tork and Uz also appear.

They were ruled by a Yabghu, with a deputy called the Kudharkin and a military commander-in-chief. By the 11th century they appear to have consisted of 22–24 hordes, and their military strength is recorded as greater than that of the Pechenegs.

After heavy defeats in Russia in the mid-11th century 600,000 of the survivors invaded the Balkans in 1064 to escape. In 1065, after initial successes against the Byzantines, they were decimated by plague and famine and defeated by Pechenegs and Bulgarians, and the Byzantines then settled many of the survivors as military colonists in Macedonia. Except for a multitude of minor tribes scattered in Asia Minor and the Near East they thereafter virtually disappeared as an independent people, though together with the Pechenegs they sometimes appear as subjects in later Cuman armies and many were finally absorbed into the Karakalpak federation. The surviving minor tribes were generally referred to from now on by the name Turcomans.

Their neighbours, the Qarakhanids, appear to have been related since they too are sometimes referred to as Turcomans, though their armies appear to have been of a heterogenous nature, even including people of Mongol stock on occasion. They were clearly influenced by Ghaznavid organisation by the early-11th century, the nucleus of their army being a small corps of Royal Ghulams, 500–1,000 being recorded in a campaign of 1007–1008 which saw an army of 50,000. The Qarakhanids were conquered by the Seljuks in 1073.

The Seljuks, who were more important after the close of this period, were themselves a Ghuzz horde. They had taken their name from a semi-legendary chieftain of c. 956 called Seljuq who had hired himself and his followers out to a Khazar prince. They were employed by the Samanids against the Qarakhanids in the late 10th century, and later by the Ghaznavids, against whom they revolted in 1037. By 1055 they had become firmly established in the Euphrates region, but continued to hire themselves out as troops to the Byzantines and others. A large part of their military strength was supplied by subject Turcoman tribesmen.

THE ARABS

From the Caliphate of Mu'awiya (660–680) Arab armies ceased to be purely Arab in composition and became increasingly multi-racial. Their forces included true Arabs, with preference initially given to those tribes which had fought for Mohammed in the religious Ridda wars; Iranians, Khorasanians, Iraqis and even Indians, inhabitants of those regions which previously formed the Sassanid Empire; Egyptians, Copts and Syrians, inhabitants of the ex-Byzantine provinces; Berbers, who were North African tribesmen, converted to Islam in the late-7th century; Mawali, these being non-Moslem troops, including Christians, or converted non-Arabs; and religious extremist groups, principally the Khawarij.

Of these the Egyptians and Syrians supplied the bulk of Arab fleets, that of Egypt being the largest and crewed in the early period largely by Egyptian Christians, who assisted without too much objection in the Arab sieges of Constantinople in 668–675 and 716–717! Otherwise non-Moslems were mainly infantry, the cavalry arm remaining principally Arab in the earliest part of this period, although the Christian Armenians were obliged to supply 15,000 cavalry on request as early as 653. Non-Moslems and Mawali were usually unpaid but were rewarded with booty.

The Khawarij lived in frontier communities raiding non-Islamic lands as part of their religious duties and were often openly hostile to the Caliphate. They were regarded as vastly superior soldiers to the average Arab and were willing to fight to the death in their fanaticism. Their dress was distinctively different from the Arabs, though it is not known in what way; however, another group of religious extremists, the Khurramis, wore red shirts, and Khawarij standards were certainly red.

In organisation the Arabs adopted many characteristics of the Byzantines and Sassanids; some tribes had been trained by these before the beginning of the Moslem era, while many Sassanid warrior-class nobles (the Asavira) who had constituted the clibanarii heavy cavalry were employed by the Arab victors after the conquest of Persia, bringing with them organisational traits as well as typically Persian armour and weapons, which survived in the East in almost unchanged form throughout this era and into the Middle Ages. However, despite attempts by Mu'awiya to organise regular army units, the Arabs continued up to the Caliphate of Marwan II (745–747) to fight in their traditional, unequal sized tribal units, which as early as 637 had however been subdivided into units of 10 men (irafas) each under a related tribal commander.

The system recorded to have then been introduced by Marwan is a straight borrowing from the Macedonian organisation described in Asclepiodotus. It was based on a unit of 8 archers or 16 spearmen called a safh almaqatir. Next came the usbah of 32 men, either 4 archer or 2 spear units. Units then progressively doubled:

Miqnab	64 men
Kurdus	128 men
Jahfal	256 men
Kabkahah	512 men
Zumrah	1,024 men
Taifah	2,048 men
Jash	4,096 men

| Khamis | 8,192 men |
| Al-askar al-azam | 16,384 men |

Although this system may never have been fully used in practice it is worth noting that the saff al-maqatir is comparable to the Byzantine lochaghia and the jahfal to the arithmos or infantry bandon. Of all these units only the kurdus appears in practice, one source claiming that it was first employed at Yarmuk in 636 in imitation of Byzantine units.

Other sources record cavalry units called khamsah (5 men), ashrah (10–20 men), tablikhanah (80 men) and alf (1,000 men); and also infantry units called katibah (500–800 men) and faylaq (5,000 men). These are partially compatible to the decimal organisation recorded elsewhere to have been employed under the Abbasid Caliphs, with units of 10, 50, 100 and 1,000 under an 'arif, khalifa, qa'id and amir respectively.

Also during the Abbasid period special naffatun (naptha troops) were attached to each of the larger archer units. They wore protective clothing consisting of padded asbestos garments, and were equipped with mangonels and catapults, as well as small pots of incendiaries to be thrown by hand.

An adoption of Byzantine practice is evident in the establishment during the early conquests of military districts reminiscent of the Themata. These districts were called Junds, 'Jund' meaning literally 'army', and the earliest 4 – Homs, Damascus, Jordan and Palestine – correspond to the pre-conquest Byzantine Syrian provinces. Each of these districts was settled by tribesmen of related clans, who were responsible both for the defence of their own district and of the whole Syrian province. They were based on fortified camps, each consisting of a circular earthwork, with 4 gates, within which tents or houses were erected. These Syrian Junds came to be the nucleus of the early Arab armies, supplying a full-time force whose members served on a rotary basis; the Jund of Kufa, operating on a similar rotary system as early as 644, obliged each man to one year's service in every 4 years, maintaining 10,000 men in the field at all times. By 741 the Junds of Horns, Damascus, Jordan and Palestine could field 6,000 cavalry and infantry each, and those of Qinnasrin, added by Yazid I (680–683), and Egypt 3,000 each, while the total strengths of the various individual provinces in the 7th and 8th centuries varied between 10,000 and 40,000 men.

All these men were listed in the Diwans, registers, and paid regular stipends for their services. Originally pay came at 40 day intervals, later lengthened to 50 or even 60 days. Some ghulams (see below) were paid more regularly, once a month, while free troops might only be paid 2 or 3 times in a year. However the latter were also allocated a large percentage of the booty of each campaign, sometimes only serving on the understanding that there was booty to be had.

Under the Abbasids 'Khorasanian' guard units, totalling as many as 30,000 men by 779, replaced the Syrian Junds as the army nucleus. However, before long mercenary slave-troops, ghulams, displaced these, equipment generally being supplied by regimental or provincial commanders. Such troops are first recorded on a small scale in 809.

Although Caliph al-Mu'tasim (833–842) is usually credited with their general introduction, purchasing 3,000 Turks as slave-soldiers at the end of al-Mamun's Caliphate and employing 10,000 of them as well as perhaps 30,000 blacks by the end of his own, they were clearly in limited use earlier than the 9th century, a black slave-soldier even being recorded as early as 625 in an incident at the Battle of Ohud, while 1,000 black slaves took part in a battle in 638 and Slav and Berber slave-troops are mentioned on occasion under the Umayyad Caliphs.

The ghulams were principally Turks but also included Berbers, Zanj, Nubians, Kurds, Daylamis, Slavs, Khazars, Byzantines, Georgians, Armenians and even Rus, though the latter may have been free mercenaries. Some were eunuchs, and the white slaves were properly called mamluks, the name under which they rose to their greatest power in the 13th century. There were strong enmities between the various distinct ghulam corps, particularly the Turks, Berbers, Nubians and Slavs, often leading to bloodshed.

These ghulam troops grew rapidly in numbers, the only restriction to the number employed being the depth of the employer's purse; figures of up to 70,000 are recorded in Arab sources during the 10th century. By the end of this period many employers, embarrassed by a constant need for cash to maintain their troops, had resorted to making grants of land, called iqta'at, to support them; this was particularly true of the eastern amirates, where the iqta' had first been introduced by the Buyids in the 10th century. That the service of the ghulam regiments was on a personal basis, however, must be emphasised – on the death of their employer they practically ceased to exist, though usually surviving in some form until members died out or found similar employment elsewhere. Either way any land grants they had held generally reverted back to their late employer's successor or replacement, for granting to his own troops. The personal tie is also evident in the practice, current from the beginning of the 10th century, whereby many, if not most, regiments bore their master's (or sometimes their commander's) name, e.g. Nasiriyyah, from al-Nasir. Other regiments might be named after their place of origin, such as the Sudaniyyah and Rumiyyah, from the Sudan and the 'Roman' lands (i.e. Byzantium) respectively.

Detachments were taken from the various regiments to form the Caliph's guards, usually 10,000 strong. In addition to this Guard there was also the Caliph's personal bodyguard of freed slaves, the al-Ghilman al-Khassa; that of the Fatimid Caliph al-Mustansir recorded c.1047 as 1,000 cavalry and infantry is typical.

Before long the provincial amirs began to employ their own slave-troops, often in vast numbers – in Egypt Ahmad ibn Tulun (himself an ex-ghulam) had 24,000 Turk and 45,000 Nubian slaves in his army in the late-9th century and elsewhere the Tulunid army is recorded as 100,000. Not surprisingly such amirs began to seize personal control of their provinces through their own ghulams, and before long the independent participation of powerful ghulam regiments in political unrests resulted in the total destruction of several, the Masifiyyah being the first in 930.

This disloyalty was contrary to the original purpose of employing ghulams, which was that their lack of personal ties would make them completely loyal to their employers. Finally, under as-Salih Ayyub (1240–1249) vast numbers of Kipchak Turks were employed, from amongst whom was formed the Bahriyyah regiment which overthrew the Ayyubids and established the Mamluk state.

The ghulam slave troops, although providing the nucleus and bulk of Arab armies, were usually supplemented by free troops such as Bedouins, generally in smaller numbers, usually paid less, and who were far less reliable on the battlefield. There were often Ghazis too, volunteers fighting for the glory of God, and loot – not necessarily in that order. Ghazis were particularly common in raiding parties, both on land and sea, and by the 10th century were widely regarded, even amongst Arabs, as bandits and corsairs rather than defenders of their faith. On occasion the eastern amirates used peasant levies, the Hashariyan, for infantry but these were too timid to be of any use whatsoever and like their Sassanid predecessors usually ran at the commencement of battle. The Saffarids (867–908) and Ghaznavids (962–1186) employed Afghan and Indian contingents, principally infantry.

Total strength of the 'regular' army under the Sufyanid Umayyads (661–684) was 60,000 men. By the reign of Marwan II it had doubled, and under Haroun al-Raschid (786–809) reached 135,000. However, under alMamun it had declined fractionally to 125,000. In 917 it is recorded as 160,000 cavalry and infantry.

Just before the end of this period, c. 1047–1054, the total strength of the Fatimid regular army of al-Mustansir (1036–1094) was recorded as 100,000 infantry and 115,000 cavalry:

infantry consisting of 20,000 Masmudis (Berbers from Morocco)

30,000 Zanj (Ethiopian blacks)

10,000 'Easterners' (Turks and Persians)

30,000 'Bought Slaves' (Sudanese blacks)

10,000 Seraiyan ('Palace Guards' of mixed origins)

and cavalry of   50,000 Bedouins

20,000 Ifriqiyans (Tunisians)

15,000 Batilis (Moroccans and Algerians)

30,000 of mixed origins, blacks and others

Medical Staff

Physicians and surgeons accompanied Arab armies from the reign of Haroun al-Raschid onwards. Camels fitted with litters were used to transport the wounded.

Artillery

The Arabs soon learnt to use artillery, probably basing their own on those of the Byzantines and Sassanids. Together with other siege equipment their engines were usually dismantled and carried in pieces on the backs of camels.

The small engines were called 'arradah, which like the Roman onager meant 'wild donkey'. The larger engines were called manganiq; unlike the Byzantine manganika these were often trebuchets, recorded as early as 665 in the siege of Constantinople, the names 'Mother of the Scalp' or 'Long-haired' recorded for a manganiq a few years later being indicative of the hanging ropes used in their operation. They also used ballistae.

ANDALUSIA

The 'Arab' invasion army which defeated the Visigoths at the Transductine Promontories in 711 numbered 12,000 men including only 300 Arab cavalry, the remainder being Berber infantry. However these were reinforced in 712 by another 10–18,000 Arabs and Syrians. In 741 they were further reinforced by the 10,000 survivors (out of 27,000) of the Syrian Junds of Horns, Damascus, Jordan, Palestine and Qinnasrin, which had been severely manhandled by Berber rebels in

North Africa. Their leader, with the Jordan contingent, settled in Cordoba, the Horns contingent settled in Seville, that of Damascus in Elvira, Qinnasrin in Jaen, and Palestine in Algeciras and Medina Sidonia. It was through these Junds, staunch supporters of his dynasty, that an Umayyad exile, 'Abd ar-Rahman, became Amir of Cordoba in 756. These Spanish Umayyads assumed the title of Caliph under 'Abd ar-Rahman III (912–961) and lasted down to 1031, after which the Caliphate disintegrated into a number of minor amirates (the Taifa kingdoms) which were steadily absorbed by the Spaniards until conquered by Murabit Berbers in 1090.

'Abd ar-Rahman I (756–788) established an army of 40,000 mercenary Berbers imported from North Africa (he distrusted the Junds), as well as a Black Guard – the first recorded regular black unit in a Moslem army. The latter at least was organised on a decimal basis, consisting of 2 units of 1,000 men, each divided into 10 companies of 100.

Thereafter Andalusian Umayyad armies comprised 5 principal elements, these being: (1) the native regulars from those districts owing military service, i.e. the old Junds whose obligations were hereditary; (2) temporary volunteers called hashid or 'recruits' who were enlisted for a single expedition; (3) religious volunteers called mujahids or al-murabitun who lived in fortified frontier communities called ribats, to whom fighting the Christians was a religious duty; (4) permanent units of foreign mercenaries, the murtaziqa, paid regular salaries; and (5) irregular foreign mercenaries called muttawi'a whose only pay, like that of the mujahids, came at the end of the campaign in the form of booty and other gratuities. In addition 'Abd ar-Rahman II, who ruled in the mid-9th century, made military service compulsory for all Andalusians, but they do not seem to have often been called on to fulfil this obligation.

Under al-Hakam I (796–822) the army was comprised chiefly of Berbers and blacks but also included Christians (the commanding officer of his bodyguard bearing the title of comes) both from Northern Spain and even beyond the Pyrenees. His famous Guard, established c. 807, consisted of 2,000 infantry and 3,000 cavalry and was called al-Khurs ('The Mutes' or 'The Silent Ones'), since none of its members could speak Arabic! In total the standing army at his disposal numbered 50,000 men, a mixture of mercenaries and ghulams. 2,000 of them were permanently posted along the banks of the River Guadalquivir on the frontier with the Christians, this force being divided into 20 units of 100 horsemen each under an officer called an 'arif.

Masudi, writing c. 940, records the total strength of Caliph 'Abd ar-Rahman III's standing army as an unlikely 100,000, which required one-third of Andalusia's total revenue for its maintenance. An alternative source records the higher figure of 150,000, adding that his bodyguard numbered 12,000 men of whom 8,000 were cavalry. It was he who introduced formal unit organisation into the Andalusian army, based on a corps of 5,000 men under an amir; within this were 5 units of 1,000, each under a qa'id, subdivided into 5 units of 200 men under naqibs, in turn comprised of 5 units of 40 men each under an 'arif. The smallest unit consisted of 8 men under a nazir.

By the mid-10th century the royal bodyguard of ghulams is recorded as 3,750 men, all 'Slavs', though in Spain the term was by this time used for Franks, Lombards and Spaniards as well as true Slavs. This Slav guard was disbanded c. 978 by the vizier Ibn Abi Amir (better known as al-Mansur, 976–1002) who distrusted its members, but Slav ghulams continued to be employed down to 1031. Nor did al-Mansur trust the native Arab aristocracy, and he resolved to totally reorganise the army by abolishing the tribal units, the Junds, on which it was still based. Many of these were thereafter exempted from military service in return for a cash payment, the money being used to hire large numbers of Berbers from North Africa plus considerably smaller numbers of Christian cavalry from Leon, Castile and Navarre. All these plus Arabs and blacks he intermixed in regular regiments without regard for family or patron so as to eliminate tribal jealousies. Al-Mansur allegedly increased Andalusia's armed forces to as many as 600,000 men (probably 60,000), the large Berber element transforming the army into a practically all-cavalry force,

The name Andalusia derives from the Arabic al-Andalus, 'The Land of the Vandals'.

CHRISTIAN SPAIN

In the early period after the Moslem conquest Visigothic organisation appears to have persisted virtually unchanged in those corners of Spain that remained in Christian hands. However, as territory was steadily regained from the Moslems military organisation underwent steady change.

A system of landholding, originally instituted by the Frankish marcher lords (who had been established in Northern Spain by Charlemagne), evolved in the 9th century in the granting of tracts of wasteland in exchange for their cultivation. These grants were called aprisiones, which tended to become allodial possessions. Nevertheless many of the landed nobility thus created were obliged to perform mounted military service for either the king or their own overlords, though others served in exchange for cash payments and yet others served simply as an obligation of their social status. The king's own vassals, irrespective of which category they individually belonged to, were the fideles or milites regis. The bands of retainers such nobles led were usually maintained at their own expense.

Up to the close of the 10th century some of the Christian states acknowledged the overlordship of the Umayyad Amir, later Caliph, of Cordoba, which gave them the opportunity to expand steadily at the expense of their Moslem neighbours, securing their gains by the construction of forts. These were garrisoned from the 10th century onwards by regular troops paid for by taxes levied from the surrounding lands. Few of these soldiers held land of their own so they were not feudal troops, particularly since the majority were non-noble. As the frontiers expanded similar non-noble mounted soldiers called caballeros villanos, freemen of sufficient income and property to own a horse, came to owe service in exchange for non-hereditable grants of conquered land called caballerias, infantry similarly owing military service for smaller grants of land called peonias; both of these types began to appear in the middle to late 10th century.

As in Andalusia military service was technically owed by all able-bodied freemen but was likewise rarely called upon, warfare being largely a matter of raids and counter-raids launched by the nobles' mounted bands, these sometimes penetrating as far south as Lisbon and Cordoba itself. However, when required infantry could be raised by a levy of one man out of every 3 by the 10th century, the other 2 of the trio paying for his rations and supplying an animal for his transport, presumably a donkey or mule since all men with horses were automatically obliged to serve as cavalry.

In addition Moslem mercenaries can often be found in Christian employ, though their numbers were smaller than in succeeding centuries. At the very end of this era we also find multinational armies fighting alongside the Spaniards in the role of proto-crusaders; Frenchmen, Normans, Aquitanians and Burgundians are encountered in this guise in 1064, and Papal and Italo-Norman contingents are also claimed by some authorities. Two sources even claim that French knights had been regularly crossing the Pyrenees to assist in the Reconquista since Sancho the Great of Navarre's reign (1000–1035).

THE SAXONS

The basis of Saxon organisation was the obligation of every freeman of 15–60 years to perform military service, constituting the Fyrd. Service was only due in the locality of each respective shire and for one day only, pay being necessary if any additional service was required. A 15 day period of service seems to have been more usual on the Welsh and Scottish borders. Being inadequately trained and ill-armed the general Fyrd, often referred to as the 'Great Fyrd', was rarely summoned except in emergencies, such as large-scale attacks.

Fyrd service was more often on a selective basis, with one man serving from each 5 hides of land. He was generally expected to have helmet, mail corselet and provisions for 2 months, or 4 shillings a hide, normally supplied by the other land-holders within the 5 hide unit in proportion to the land they held. However, the size of a hide varied from region to region and was not even used in the ex-Danelaw, where it has been estimated that one man served from each 6 carucates (an unknown land measure), or Kent, where service was assessed in sulungs. Towns were assessed at 1–20 men depending on their size in 5 hide units. Unlike the Great Fyrd this 'Select Fyrd' served beyond its own borders and even overseas under Cnut. The Tribal Hidage, a late-10th century copy of an earlier original, lists the total hidage of Mercia, Wessex, Kent, Lindsey, Elmet, Hwicce, East and South Saxons, East Angles and various smaller regions at over 230,000, giving a Select Fyrd service for the listed areas as well over 45,000 men at one man per 5 hides.

By the 11th century thanes (lesser noblemen) usually held estates of 5 hides of land, so that they probably constituted the bulk of the Select Fyrd. They were also obliged to enforce the military service of the other men on their estates and took command of the local contingents. If no thane were present within a 5 hide unit then the military service was performed by one of the upper-class peasants, called variously cnichts, radmanni or geneats.

Alfred the Great (871–899) reorganised the West Saxon Select Fyrd so that it served at only half strength, the other half remaining at home to continue with agricultural chores. The second half replaced the first when their period of service had expired, thus theoretically doubling the period for which an army could be maintained in the field. However, the first part did not always wait to be relieved before disbanding! The first mention of this split Fyrd appears under the year 893 in the Anglo-Saxon Chronicle; it is last mentioned in 920.

The service of the Select Fyrd was for a period of 60 days. However, this service was apparently not an annual obligation but an obligation in time of war, so it might be – and on occasion was – summoned more than once in a year; the Chronicle records the Fyrd being called up 5 times in 1016. Obviously under such circumstances the full service of

60 days was not anticipated on each subsequent summons. Failure to serve usually resulted in a fine of 40 shillings or 100 shillings for Great or Select Fyrd respectively, while a thane could lose his lands. Desertion could invoke a death penalty if the king were present in the army. Organisation was in shires and, later, in earldoms. Lesser organisation may have been decimal, based originally on the hundred of land. This would similarly give rise to a unit of 20 men in the Select Fyrd.

As well as Fyrd service, other military obligations involved work upon bridges and fortresses, sometimes dismantling those of the enemy. Garrison duty in fortified burhs was required in some regions; 2 related documents record that an acre's breadth of wall should be maintained and manned by 16 hides, each hide represented by one man. Garrison duty appears to have exempted those who took part from Fyrd service.

In addition to the Fyrd levies, Saxon kings and nobles were accompanied from the earliest times by a personal retinue or bodyguard of warriors, usually referred to as a Hearth-troop or Hird. These warriors were lesser noblemen called successively eorls, gesiths or thanes from the 7th to the 11th centuries, and distinguished as either dugud, 'veterans', or geogud, young inexperienced warriors. Those noblemen who served in the king's retinue were distinguished as King's Thanes. These the king often supplied with equipment, armour and weapons as gifts, though they were returned on the retainer's death unless he died in battle, upon which they passed to his family. This was the heriot, still in existence in the 10th and 11th centuries. A 10th century source records the heriot of an ealdorman as 4 swords, 4 byrnies, 4 helmets, 4 saddles and trappings, 8 horses, 8 spears and 8 shields, plus 4 gold armbands; in Cnut's time the heriot of a thane consisted of a horse, saddle, sword, spear, helmet, shield and byrnie, or an amount of gold, and a King's Thane 4 times as much except for saddles and swords of which 2 were required. These amounts can probably be taken as average heriots.

The ealdorman was senior to the King's Thane, being an upper-class thane living on his own estate rather than serving in the king's retinue. During the 9th and 10th centuries this title gradually gave way to the Scandinavian jarl, or rather its Anglo-Saxon equivalent eorl (earl).

Mercenaries were another source of troops. Welshmen are occasionally mentioned in this context, but Vikings provided the bulk of such troops. Large numbers were employed under Ethelred the Unready under such notable leaders as Olaf Tryggvasson and the Jomsviking Thorkel the Tall. There were Scandinavian mercenaries at Stamford

Bridge, and possibly Danes even appeared in the Saxon army at Hastings in 1066.

Most famous of all the Viking mercenaries were the Huscarls, a permanent body of royal household troops based on the Jomsvikings and living by a strict military code. Flateyjarbok claims that Swein Forkbeard introduced them into England prior to his death in 1014, though they may have existed in Saxon employ late in Ethelred's reign in the form of the contingents of Thorkel the Tall and others. They were divided into 2 corps based in London and an unknown northern site called Slessvik, almost certainly near York. Other Scandinavian sources, however, record that Cnut was responsible for their introduction, probably c. 1018. The later Danish chroniclers Sven Aggeson and Saxo Grammaticus record the strength of the Huscarls as 3,000 and 6,000 men respectively, Saxo stating that they were distributed amongst 60 ships, presumably at 100 men per ship. However, Sven's figure is more convincing, particularly since it can be tied in with the 40 ships retained by Cnut in 1018 if an average of 75 men per ship is assumed.

Together with the Hirdrnen and the other Scandinavian mercenaries, the lithsmen and butsecarls, who all came to be included as Huscarls in the more general sense, they were paid for by the Danegeld or Heregeld, the Army Tax, levied at a rate of 1–2 shillings on the hide. This tax was introduced in 1012, abolished in 1051 and then apparently reintroduced late in the reign of Edward the Confessor (1042–1066). Additional payment came from special taxes specifically for the payment of mercenaries, fines for failure to serve in the Fyrd, and voluntary payments in lieu of military service, the latter becoming known in the post-Conquest period as scutage.

The Huscarls were at first usually near the king, though by 1066 they were sometimes supported by grants of land, upon which they might reside. Edward the Confessor used the Huscarls as garrison troops at strategic points, while during his reign the greater earls began to imitate the royal bodyguard by raising their own bodies of Huscarls; Earl Tostig is recorded to have had 200 of his Huscarls killed by Northumbrian rebels in 1065 while others escaped alive, suggesting a minimum total strength of 250–300. The royal Huscarls probably remained around 3–4,000 strong. They were the nucleus of the army, improving morale and bolstering the Fyrd levies.

Armies were generally led by the king himself, otherwise by his deputy, usually an earldorman or earl though sometimes a bishop. However there is one recorded instance when an army not only refused to fight but even disbanded because the king was not present. In later times an earl would lead a force composed of the Fyrds from several shires, each commanded by its own shire-reeve.

The Navy

Because of the frequency of Viking raids an important element in England's defence was the fleet, particularly from the late-9th century. A fleet is mentioned as early as the reign of Edwin of Northumbria (617–633), and even prior to the reign of Alfred the Great Saxon ships had been capable of defeating the Vikings at sea. However, the ships designed and introduced by Alfred were almost twice as long as the Viking ships (some having 60 oars or more), as well as being higher-sided and of a generally different design to either Frisian or Scandinavian vessels. At first they were crewed largely by Frisians.

These ships, and usually the crews too, were obtained by the Select Fyrd system. Each unit of 300 (or 310) hides, called a ship-soke, was expected to produce a ship when requested; on the basis of the 5 hide system it would have also produced a crew of 60 (or 62) men, though since this is insufficient to man the vessel we should perhaps assume that for naval service each 5 hides provided 2 men, which would give us a more realistic crew of 120–124 men. Service was for 60 days as on land. The 3,600 ships recorded by Florence of Worcester to have been mustered annually by Edgar (959–975) probably represents the total number of vessels that could be raised by this system; Edgar divided them into northern, eastern and western fleets, which sailed back and forth along the English coastline throughout each summer. This practice of mustering the Fyrd fleet even in peacetime died out under Ethelred the Unready. Cnut may have raised some 350 ships by this Fyrd levy in 1026, and 40 years later Harold appears to have mustered 700 ships by the same means in the fateful summer of 1066.

In addition Edward the Confessor made an agreement with such southern seaports as Dover, Sandwich, Romney, Fordwich, Hastings and Hythe for naval service. They were exempted from the obligations of the land Fyrd but had instead to provide a large number of ships. Domesday Book records both Dover and Sandwich owing the service of 20 small ships (each crewed by 23 men) for 15 days annually. The service of the other ports was probably similar.

Mercenary ships were also employed; in 1012 Ethelred took Thorkel the Tall into his service with 45 ships. Cnut maintained 40 such Danish ships and under his sons a mercenary fleet continued to be manned by Danes, as were Hardacnut's 60 ships recorded in 1040. Even Edward the Confessor maintained 14 Danish ships, though he dismissed 9 in 1049 and the last 5 in 1051. However, even in 1066 Scandinavian mercenary seamen, called lithsmen, were still being employed. These, like the butsecarles, were amphibious warriors who fought on land or sea as required, those recorded in 1066 being in Harold's army which marched to Stamford Bridge. Merchant vessels and captured Viking ships were also pressed into service when needed.

THE NORMANS

The Duchy of Normandy was settled by Vikings, probably Danes, when the French king Charles the Simple granted it to Hrolf Gange in 911 so that he might protect it from other Viking raiders. By the end of the 10th century the Normans had discarded many of their own ways in favour of the French, apparently supplying Charles with a contingent of cavalry as early as 923, though at the same time Duke Richard I was still described as a 'pirate chief' even as late as 996!

Their organisation was feudal and substantially French, noblemen supplying troops to the Duke who in turn supplied a contingent to his overlord the King of France, a duty which ultimately became little more than nominal. They fought in small units called conrois, each consisting of a nobleman and his knights and retainers, usually about 25 men and rarely more than 40. (Interestingly Norman mercenaries revolting against the Byzantines in Italy similarly organised themselves in units of 25.)

The number of troops such a feudal vassal could raise actually depended, as in France, on the amount of land he held. The knights required were generally in multiples of 5, who were usually accompanied in addition by their lesser retainers fighting either as infantry or less well-equipped cavalry – the following of Robert Guiscard when he first departed Normandy in the mid-11th century is recorded in a Byzantine source as 5 cavalry and 30 infantry, which can be taken as typical in its proportions. Often only the knights were apparently summoned, which may explain the absence of Norman infantry in most sources. The Normans preferred auxiliary infantry – Italian militia, Saracen mercenaries and Saxon fyrd are all recorded in the immediate post-1066 period, the 2 former even appearing on occasion prior to that date. As in France, however, infantry could be raised by the retro bannus or Arriere-Ban, a general levy of able-bodied freemen comparable to the Saxon Great Fyrd and likewise not obliged to serve beyond the borders of its locality; smaller numbers of better quality infantry were obtainable by a selective levy supplied by the towns. The Arriere-Ban was organised in regional contingents apparently under parish priests.

The service due to the Duke by the nobility was only obligatory within the Duchy itself so that for the greatest Norman enterprise of all, the invasion of England in 1066, Duke William had to employ large numbers of mercenaries. Normandy itself thereafter remained part of the English kingdom until its loss to the French in 1204.

Often overlooked is the Norman enterprise in Italy, where the first Norman mercenaries were fighting with an Apulian rebel leader, Melus, from c. 1015 until the Battle of Cannae against the Byzantines in 1018, when 250 Norman knights were involved. Thereafter Normans took service as mercenaries with most of the southern Italian states, principally Salerno, Capua, Beneventum and Naples, and with the Byzantines in Sicily from 1038 when Maniakes hired 500. They revolted against the latter in 1040, joined another Apulian rebellion and were 2,000 strong in the army which defeated the Byzantines at Monte Maggiore in 1041.

Sicily itself was conquered from the Moslems by the Normans in an almost leisurely series of campaigns which commenced with raids in 1060 and 1061 and finally ended in 1091.

TACTICAL METHODS

THE BYZANTINES

General

Byzantine tactics were essentially based on the use of cavalry, the role of their infantry being defensive throughout this period, mainly acting in support of cavalry.

The basic rule of their tactics was never to form up in a single body but always in 2 lines or preferably 3, with flankguards and reserve. This enabled the delivery of a number of successive shocks in battle and discouraged attacks from the rear. The late-6th or early-7th century Strategicon gives thorough details for the basic formation, with the front line a minimum of three-eighths of the total force, second line one-third, a small reserve of one-tenth, and flankguards of one-fifth. The first 2 lines were to be separated by about 400 metres and both were to consist of distinct centre, left and right divisions with space between them so that the first could retire through the second if hard-pressed. The second line could either act in support of the first or turn to face an enemy approaching from the rear (particularly useful against the envelopment tactics of the Turks). It was the failure of this second line to perform its duties that resulted in the disastrous defeat of Manzikert in 1071 (for which see *Armies and Enemies of the Crusades*).

Flankguards consisted of detached units thrown out on the wings and preferably concealed. Their tasks were to outflank the enemy and prevent similar attempts on his part, or to charge out into his rear once he had advanced beyond their position or was engaged frontally. An extra detachment was usually flung far out on the right for added protection of the unshielded flank.

The front line of cavalry was to be 8 deep at the centre and 4 on the flanks, though first-class troops needed only to form up 5 deep. The later Tactica of Leo VI (c. 900) states that 10 deep was the safest and most solid formation and 8 deep the minimum, though he adds that an ideal unit, probably such as those of the Tagmata, need only draw up 4 deep. The mid-10th century Praecepta Nikephori advises 5 deep formations.

The tactics of the front line were for the archers to advance in open order and skirmish, or cover the close order advance of the lancers; the archers always retired to the lancers if threatened. The archers went under the name cursores and the lancers defensores. Later, when

Asiatic light cavalry auxiliaries performed the functions of cursores, they were often used to draw the enemy into ambush by feigned flight. These auxiliaries included Avars, Turks, Bulgars, Magyars, Pechenegs and Seljuks, whose traditional tactics made them ideally suited for the job.

Super heavy cavalry, klibanophoroi, were reintroduced by Nikephoros II. If present on the battlefield they drew up in a wedge formation, the first line being of 20 men, the second of 24 and so on, each line wider by 4 men; the final line (the twelfth) could consist of as many as 64 men, which gives a maximum unit of 504 – in fact the ideal unit is recorded in the Praecepta Nikephori to be '500' men, though 384 (10 ranks) was regarded to be sufficient. Ranks 5 back were to include archers if possible, a unit of 500 having 150 archers and one of 300 having 80. The flanks of the base of the wedge were to be protected by 2 lines of ordinary cavalry. Klibanophoroi advanced in close order, never faster than a slow trot, and were not to join in the pursuit of a routed enemy.

Infantry tended to form up as a second line behind the cavalry, relying on them to break the enemy and then following up, or else they formed the centre of the line with wings consisting of cavalry. The Strategicon says infantry could form up 4 or 8 deep, though 16 was more usual. The archers would shoot overhead against an advancing enemy while spear ranks 3 and 4 threw martiobarbuli then spears. On contact with the enemy all spearmen discarded their long spears and fought with swords. If charged by cavalry the front ranks braced themselves by pushing their spear butts in the ground and were supported from behind by the shields of the hind ranks. However, against infantry they could advance with confidence, their heavy armour, close formation and cavalry support giving them the advantage. Archers stood behind the spearmen (never in front), were interspersed with files of spearmen, or stood on the flanks, a position otherwise taken up by light infantry, archers or javelinmen. Servants armed with slings could be positioned on the extreme wings.

On the march great use was made of patrols, guides, and advance, flank and rear guards. The advance guard units were usually of cavalry, whose job was to cover the infantry, but in difficult terrain the advance guard consisted of infantry 2 or 3 days ahead of the main body. If the army had to traverse a pass light infantry armed with javelins and bows were sent ahead to take up vantage positions. Javelin-armed psiloi were preferable in wooded areas, archers in mountains. Infantry unable to otherwise keep up with the cavalry were to ride mules.

At the end of each day's march fortified camps were erected, usually a number of small ones rather than a single large one. These were usually square, surrounded by an embankment and ditch. If possible, the regimental wagons were drawn up as a laager round the outside of this, or else a stockade or caltrops, in this instance similar to later chevaux-de-frise, were erected instead. Outside these main defences small pits were dug with a sharpened wooden stake in each.

The Byzantine battle cry was 'Deus Nobiscum', shouted by the officers, to which the men shouted back 'Kyrie Elesion'. The earlier Strategicon records the officers shouting 'Adjuta' and the men replying 'Deus'.

The surviving Byzantine military manuals concentrate, however, on tricks, ambushes, raids, patrols, spies and the cutting of lines of communication rather than pitched battles, regarding such strategems as preferable.

Against Arabs

Fighting the Arabs was principally a matter of containing raids which varied in scale. Once within Byzantine territory they were permitted to pillage, the civilian population having been evacuated in advance. As they looted and raided they were shadowed by cavalry and any stragglers cut off. In addition, small decoy bodies of 100 men were used to draw foragers into prepared ambushes. Meanwhile infantry seized the mountain passes in the Arabs' rear.

The Arabs were to be attacked when they had loaded themselves down with loot or had slowed down to negotiate a pass. If they had to withdraw through one of the infantry defended passes they could be shot down en masse by the light infantry archers and javelinmen, and most of the successful actions against Arabs involved the cornering of a raiding force in a pass as it tried to withdraw; Acroinon in 738 was such a battle, where a cornered Arab army of 20,000 was virtually exterminated. Night attacks were preferable, as were attacks during bad weather, rain or cold tending to dispirit them.

Generally Arab raiders avoided pitched battles, but if forced to stand in the open they were generally no problem, though disastrous battles such as Amorium in 838 proved that the Byzantine cavalry were not invincible; however, conditions there were exceptional, the Byzantines having fought a half-day engagement before being surprised by the Arab cavalry. Normally the Arabs' single cavalry formation could not stand up to the successive charges Byzantine formations permitted, and man for man their horsemen were no match for the Byzantines in close combat and need only be feared if numbers favoured them.

Archers were to aim for the Arabs' horses since they were proud of them and would avoid having them killed even if it meant running away; and once broken or routed they lacked the organisation to reform or rally.

Frequently a counter-raid by land and sea was launched against Arab Syria and Cilicia.

Against Slavs

Lacking large numbers of cavalry the Slavs needed only to be feared in mountainous or wooded country where their lightness of arms was to their advantage and they could harass the flanks and rear of Byzantine columns with arrows and javelins. Sentries needed to be posted with care against ambush.

They were best attacked in winter when there was little foliage to act as cover and snow gave away their tracks and betrayed their ambushes or, in the case of marsh-dwellers, because the waters were frozen, permitting the Byzantines easy access across the ice to the villages of the Slavs and preventing them from taking refuge amongst the bogs and reed-beds. In the open they could easily be ridden down by cavalry, since in general they lacked both arms and effective organisation.

Otherwise their various rival communities could be played off one against the other.

Against Turks

Under this heading the Byzantines included most of their Central Asiatic nomad enemies, but particularly the Magyars. The best formation against Turks was to have a front line of infantry with cavalry on the flanks. Special care had to be taken against flank and rear attacks, and if possible the formation was to have its rear secured on a marsh, river or defile.

On an open field Turks could be ridden down by the heavy cavalry, who were therefore to close with them at once rather than attempt an exchange of fire in which the Turks would fairly certainly come off best; a mid-11th century source records how Pechenegs 'shot down the Byzantines' horses with a mass of arrows' and 'panicked the horses of their adversaries by the wounds that they inflicted and forced the Byzantines to flee ignominiously'. The Byzantines' infantry and cavalry were therefore never to entirely separate themselves from each other, especially since the Turks could not break Byzantine infantry and particularly feared the infantry archers, whose bows outranged their own.

Routed Turks were only to be pursued with extreme caution since it might be a feigned flight as bait for an ambush.

Turks were best attacked in February or March when their all-important horses were in poor condition after the hardships of winter.

Against Franks and Lombards

The European mode of warfare was basically all that Byzantine warfare was not, being unscientific and impetuous. Only the charge of their cavalry had to be avoided at all costs, though even then an attack on the flank or rear of the unwieldy mass in which they fought could rout them. They could also be drawn into an ambush by a feigned flight and were incapable of fighting over difficult ground. Since they were poor on sentry and reconnaissance work, and did not generally fortify their camps, night attacks could be particularly successful.

However, the best way of all to defeat a Frankish army was by attrition, wearing them down by skirmishes and hunger; they were insubordinate and their commissariat and morale were bad, so that a prolonged campaign usually disheartened them and caused many to desert. They might also be bribed.

Against Normans

Together with other Europeans the Normans are classified in Byzantine sources as Kelts, Latins, or 'Franks'. The Byzantines were uneasy fighting against them and, as against the Franks, could not withstand the initial charge of their heavy cavalry, which they regarded as irresistible. This advantage was probably a result of the Normans using spurs, which gave them considerably greater control over their horses. A later source claims without too much exaggeration that one mounted 'Frank' was worth 20 Byzantines!

The Byzantines' principal aim was, therefore, to break the first and decisive charge before impact. The Alexiad of Anna Comnena records various strategems utilised to this end by Alexius I, including the use of caltrops and of light wagons, propelled from underneath by heavy infantry, to disorganise their line. Light infantry archers and Turk horse-archers were also used to disrupt the Norman line by shooting down their horses, leaving them helpless on foot where, according to Anna, their 'huge shields' and 'spurs on their boots' impaired their ability to fight.

As an example of the way; n which these elements could be combined, one plan involved caltrops being used to break the first charge while the Byzantine heavy lancers were to advance, split to left and right to bypass the caltrops and, while the Normans were preoccupied by a continuous stream of arrows from light infantry positioned well out of reach, charge simultaneously into both their flanks. (Unfortunately the Normans discovered this plan before it could be executed and, anticipating the flank attack, refused with their centre and, avoiding the caltrops, charged the Byzantine flanks and routed them!)

Naval Tactics

The Byzantines' main maritime adversaries for most of this period were the Arabs, whose ships were generally slower and seamanship generally poorer. Because of this the Arabs often chained their vessels together Viking fashion to provide sturdy fighting platforms and frustrate the superior Byzantine seamanship, a tactic that appears to have been used for the first time at the Battle of the Masts in 655. The standard Arab galley, based closely on the Byzantine dromon, had 2 banks of oars, 25 a side with 2 men on each oar giving a total of 200 oarsmen, all armed; in addition there were deck fighters. Others were probably more like pamphyla with only one man on each lower bank oar.

As on land, battle was to be avoided unless no other course of action remained or the enemy was decisively outnumbered; it was preferable to leave storms and rocks to destroy an enemy fleet.

If battle took place, then it was to be off an enemy shore rather than a friendly one, so as to discourage desertion! The advised formation was the crescent, heavy ships on the wings and lighter ships in the centre. The wings were to close round behind the enemy fleet so that it was completely encircled, at the same time attempting to disable as many vessels as possible by shearing off their oars or attacking them with Greek Fire, a combustible mixture directed by siphons against enemy vessels and igniting on contact with water; it is described in greater detail under 142 in the dress and equipment section. Leo's Tactica also advises the use of feigned flight, apparently as effective on water as on land. Disabled vessels could then be rammed or attacked and boarded by the lighter ships, which were far more manoeuvrable in close combat. All movement was by oar. The fleet was controlled by flag signals during daytime and by coloured lights at night.

Venetian ships employed by the Byzantines at Durazzo in 1081 and Passaron in 1084 appear to have employed much the same tactics; their formation was the 'sea harbour', where the large ships were all chained together in a crescent with the smaller ships gathered in the centre before them.

Another tactic, specifically recorded to have been used by the Venetian fleet at Durazzo and by Belisarius 5 centuries earlier at Palermo, was the hoisting of manned ships' dinghies to the mastheads, from which vantage point the sailors or marines could shoot down at the enemy; Leo indicates that the same dinghies could be used for boarding by being hoisted by a winch onto the decks of the enemy ships!

In addition Leo's Tactica advises the throwing of pots of powdered quicklime, which gave off a thick choking dust, caltrops (in this instance iron-spiked wooden balls covered with pitch and sulphur and set on fire), and baskets of live scorpions! The Byzantines apparently also had a secret device with which they could fill enemy ships with water – probably some sort of pump and hose.

THE SUB-ROMANS

The tactics of the Roman successor states in Gaul and Britain were undoubtedly evolved from those of the late Romans. The infantry seem to have formed a steady line of 'clusters' or hollow squares around which the few cavalry operated as a fluid attacking force; the tactics of the latter undoubtedly included the feigned flight and were probably based primarily on the use of javelins.

These cavalry were a minority of warrior aristocracy. Their importance in Britain lay in the fact that their main enemy, the Anglo-Saxons, fought exclusively on foot. An indication of the potential of even a few heavy cavalry against undrilled foot-soldiers can be found in Sidonius Apollinaris, who records that at Clermont Ferrand c. 471 a certain Ecdicius, a sub-Roman Gallic chieftain, defeated several 'thousands' of Gothic infantry with only 18 such horsemen! Cavalry were also useful in cattle-raiding.

Of tactics in general, the 2 recurrent themes in British sources are dawn attacks and the defending of fords, guarding a ford in battle being an honoured position. The sub-Roman Britons seem to have concentrated on river defences, many of their battles against the Saxons being fought at river crossings; indeed, the expansion of Wessex into the West Country is a history of battles fought at fords.

One description of sub-Roman tactics in action comes from the 12th century chronicler Henry of Huntingdon. Allegedly describing the Battle of Beran-birig (Barbury Castle) in 556 he speaks of the British forming up in 3 lines, each line divided into left, centre and right, with spear-armed infantry in the first line, archers in the second and cavalry in the third. One suspects, perhaps justifiably, that these tactics are based on those of Henry's own day, but at the same time there is other evidence that he had access to old chronicles otherwise unknown to us, and it is worth noting that he correctly describes Saxon tactics when he speaks of their attack at this battle being launched in a single, great body – undoubtedly the traditional shield-wall.

THE SCOTS

As with the Picts and later mediaeval Scots, Scots armies of this period consisted chiefly of unarmoured spearmen. They formed up in close-order clumps flanked and/or preceded by missile-men armed with bows or javelins.

By the 10th century, if not earlier, they were little different from the Saxons; certainly those Scots present in the Celtic-Viking army at Brunanburh in 937 fought in a shield-wall formation combined with the Strathclyde Welsh and in the battle they are in no way distinguishable from their Viking allies in tactics.

The lightly armed Galwegians appear to have preferred a wild charge, discharging a shower of darts before impact.

THE IRISH

At the beginning of this period the Irish were still sea-raiders, the name 'Scotti' itself possibly deriving from a word meaning to raid. Their seamanship served them in good stead through the Viking era when several naval victories against the invaders are recorded.

Prior to the Viking invasions warfare seems to have usually been on a small scale, principally involved with the collection by force of tribute from client kingdoms – generally in the form of cattle-raiding. The burning of monasteries, abbeys and churches seems to have been a standard part of such campaigning, and the monasteries were not above arming their monks and fighting back!

Large battles were rare but not unknown and usually involved armies numbering only in hundreds, the losing side fleeing on the death of its leader. The small, light Irish weapons were ideally suited to this type of warfare. On occasion a set-piece battle might take place with considerably larger forces involved; an Irish source records as many as 3,000 dead in such an engagement in 561.

By the 10th century at the latest Irish tactics seem to have been copied from the Vikings; units were drawn up in large phalanxes and opened the battle with a shower of javelins before drawing sword and making a wild charge – they made no use whatsoever of the bow in warfare, relying on their light darts for missiles. The chronicle called 'The War of the Gaedhil with the Gaill' records that the Irish at Clontarf formed up in a solid phalanx packed so tightly that 'a 4-horsed chariot could run from one end to the other of the line on their heads so compact were they'; at the same time individual 'battals' and 3 distinct lines are mentioned, while Njal's Saga speaks of the Irish formed up as centre and wings.

Probably now as later they also made considerable, and highly successful, use of ambushes in difficult country; in woods they would obstruct pathways by 'plashing' the undergrowth into barricades, and in marshes they dug ditches, both intended to slow the enemy down so that he could be harassed with missiles or attacked from both sides. In 1103 Harald Hardrada's grandson, King Magnus Barefoot, was killed in such an ambush in a bog in Ulster.

Chariots may still have been in use in warfare at the beginning of this period. Cavalry were unknown until the 14th century except among the Scandinavian settlers, who are recorded as using cavalry on odd occasions such as at Sulcoit in 968 and by a body of Dublin Vikings in a campaign of 1000–1001.

THE VISIGOTHS

Visigothic tactics appear to have been similar to those of the Franks, making considerable use in particular of the heavy cavalry charge, the feigned flight, javelin-armed light cavalry and bow and spear-armed infantry; they were held in high repute as archers and slingers, though the bow was only a secondary weapon to them (even so, the Arabs captured large numbers of bows during their invasion in 711).

THE LOMBARDS

Though grouped with the Franks in Leo's Tactica the Lombards, in their early period at least, fought differently to them, relying on cavalry as they did to a much greater degree.

A Byzantine manoeuvre, the 'Italian', recorded in the Strategicon is probably based on the Lombards' main battle formation. Here the cavalry formed up in 2 continuous lines a fair distance apart, each line several ranks deep. The second line followed each movement of the first, by its presence preventing an encirclement as well as acting as a reserve.

Otherwise they probably fought in a similar fashion to the earlier Goths, supported by a potentially large number of infantry archers whose usefulness was probably restricted by their inability to keep up with the cavalry. The cavalry themselves were, like those of the Franks, prepared to dismount and fight on foot in really desperate situations.

THE FRANKS

The Franks formed up in dense, close order masses, with men from the same estates or towns standing together and feudal vassals gathered round their lords. Both infantry and cavalry drew up in such divisions.

Their main disadvantage was the inability of the men to carry out any complex manoeuvre, since lacking any regular training or drill they were likely to lose formation. Because of this general unwieldiness they were particularly susceptible to attacks in flank or rear. The Byzantine manuals categorise the Franks as headstrong, with no respect for strategy, precaution or foresight and displaying contempt 'for every tactical command, especially the cavalry.'

The wild charge of their cavalry, however, was formidable, though it had not yet developed into the mediaeval shock charge with couched lance, the Franks relying just as much, or even more, on their swords as their spears, especially in close combat. Their mounted troops were also quite prepared to dismount and fight on foot if necessary, and the Byzantine Tactica records that in a cavalry action a hard-pressed force might dismount and stand back to back in a shield wall to face the enemy. It would seem apparent, therefore, that good quality troops fighting as infantry were capable of standing up to Frankish cavalry, though admittedly after the initial shock of impact was spent. However, Viking infantry certainly withstood Frankish cavalry on several occasions.

Against Asiatic horse-archers tactics were slightly different. The 10th century chronicler Liudprand of Cremona records that, fighting the Magyars at Meresburg, King Henry ordered that his cavalry should maintain strict formation, use their shields to protect each other, and that after thus withstanding the Magyars' first volley of arrows they should close with them fast before they could discharge a second volley, advancing in a level line in close formation. Tactics against the earlier Avars may have been similar.

Lighter cavalry, notably Gascons and Bretons but also East Franks and Saxons, are recorded as using the feigned flight in 9th century sources, though the Byzantine Tactica lists this tactic as one which could be used with notable success against Frankish troops! The Visigoths certainly used it against them successfully as early as the 6th century.

The infantry masses probably resembled the Saxon or Viking shield-walls; at Tours in 732 the Franks are specifically described by one chronicler as 'motionless as a wall; they were like a belt of ice frozen solidly together'. However, they often formed up in a number of individual bodies rather than a single solid phalanx. Javelinmen and archers seem to have normally either formed the rear ranks and fired overhead while the front ranks charged, or else preceded the main body. Evidence also suggests that light cavalry might precede the main mass of heavy cavalry as skirmishers.

However, other than for siege work and the defence of fortresses, where from the later-10th century the crossbow excelled, archers were never present in large numbers in Frankish armies except during Charlemagne's reign. Under any circumstances Franks were reluctant to flee.

THE VIKINGS

The origin of the word 'Viking' is not clear but it could mean 'lurker in a fjord', an apt description of a northern pirate! They were known by more various names to their victims, including Lochlanns, Dubhgaill, Finngaill, Madjus, and more generally Danes, Norsemen and the Heathen. In the East the Vikings came to be known to the Byzantines and Slavs as Rus, or Rhos, and Varangians. Their recorded raids lasted from 789 (though there is some evidence that Scandinavian vessels may even have been raiding Britain as early as the 7th century) until well after the close of this period, though from the end of the 11th century they were on a minor scale, and the Viking 'era' is usually taken to have ended with the Battle of Stamford Bridge in 1066. During this period they are recorded at various times serving as mercenaries in Russian, Byzantine, Slav, Khazar, Frankish, Saxon, Scots, Irish and even Arab armies.

On land they fought primarily on foot, though cavalry were evidently used on occasion, as at Sulcoit in Ireland in 968, and by the Danes in operations against the Wends in the later-11th century, while the chronicler Abbo of Fleury implies the use of a large body of Viking cavalry, fighting separately from their infantry, at the Battle of Montfaucon in 888. However, those at Sulcoit at least may only represent Vikings who rode to battle and were attacked while still mounted; they appear to have been only 100 or 50 men in a combined Viking-Irish army which was large enough to suffer 1,200 or 3,000–7,000 casualties.

Horses were more often used in cross-country raids, rounding up taking place either in the neighbourhood of their encampment or after

Viking victories, when the horses of the defeated Saxon Select Fyrd or Frankish cavalry could be gathered. Asser even records the Danes bringing captured Frankish horses with them into England in 885 and 892, predating by a century and a half the famed horse-transporting of the Norman invasions of Sicily and England.

In battle the army formed a shield-wall akin to the Saxons', normally in one large phalanx apparently about 5 men deep at least. On occasion it would split into 2 or more divisions, as at Ashdown and Meretun in 871, Corbridge in 918 (where of 4 divisions one was held in reserve in a concealed position) and Clontarf in 1014 (though the latter was a heterogenous force). How close-packed the shield-wall formation was is uncertain, but it seems unlikely that shields were overlapped. Literary evidence indicates quite clearly that hand-to-hand combat involved a variety of almost acrobatic skills, with much twisting, dodging and leaping back and forth, which it is hard to imagine being possible in the cramped and rigid formation that overlapping shields would seem to dictate, and the effectiveness of long-handled axes, a favourite Viking weapon, would have been particularly restricted. On the other hand the experiences and observations of a present-day 're-enactment' association, the Norse Film and Pageant Society, who use accurate reproductions of Viking weapons, would indicate that the axe could be swung in a remarkably small space without braining one's compatriots, and they claim that in close combat any extra room required for a good swing was best found by pushing into the enemy formation rather than standing in line in one's own ranks; this certainly fits with the contemporary evidence for battlefield acrobatics described above. Interestingly a 10th century hogback tombstone in Gosforth, Cumbria, carries a relief of a shield-wall where the shields are overlapping up to about half their width, which gives a frontage of only about 1½ feet per man, and the 9th century Oseberg Tapestry too shows a shield-wall of partially overlapping shields. Probably, in fact, shields were interlocked to receive the impact of the first charge (as Snorri tells us the Norse shields were at Stamford Bridge, 'overlapping in front and above'), but the formation loosened up automatically both in advance and melee.

The Vikings' main variation on the simple phalanx was the svynfylking, a wedge-shaped formation which could be used singly or in multiples joined at the base, the whole line resembling a zigzag. Sword and axemen formed the front rank, then spearmen, and behind them archers, slingers and javelinmen, who normally opened the engagement with a hail of missiles to weaken their opponents' shield-wall. When a circular shieldwall was formed the archers remained in the open centre. Commanders appear to have been protected by a separate shield-wall of bodyguards whose job it was to deflect missiles.

Sources indicate that if they were present cavalry would form up as a single body behind and distinct from the infantry.

Vikings were usually uncomfortable fighting against cavalry, though they seem generally to have succeeded in retiring in good order and even of rallying and winning the day. The Battle of Saucourt in 881, where they lost 8–9,000 men, was their first decisive defeat at the hands of Frankish cavalry, and even that was a close thing; when their first attack seemed successful the Franks had broken ranks to plunder, and a Viking counter-attack nearly broke them before a second charge forced the Vikings to withdraw (once again apparently in good order, despite their heavy losses). A rare instance of Vikings facing early mediaeval cavalry is recorded in Heimskringla, when in 1151 a raiding force in Northern England defeated mounted knights and supporting infantry by their use of archery.

When raiding the Vikings developed a habit of beaching their ships on a small island or in the curve of a river and throwing a stockade up on any side which could be approached by land. This camp was usually left with a garrison since the Vikings were always highly concerned about their lines of communication, and failure to adequately protect the line of retreat to their ships, as at Clontarf (where they seem also to have misjudged the tide), could result in utter rout and heavy losses. These camps were sometimes used as a refuge when the raiders were faced by a superior enemy force, and were rarely attacked successfully, the besiegers usually dispersing after a period of inactivity. However, a chronicle of 891 records an army of East Franks dismounting, scrambling across the outer ditch and hacking a breach through the stockade of such a camp with their swords and axes to rout the occupants, driving them back into the river behind.

At sea the Vikings made no use of ramming tactics, preferring to make a naval action as much like a land battle as possible. Thus the fleets were arranged in lines or wedges with the bigger or better-manned ships in the centre of the line. These were often roped together gunwhale to gunwhale to form large floating platforms. The prows of longer ships extended in front of the line and for this reason some, called bardi, were armoured with iron plates at stern and prow, from where most fighting took place; it was from the forecastle that Berserkir fought if present. Others had a series of spikes called a comb or skegg round the prow to hole enemy ships venturing close enough to board. On the flanks of the platform, and often in reserve were numbers of individual ships, whose tasks were to skirmish with their opposite numbers, attack the enemy platform, or pursue the enemy in flight. Masts were lowered in battle and all movement was by oar.

The main tactic was to row against a vessel, grapple and board it, and clear it with hand weapons before moving on to another vessel, sometimes cutting the cleared ship loose if it formed the wing of a platform. (Heimskringla records an incident where a high-sided Saracen dromon was boarded by axemen hacking entrances through the hull sides!) The platforms were attacked by as many ships as could pull alongside, but they could be reinforced by their own individual ships putting extra men aboard. On many occasions ships were subjected to a barrage of arrows as a prelude to boarding. To counter this each oarsman was often protected by a second man, who deflected missiles with his shield. This practice probably explains the considerable increases in ships' complements in battle, especially since a third man per oar is mentioned as being told off to fight.

Some ships carried supplies of stones and other spare weapons, such as spears and iron-shod stakes, all being used as missiles. Stones were often dropped from high-sided ships onto (and through!) the decks of vessels attempting to board. They also used fireships and are known to have sunk vessels as blockships.

Their sea battles were not limited to squabbles amongst themselves – Irish, Saxons, Franks, Arabs and Byzantines were all engaged in naval actions with them and all at one time or another secured the victory.

One other feature of northern warfare which should be mentioned was the hazelled field, belonging more properly to the preceding era but surviving on occasion well into the Viking age. This was basically a battle by appointment in a prepared battlefield fenced in on all sides with hazels. Once invited to fight in a hazelled field it was apparently a disgrace to refuse, or to ravage the opponent's territory until the battle had been fought. The hazel fences also tended to hinder the flight of either party! The Saxons were not unaware of this custom, since according to Egil's Saga the Battle of Brunanburh in 937 took place in a hazelled field prepared by King Athelstan so as to delay the allied invaders from pillaging for just long enough to allow him to gather an adequate army with which to face them!

THE RUSSIANS

Warfare to the Rus was chiefly a matter of internal struggles or raids against neighbouring Slav tribes for tribute and slaves. There were also fairly regular campaigns against various Asiatic peoples. Raids were nearly always by boat down the rivers and waterways of Central Asia, their ships constituting the only real navy of the area (with the possible exception of that of the Khazars). Certainly ships are never far away whenever we find the Rus in battle.

Most fighting was done with spear, sword, axe and javelins; some men also carried bows, archers being present in most battles. They fought chiefly as infantry in the traditional Scandinavian manner, forming a shield-wall in one or more divisions with spearmen in the front rank, javelinmen in the second and whatever archers were available in the third. The Byzantine chronicler Leo the Deacon records the advance of such a shield-wall at Silistria in 972, describing their close order, steady formation and levelled spears. In one of the various engagements Svyatoslav even formed his men up in squares with their archers in the centre, apparently a common Russian tactic, and advanced in this formation in an attempt to frustrate the Byzantine cavalry attacks. The Byzantines' answer was to engage the squares frontally with infantry, their slingers and archers picking off any Rus who exposed himself, while the cavalry charged in on their flanks.

Archery was probably supplied chiefly by Slav and Asiatic auxiliaries, the latter also supplying the bulk of Russian cavalry in the 9th and 10th centuries. Such auxiliaries usually formed up separately within the army – for example in 971 Svyatoslav's army contained, in addition to Rus, divisions of Pechenegs and Magyars and a smaller contingent of Bulgars. Other additional troops might be supplied by Varangian mercenaries, who seem to have usually held the centre of the line when present.

The Rus themselves were not horsemen, though by the mid-10th century at the latest chieftains, and therefore probably their immediate bodyguards, are often to be found fighting on horseback, and horses were regularly used to ride to and from battle. Their general inability to fight as cavalry is remarked upon by Leo the Deacon, who says the Rus were 'a foot-soldiering nation who could not even ride' and records a singularly unsuccessful Russian cavalry sortie during the fighting at Silistria. Even in the 11th century a Moslem author, Marvazi, records their lack of horsemen, though he credits the average Rus warrior as being the equal of several men of any other nationality.

By the 11th century the Rus had certainly taken to fighting on horseback, however, and appear to have been notably successful against Asiatic horse-archers, usually closing with them fast and routing them in hand-to-hand combat, sometimes even before they could let off a single volley of arrows. By the end of the century infantry are occasionally absent altogether from battle descriptions.

THE SLAVS

Our main sources of information on Slav tactics are Byzantine manuals, the Strategicon and Tactica, which are chiefly concerned with the southern and eastern Slav tribes. They speak of the Slavs having hardly any cavalry and fighting on foot, which is certainly true of the 6th and early-7th centuries though greater numbers of cavalry appeared under Avar influence. Many of these fought in Avar fashion with sabre, lance and bow.

However the Antes, the Byzantines' principal opponents in the early period, were especially skilled at fighting in hilly country and were specifically employed by them in this context. The Tactica of c. 900 still records the Slavs as being at their best in the forest-covered mountains and narrow passes, specialising in surprise attacks and forest ambushes, particularly at night, and in skirmishing with missiles from inaccessible positions. The missiles usually included arrows, javelins, axes, rocks and stakes. In the words of a later chronicler, 'The Slavs are exceedingly skilled in making clandestine attacks'; this chronicle and others are full of references to ambushes, and successful skirmishes against unwary foragers and stragglers. Such attacks were executed by both infantry and cavalry.

Leo records that if caught in the open Slavs could be ridden down, though he fails to record their tactics for a set battle. Later sources refer to wedges and multiple lines several ranks deep, without distinguishing between cavalry and infantry. Western Slav cavalry, principally Poles, appear to have used the same tactics as their European counterparts, though their combination of heavy cavalry with Turk auxiliary horse-archers must have given them a slight edge. Pechenegs and Magyars are especially recorded in this context. However, even in the 10th and 11th centuries many of the lesser independent tribes, particularly amongst the Baltic Slavs, still fought mainly as infantry, with few horsemen.

Against Magyars, Pechenegs and other raiders they constructed fortresses into which they withdrew in winter, Asiatic nomads being generally poor at any kind of siege-work (despite having siege-engines, Magyars attacking Augsburg in 955 had to be driven forward by whips!). The Slavs themselves also raided, using their monoxyla along the rivers and the Adriatic coastline, each capable of carrying at least 10 men, those of the Croats carrying up to 20 or 40 men. In the Baltic raiders and pirates were as often Slavs as Vikings!

ASIATIC HORDES

Asiatic tactics were based on 3 main factors – horse-archers, ambushes, and the feigned flight. They had a dislike for close combat, particularly against heavy cavalry, but were nonetheless prepared to carry out a charge whenever an opportunity presented itself.

The accuracy of their archery is testified by early Arab sources, which credit them with the ability to mow down a thousand horsemen with as many arrows, of being as deadly in retreat as attack, and of being able to fire 10 arrows in the time it took a Khawarij Arab to nock one! The one real enemy of such tactics was rain, which rendered their bows useless, and there are a number of recorded instances of Turk armies being routed in battles during rain storms in both the East and the West – damp bowstrings are offered, for instance, as an excuse for the Magyars' decisive defeat at Lechfield in 955.

Pack animals carrying spare arrows generally accompanied their armies on campaign and presumably in battle. Contemporary sources also suggest that training and practice of a kind took place, both in archery and tactics.

On the battlefield they formed up in small, scattered sections rather than a single unit and rode across the enemy front and round his flanks discharging volleys of arrows, looking for any weak point in his formation, concentrating on it, and preferring to withdraw if there was no such weakness apparent. Faced by superior numbers they could disperse with amazing speed. Sometimes they may have formed up in wedge-shaped masses as did the earlier Scyths and Huns.

The feigned flight was used to draw enemy cavalry in pursuit, thus disorganising them, often luring them into a pre-planned ambush where they were attacked in flanks and rear while the decoy body would turn in the saddle and fire volleys of arrows into their front before charging in amongst their confused ranks and routing them in hand-to-hand combat. The charge was usually accompanied by loud clashing of cymbals, braying of horns, and fearful wolf-like howls (Liudprand of Cremona records the Magyars' cry as 'Hui, hui!').

When raiding they would split into small parties of 100 or so, though if suddenly faced by a larger enemy force while divided thus they could apparently easily reassemble 'in some strange fashion'; the Magyars at least achieved this by smoke signals.

It seems reasonable to assume that at least on occasion those heavy cavalry present in Asiatic armies, normally the chieftains and their immediate bodyguards, would have acted similarly to those of the Jurchids, recorded in the early-12th century, and the later Mongols, charging at the enemy once he had been adequately disorganised and weakened by the horse-archers. .

The Pechenegs added a new dimension to these basic Turkic tactics by utilising their laager of horse or oxdrawn wagons. Alans, Turks, Avars, Khazars, Bulgars, Pechenegs and Cumans are all recorded as being accompanied on campaign by wagons, like the earlier Goths and Huns, and of forming them up, tied together with ropes, as a defensive circle round their camps. Felt or leather tents were set up inside the laager and sometimes a ditch was dug around the outside.

Although such wagons were the Asiatic norm, it was the Pechenegs who first began to utilise them as a tactical element. In battle the laager provided a refuge in which their cavalry could rally, charging in and out through oblique openings in the ring of wagons. At the same time any enemy who approached too close ran the risk of being lassoed or hooked from his saddle with grappling irons by the women and dragged inside, to be either killed or held for ransom. The Alexiad even goes so far as to say that if the Pechenegs risked a battle without the support of their wagons they were sure to lose. They even used abandoned wagons as decoys in their preplanned ambushes.

The one disadvantage of the laager must have been that it was stationary, allowing a more mobile enemy the advantage of performing feigned flights directly away from its position – though only if the Pechenegs were gullible enough to allow themselves to be drawn away from their sanctuary (and the stupidity of the Pechenegs was apparently proverbial!). There are, however, no recorded instances of this tactic to my knowledge, though practically the only surviving records of any events on the steppes are those of outsiders – whose presence would have been unlikely at an engagement between 2 rival bodies of Asiatic nomads.

On the other hand, the laager would have presented a formidable obstacle to Asiatic horsemen, whose traditional tactics would have been somewhat frustrated by it. There is a recorded instance at the Battle of Tel Afar in 1042 where Ghuzz horsemen, having initially beaten an Arab force and pushed it back into its encampment, found themselves severely hampered and unable to use their bows in the confined spaces amongst the tents and wagons, and they were soundly beaten in the ensuing hand-to-hand struggle. An attack on a wagon laager would have undoubtedly had similar results; those successful assaults on laagers recorded in contemporary sources were invariably carried out by infantry, which of course the Asiatics generally lacked.

The Russians had adopted the wagon-fortification from the Pechenegs or Cumans by the 12th or 13th century at the latest, calling it by the name gulaigorod, 'walking fortress'. The Hussites perfected the technique in the 15th century, and in general the Pecheneg wagons probably resembled those of the Hussites. See the description under 148 in the dress and equipment section.

The Khazar Khagan used a wagon positioned in the midst of his army as his command post on the battlefield. However, by the 10th century Khazars no longer always used wagons to fortify their camps, Marvazi recording that each Khazar horseman carried 20 short stakes for erecting a palisade round the camp each night, against which they leant their shields for added protection; he adds that a palisade of this nature could be erected in less than an hour.

Khazars preferred to use their subject levies for the brunt of the fighting, dissuading these from running away by a simple regulation that all those who did so were to be executed and their commanders hung or crucified!

The Avars likewise preferred to use their subjects. Under the year 623 the Frankish chronicler Fredegar records an Avar custom of staying in camp, though fully armed, while their expendable Slav subjects did the fighting; if the Slavs won the Avars would advance to pillage, but if they were hard-pressed then the Avars backed them up.

The Bulgars, fighting more of a defensive war against the Byzantines, preferred to stay in the mountains and avoid pitched battles unless the enemy could be ambushed or trapped in a valley or pass, normally by the erection of a palisade at either end. If they captured a Byzantine fortress they would dismantle its defences, massacre or enslave the population then withdraw rapidly. Their general tactics are not listed in the Tactica of Leo but he groups them as 'birds of a feather' with the Magyars, who employed the standard Turkic tactics. However, the Bulgars appear to have made somewhat less use of the bow than most other Asiatic hordes.

Some Turk armies made limited use of infantry, usually Slav auxiliaries though Pechenegs and Cumans had infantry of their own and Khazars were prepared to dismount and fight on foot when necessary. There is no indication how such infantry were used, though they would undoubtedly have been principally archers and javelinmen. Probably many of them garrisoned the wagon-laagers during battle.

Lastly, an observation made in Byzantine sources was probably as true of Asiatic hordes in general as it was of those serving as mercenaries in Byzantine armies; this was that their efforts in battle tended to be concentrated more on looting the enemy camp than on physically defeating their opponents. There are recorded instances of Asiatic auxiliaries whose orders had put them in the rear of the enemy diverting their attentions to looting baggage or camp and, having taken what they wanted, dispersing without another thought for the battle – leaving their employers decisively in the lurch.

THE ARABS

After the Ridda wars the early Arabs relied principally on cavalry, and the great speed at which Arab armies could move is particularly noted in the Byzantine military manuals. They often rode mules or camels on the march and led their horses, mounting them only for battle, while infantry rode on the cruppers of the cavalry mounts or had mounts of their own, usually camels.

The camels were particularly useful in desert regions where they were valuable because of their ability to store water for a number of days, supplying the men with fresh meat and the horses with water when slaughtered. On occasion they were ridden in battle by Arabs and other Easterners, though this was exceptional. The Arabs were also aware of the general dislike horses have for camels; at Qadisiyya (637) some camels were disguised in hoods and hangings and concealed amongst their cavalry to frighten the Sassanid horses. Leo too remarks upon such use of camels by the Arabs.

The cavalry usually formed up in a single phalanx 5 men deep, described in Leo's Tactica as 'a solid oblong' and a 'safe' formation, which was not to break either in attack or defence; he says that the Arabs would withstand attack in good order, waiting until the enemy had exhausted themselves before counter-attacking. They charged as a dense, wild mass, sometimes preceded by skirmishers, and if this attack failed they were likely to become discouraged and a rout could ensue. Early sources describe the recognised formation as the ta'biya or khamis, the 'five', consisting of centre, wings, advance guard and rear guard, each comprised of related tribal contingents. In addition there were detached light troops and scouts. Spacing of units was dictated by circumstances but normally the centre and wings formed an unbroken phalanx. This formation was evolved by Mohammed himself as early as the Battle of Badr and remained in use, with variations, throughout this era. The centre was usually formed of elite troops or, later, ghulams. Baggage was kept with the rearguard (saqa). Under Marwan II and thereafter the main divisions of the khamis were subdivided into smaller, more flexible units called karadis (singular, kurdus); these usually drew up fairly close together so that they could be mutually supporting.

Feigned flight was one of the Arabs' traditional tactics and is even mentioned indirectly in the Koran. Ambushes were often used in connection with the feigned flight and were in themselves another major Arab tactic; ambushes were best executed at dawn, the coldest hour of a winter day, or the hottest hour of a summer day, the cavalry charging in small independent groups. Arab sources also record cavalry turning either enemy flank, while the seizure of positions to the rear of the enemy was a common practice. Night and dawn attacks on the enemy camp were also popular. Night attacks were traditional and carried out by bands of men on foot, supported by archers firing into the camp from outside. Dawn attacks were by cavalry.

Infantry are mentioned in early sources as being drawn up in 8 or 11 ranks. Archers were usually positioned on the wings to prevent out-flanking or interspersed with the spearmen. The 8 or 11 ranks suggests a close affinity to Byzantine formations, the 8 ranks as half a lochaghia, the 11 ranks possibly as the spearmen of the lochaghia (minus one – an officer?), with archers probably formed up in the front row, as a screen before the main army, or on the flanks. Under the Abbasids the use of infantry declined somewhat except where geographical conditions proved unfavourable to cavalry, for example in the Iraqi marshlands. However, the infantry were generally an unreliable rabble. Their principal weapons were sword and spear, or bow or javelins. Cavalry relied on the lance but fought with sword or mace in the melee following the initial charge. Cavalry sometimes dismounted and fought on foot, particularly under the Abbasids, as at the Battle of Zab where they knelt with outstretched lances to receive the Umayyad charge.

On the march the Arabs followed Byzantine practice, with advance, rear and flank guards screening the main body, each with its own commander. The cavalry always preceded and screened the infantry units, the vanguard consisting of specially chosen elite cavalry. The main body included the baggage, which since it contained large quantities of loot tended to gradually slow the Arabs down, as both the Franks and Byzantines were well aware. (The attempts made by some commanders to discourage the accumulation of too much loot because of the dangers of reducing mobility could never have been overwhelmingly successful, and any restrictions imposed on booty would have seriously affected the morale of the army, since it was largely for this that they fought). The baggage itself usually included some wagons but consisted chiefly of a train of camels carrying food, spare equipment, loot, siege-gear and the like; as an indication of the size of such a baggage train, the army which marched on Amorium in 838 was accompanied by perhaps 50,000 camels, 20,000 mules and 30,000 camp followers, while a Saffarid amir campaigning in the early-10th century required 1,000 camels merely to transport cooking equipment!

The Arabs' battle-cry was 'Allahu Akbar' (God is greatest).

Elephants

Elephants continued to be used in eastern armies by the Saffarid, Ghaznavid and to a more limited extent Buyid amirs, whose encounters with Indian troops with elephant contingents numbering in hundreds led to their adopting them into their own forces during the 10th century. Ghaznavid armies reviewed in 1023 and 1031 contained as many as 1,300 and 1,670 armoured elephants respectively.

The Arabs had first encountered elephants when fighting the Sassanids and were initially terrified by them. The Sassanids often used elephants to open an attack, sometimes protecting them with heavy infantry and usually following them up in column. The Arab horses refused to go near them, so that the cavalry had to dismount and face them on foot, stabbing at the elephants' eyes and trunks with their long lances or ducking between their legs and cutting the girth straps that secured the howdahs on their backs.

Ghaznavid elephants were fully-armoured with the head piece at least being of iron, while a poem records the body as protected by a coat of scale armour (Indian war-elephants of a slightly earlier date are described as having bodies armoured by bands of cork and iron and the trunk by a curved sword, the latter possibly meaning that it wielded the weapon in its trunk, a trick also claimed by considerably later sources). Their most vulnerable point was the underbelly, against which the enemy therefore concentrated. They did not use howdahs, 4 mailed crewmen with spear or bow usually being mounted on their backs and secured by straps. Sometimes the elephants were fitted with rams for use in siege work, though often they would have used their armoured foreheads for ramming doors.

In battle they were normally placed in front of the main body to throw the enemy cavalry into panic, a particularly successful tactic when employed against the Asiatic Qarakhanids, Turcomans or Ghuzz, who were almost entirely cavalry! They were deliberately enraged by the beating of drums and the jangling of the hanging bells and ornaments of their armour before being led to a charge, usually against the centre of the enemy line. They were also used as mobile command posts for senior officers.

THE SAXONS

The Saxons, it is always said, fought on foot. The chronicler Florence of Worcester states quite specifically that it was 'contrary to the custom of the English to fight on horseback'. Wace, although writing in the 12th century, also records the tradition that the Saxons 'did not know how to fight with the lance or how to bear arms on horseback', and though this may be intended as an insult, it may also be intended at face value. Either way it would seem to indicate that as mounted soldiers they made good infantry. The one undisputed record of their entering battle on horseback in this period is of the Battle of Hereford in 1055, where their performance was singularly unimpressive.

The 13th-century account of cavalry attacks by Saxons at Stamford Bridge in 1066 recorded in Heimskringla is usually discounted as a jumbled confusion with Hastings, or with the tactics of author Snorri Sturlusson's own day, though there are admittedly many elements of his story that ring true; for instance, his Saxon cavalry throw their spears javelin-fashion as was the usual practice in the 11th century rather than charging home with them couched as was usual in his own day. Knytlinga Saga also records 11th century Saxons fighting mounted but again is of 13th century date. However the Saxons certainly used horses for transport to and from battle, and the pursuit of fast-moving (mounted) Viking raiding parties up and down the length of England in the late-9th, 10th and 11th centuries would have been impossible without them, their presence being confirmed by the Anglo-Saxon Chronicle. The first certain mention of a mounted Saxon force is in the Nechtansmere campaign against the Picts by Ecgfrith of Northumbria in 685, while Beowulf and other early works often refer to mounted warriors.

But the question as to how much this and other evidence proves or does not prove the existence of Saxon cavalry is a thorny and much-debated one. It is fair to say, however, that there is a fair amount of material that could be interpreted as evidence that at least some Saxons fought mounted, though none of it is conclusive. There seems little doubt that in certain situations, such as the pursuit of a mounted or routed enemy, they would have had little choice but to fight on horseback (after all, you wouldn't expect your enemy to oblige you by dismounting – he would just keep riding), and in 1016 Edmund Ironside's troops are specifically recorded overtaking and killing mounted Danes. Having had 3 years to digest all the evidence since the first edition of this book appeared, I now feel fairly confident that by the 11th century at the very latest Saxon armies in the field occasionally did include some cavalry. One can assume that their tactics would have been the same as those of their Norman counterparts, just as Snorri describes them.

Probably only kings, nobles, the Select Fyrd and Huscarls possessed horses anyway, though a 10th century law of Athelstan states 'that every man is to have 2 mounted men for every plough', which undoubtedly refers to military service. The driving away of horses prior to battle indicated that there was no intention of flight.

The standard infantry battle-formation throughout this era was the shield-wall, the 'bord-weal' or 'scyld-burh'. The whole army formed up in one massive phalanx several ranks deep with the better-armed men in the front ranks, though on occasion it could form up as 2 divisions, as at Ashdown and Brunanburh, while one chronicler records as many as 7 divisions at Stamford Bridge. The same comments on density of formation apply here as in the section on Viking tactics. Florence, describing the advance of a shield-wall at the Battle of Sherston in 1016, speaks of the pace being slow and steady so as not to lose formation. Once in motion its progress could probably be likened to a steam-roller.

The Saxons made some, but not extensive, use of the bow; there were, for instance, some (though perhaps not many) archers at Ashdown in 871, as well as at Maldon in 991 and Stamford Bridge in 1066 if we accept Snorri's account. The battle station of archers is not certain though they appear to have stood in the shieldwall, either as a second rank shooting past the first or a hind rank shooting overhead. They may have sometimes fought in units distinct from the spearmen. However, the bow was used as much in close hand-to-hand fighting as in a longer range exchange of fire.

Though there were attempts at outflanking or turning flanks there was basically an alarming absence of tactical sense. Volleys of spears, javelins and arrows opened a battle, usually at close range, but once opposing shield-walls collided it was merely might, determination and often numbers which decided the day, the loser generally suffering considerably in the rout.

However, in the early Saxon period and as late as the 10th century it was regarded as a disgrace for retainers to leave the field of battle alive if their lord had been killed, unless the victory was theirs. Such men as did were declared 'nithing' and no longer existed in the eyes of the law. The same ruling applied in Scandinavian lands. Although this custom is still recorded at the Battle of Maldon in 991, it had by the 11th century generally become obsolete and thanes and Fyrd alike could flee with impunity. However, the heavy slaughter of Vikings at

Stamford Bridge in 1066 was a result of their resolution to die with their king.

Saxon battle-cries recorded by Wace to have been used at Hastings were 'Olicrosse' (Holy Cross), 'Godamite' (God Almighty), and 'Ut, Ut!', literally 'Out, Out!'. He also records what appear to be two Saxon traditions when describing their battle formation – that whenever Kentish men accompanied the king in battle theirs was the right to strike the first blow, and that it was the right of Londoners to guard the king's person and standard; the latter is also implied in the Chronicle.

THE NORMANS

As with the Franks, the main tactic was the charge of the heavy cavalry, a charge so powerful as to be all but irresistible; Anna Comnena remarks that a charging 'Frankish' horseman could make a hole 'through the walls of Babylon'! Against another body of cavalry victory or defeat depended simply on the ability of the forces involved to withstand the shock of impact, success or failure often being decided in the first charge.

A close formation of heavy infantry stood more chance of survival, since if they stood firm they could not be ridden down but only slowly reduced in a hard slogging match, as proven by the Swabians with their two-handed swords at Civitate and by the Saxon Huscarl axemen at Hastings.

In addition the Normans used the feigned flight, though its use at Hastings has curiously often been doubted. It would appear that they adopted this tactic from the Bretons, who were using it in the 9th and 10th centuries with considerable success and amongst whom it can be traced back to Alan troops settled in Armorica in the 5th century. William of Poitiers, who also records the Bretons training in peacetime, ascribes the first feigned flight at Hastings to the Breton contingent, the second to the Normans.

The training which the Normans, like the Bretons, seem to have carried out even in peacetime probably included the feigned flight, and its successful use by them is recorded on two other occasions during this period, at Arques in 1053 and Messina in 1060, and also a few years after Hastings at Cassel in 1071.

Another tactic undoubtedly adopted from the Bretons was the use of javelins, the traditional Breton method of attack being to charge at the enemy in small bands, avoiding the impact of his direct charge by discharging a volley of javelins and then veering away; if these skirmishing tactics were successful in causing confusion or even a breach in the enemy formation then they might charge home and exploit their success with hand weapons. The Bayeux Tapestry shows a large number of knights throwing their lances javelin-fashion. A 9th century source records that the Bretons were backed up in action by cartloads of missiles from which they replenished themselves with javelins as the need arose; it is not inconceivable that this practice continued into the 11th century. A 10th century source says they and the Frisians were also accurate throwing javelins behind them when in flight.

Infantry, if present, usually took little or no part in pitched battles though they were employed successfully in sieges (though for assaults dismounted knights were used). Hastings was the only battle of this period in which it is recorded that 'Norman' infantry played a specific role, advancing in 2 lines ahead of the cavalry, archers in the first line preceding heavy infantry; these were almost certainly largely mercenaries. Infantry are recorded on other occasions – 500 infantry are recorded with 700 cavalry in Italy in 1041, Calabrian infantry appeared in the Norman army at Civitate in 1053, peasant infantry of the Arriere-Ban were summoned in 1058, while Saracen, Italian and other auxiliary foot-soldiers fought for Robert Guiscard in 1081 until by 1084 he could apparently raise 30,000 infantry to only 6,000 cavalry.

The Normans' battle-cry, recorded in various sources, was 'Dex Aie'. That of the French was 'Montjoie', the Flemings 'Azraz!' and the Angevins 'Valie'.

MAJOR BATTLES OF THE PERIOD

Due to space limitations only a selection of the most significant and decisive battles can be included, and only a brief description of these. Some important battles have been omitted because their details are obscure, and few tactical details are available even for many of those that have been included. Because of the Vikings' preference for sea warfare a few naval battles have also been included.

VIMINACIUM 601

Campaigning beyond the Danube the main part of a Byzantine army, having been sent ahead by its commander, Priscus, was attacked in its encampment by an Avar army under Bayan including Sclavini, Gepids and other subject nations. Informed of the attack Priscus advanced and joined his troops, first sending all the Byzantine rafts and boats back over the Danube to prevent flight.

The Byzantines then marched out of camp in 3 bodies to confront the Avars, each body formed up in a square to frustrate the Avars' tactic of attacking from all directions. After a battle lasting until nightfall the Avars withdrew, having lost 4,000 men to the Byzantines' 300, and the Byzantines returned to camp.

7 days later Priscus again marched out to face the Avars, this time forming his 3 divisions in crescents which enclosed the Avar cavalry when they attacked, forcing them to withdraw with losses of 9,000 men.

After another 6 days the Avars mustered for a further attack, and the Byzantines again faced them in 3 divisions while the Avars themselves unusually remained in one body, probably hoping to avoid a repeat of the earlier disasters. The Byzantines managed to secure a height from which, extending both flanks, they charged down and routed the Avars, forcing them back into a marsh behind their position. 15,000 were killed or drowned, including 4 of Bayan's sons.

The Avars then withdrew to the River Theiss, where Priscus followed up his victory by defeating them a fortnight later. 4,000 Byzantines then crossed the river, massacring 30,000 Gepids in 3 towns, and 20 days later again defeating the Avars on the Theiss, killing 3,000 Avars, 8,000 Sclavini and 6,200 others.

HALYS 622

Having outmanoeuvred the Sassanids and slipped past their defensive positions in the fortified mountain passes, an inexperienced but well-trained Byzantine army under the Emperor Heraclius proceeded to advance into Kappadocia. The Sassanids, under their great general Sahrbaraz, were therefore obliged to abandon their positions and set out in pursuit.

His army being low on morale and becoming weakened by unsuccessful skirmishes, Sahrbaraz decided to force an engagement before it was too late. Just before dawn he drew up his torces in 3 divisions before the Byzantine camp, concealing an elite cavalry unit in a ravine on one wing with orders to charge into the Byzantine flank once it was engaged.

Heraclius, however, was aware of the Sassanid dispositions, probably being informed of them by deserters during the night. He accordingly arranged his own army in 3 divisions and despatched a unit of light troops to lure the Sassanid flank unit into the open. This they did by feigning flight. The Sassanid unit, thinking that the whole Byzantine army was in rout, charged out of concealment only to find the Byzantines formed up and waiting for them; they were put to flight by a detachment under Heraclius himself.

Sahrbaraz, apparently unaware of this development, now ordered a general advance; but the rising sun was in their eyes and their formation was disorganised over broken ground, and finding in addition that the Byzantines were formed up ready for them the Sassanids panicked and ran. Few escaped the close Byzantine pursuit, and the Sassanid camp was captured intact.

NINEVEH 627

The Byzantines, under Heraclius, started this final campaign against the Sassanids with 70–80,000 men, plus the remaining part of 40,000 Byzantine-trained Khazar heavy cavalry who had joined them at Constantinople. At the time of battle the total force seems to have numbered 70,000, most of the Khazars having deserted. The Sassanid army which faced them was 12–50,000 strong, though of unreliable quality. Further reinforcements were constantly arriving, some coming in even after the battle.

The armies camped close together and the Sassanids, realising they could not avoid battle, deployed in close formation in 'their customary 3 columns', facing the sunrise. Their best troops, presumably clibanarii, formed the first 2 ranks. They had no elephants.

Razatis, the Sassanid commander, then challenged Heraclius to a personal combat. Heraclius got 2 slight wounds but killed Razatis, and the Byzantines attacked, having a big advantage from the sun in the Sassanids' eyes. Heavy fighting continued for 8 or 9 hours, by the end of which the Sassanids had lost 28 standards and perhaps as many as 50,000 men, including most of their officers (the Byzantine chronicler Theophanes says all). However, the survivors withdrew to their camp in good order in the small hours and then took to the hills and escaped. Theophanes claims that the Byzantines lost only 50 men!

The Byzantines followed up, capturing the new Sassanid capital of Destigerd (where 300 captured Byzantine standards were recovered) and marching on towards the old capital Ctesiphon. But encountering a wide canal defended by an army this time including 200 elephants Heraclius decided to withdraw into winter quarters.

Early the next spring the Sassanids overthrew and killed their king, Chosroes, and the new king, surrounded by generals in revolt and with the kingdom collapsing into anarchy, made peace with the Byzantines.

YARMUK 636

After a series of engagements over several weeks the Byzantines, under Theodorus and Baanes, faced 24–50,000 Arabs under Khaled ibn al-Walid on the banks of the River Yarmuk. The Byzantine army of 60–110,000 (or according to some Arab sources 240,000) contained Ghassanid Arab auxiliary cavalry as well as Slavs, Syrians and Armenians. However, the Byzantine units had come to blows with their Armenian allies the day before, while the Ghassanids' loyalty was in doubt and they in fact deserted to the Moslems during the battle.

At first the Byzantines had the advantage, isolating the Arab left flank, but they were eventually repulsed, as were 2 further charges. Finally, with a sandstorm blowing in their faces, the Byzantines were forced back by a fanatical Arab charge and routed. Their line of retreat having been cut by the Arabs' seizure of a bridge to their rear, they attempted to escape westwards across the deep ravines of the Yarmuk and its tributaries, where thousands died falling from the high cliffs and precipices and others were slaughtered by the pursuing Arabs.

Byzantine losses are recorded as 40–70,000, including Theodorus, while those of the Arabs amounted to only 4,030.

QADISIYYA 637

A 3-day battle between 16–30,000 Arabs under Sa'd ibn Abi Waqqas, and perhaps 60–120,000 Sassanids under Rustam, including 33 elephants. However the Sassanid army was of low quality, containing only 30,000 regular troops. They drew up in 13 lines, the Arabs in only 3 lines.

On the first day the Sassanids withstood the Arab cavalry charges then counter-attacked with their elephants. The Arabs were pushed back before several elephants were disabled or neutralised by men ducking between their legs and cutting the girth-straps that secured the howdahs on their backs.

The elephants made no appearance on the second day, and when they were used again on the third day Syrian reinforcements, freshly arrived and probably originally Byzantine-trained, dealt with them by attacking on foot with lances and stabbing at their eyes. Two elephants thus blinded stampeded the rest through their own lines.

The Sassanids were harassed throughout the third night by large-scale Arab attacks, and on the morning of the fourth day, with a sandstorm beginning to blow in their faces, they were routed. Rustam was killed in the pursuit, and many Sassanids were drowned in the Euphrates and its marshes. Thirty units (probably the regular troops) stood and fought to the last man, while only 2 units managed to withdraw in good order. The royal standard (a leather apron encrusted with precious stones) was captured by the Arabs, who lost 7,500 men, 6,000 of them in the night attack and final assault.

NIHAWAND 642

In this final engagement the Sassanids were totally defeated by 30,000 Arabs.

The Arabs launched their first attack in the late afternoon but their commander, al-Muzani, was killed and they were repulsed. For 2 more days they launched unsuccessful attacks, their cavalry being severely hampered by fields of caltrops spread by the Sassanids. Eventually on the third day the Arabs feigned a retreat, and the Sassanids, drawn in pursuit through their own caltrops by the decoy body, were ambushed by the main army.

Possibly numbering 150,000, the Sassanids fought fiercely, many of their levies being chained together to prevent flight, but after sustaining heavy losses those that could fled. This battle became known to the Arabs as the 'Victory of Victories'.

Except for the small province of Tabaristan on the edge of the Caspian Sea, Sassanid Persia was completely overrun by the Arabs by 649.

TRANSDUCTINE PROMONTORIES 711

With the help of one Count Julian, probably governor of Byzantine Ceuta, the Arabs succeeded in ferrying an invasion force of 7,000 Berber tribesmen and 300 Arab cavalry across the Straits of Gibraltar to conquer Spain. Shortly before joining battle with the Visigoths a further 5,000 Berber reinforcements arrived. The Visigothic army under King Roderick, containing a large number of cavalry, is reputed to have been 90–100,000 strong but was probably much smaller. The armies met on the banks of the River Lakka, possibly the Guadalete or the Salado.

The wings of the Visigothic army, commanded by Sisbert and Oppa, 2 disaffected relatives of the previous king, deserted at an inopportune moment in the battle and the centre, under Roderick, stood for only a short while unsupported. It broke after suffering severe losses, Roderick apparently drowning in a marsh while trying to escape.

Visigothic casualties in the battle were high enough to mount nearly all the Berbers on captured horses, and many more were killed in a 3-day pursuit. Arab losses were also heavy, though the recorded figure of 16,000 exceeds their total strength!

By 716 most of Spain had become an Arab province.

TOULOUSE 721

An Arab army was destroyed by a mixed force of Aquitanians and Franks under Duke Eudo. The battle was short-lived, the Arabs being surrounded and routed soon after its commencement. They were slaughtered in their flight, their commander al-Samah being amongst the fallen. The Franks lost only 1,500 men while the Arab losses were evidently far greater, the contemporary estimate being an impossible 350–375,000!

MARJ ARDABIL 730

Following Arab attacks on Khazar territory in 728 and 729 the Khazars launched a counter-offensive through the Darial Pass in 730 with an army of 30,000 under Barjik.

The Arab army, under Jarrah, first engaged them near Warathan in an attempt to relieve the town from a siege. In this he appears to have been unsuccessful; the Arab army was probably far inferior in strength since detachments had been despatched to garrison or defend other regions from the Khazars.

Jarrah therefore withdrew to Ardabil. Here he was advised to take up a defensive position with his rear protected by Mount Sabalan, but he resolved instead to force a general engagement with the Khazars. Both sides drew up their forces on the plain of Marj Ardabil. The Arab army, almost certainly inferior in strength to the Khazars, was high in morale but probably low in quality since it contained a large number of volunteer irregulars and levies.

2 days of fierce fighting ensued, the Khazars' superior numbers giving them a decisive advantage by the end of the second day, by which time most of the veterans in the Arab army had been killed. When night fell a great part of the less reliable levies slipped away, leaving Jarrah with only a small number of men to resume the fight on the third day. These rallied under Jarrah but were massacred by the Khazars, only 100 managing to escape.

Jarrah himself was amongst those killed in the battle, and his head was cut off by the victors. Paradoxically it was his head that was the principal reason for an Arab victory shortly afterwards at Baylaqan. This was because Barjik, the Khazar commander, had the head displayed on his command wagon, and this so incensed the Arabs that they launched a fanatical attack directly against him. In the ensuing engagement Barjik may have been killed, and his 100,000 strong army was routed with heavy losses by the smaller Arab force.

TOURS 732

Having defeated Duke Eudo and destroyed most of his army near Bordeaux, an Arab raiding force under 'Abd ar-Rahman, said to have been 70–80,000 strong, began to lay waste Aquitaine. Eudo, however, managed to reach Charles Martel, the Mayor of the Palace, who summoned a Frankish army and set out in pursuit of the Arabs.

Slowed down by plunder, the Arabs sent their wagons on towards Poitiers while they faced the Franks for 2 days to cover it, during which the latter were awaiting reinforcements. The Arabs then withdrew but near Poitiers caught up with their baggage train and resolved to stand and fight to cover its withdrawal.

The Franks, who appear to have pursued on horse but fought mainly as infantry, formed a phalanx in close order on high ground and withstood the repeated Arab cavalry charges, until late in the day when a body of Aquitanian cavalry under Eudo had charged, got round the Arabs' left flank and had begun to pillage the plunder in their camp. When some Arab cavalry units fell back to defend the camp the rest of their army thought they were running away and began to withdraw in confusion, and in the ensuing chaos 'Abd arRahman was surrounded and killed by Austrasian spearmen. The Arabs, discovering themselves to be leaderless only when they had reached their camp, then broke and fled.

The Franks did not pursue, but gathered together the Arabs' abandoned plunder and withdrew across the Loire. Arab sources, incidentally, record this as a 2-day battle.

RONCESVALLES 778

A Frankish expedition against Spain under Charlemagne was ambushed as it returned through a pass in the Pyrenees by the Basques, whose light arms, knowledge of the terrain and advantage of surprise allowed them to attack and slip away again unhindered. The Frankish rearguard was particularly badly mauled, possibly even wiped out, and many of the commanders were killed, including the Seneschal, the Count of the Palace and the Breton Markgraf Hruotland, the famous and semi-legendary Roland. The Basques withdrew after plundering the baggage train.

PLISKA 811

A Byzantine army under Nikephoros I marched against the Bulgar capital of Pliska, wiped out the several thousand Bulgar defenders and sacked the city. Nikephoros then advanced in pursuit of Khan Krum into the mountains, where the Bulgars trapped them in a narrow pass by erecting palisades at either end. For 2 days the Bulgars made no move, but on the third day they made a dawn attack on the rear of the Byzantine camp.

The Byzantines, encamped haphazardly, were routed and suffered heavy losses, their cavalry being stampeded into a river where hundreds drowned. Nikephoros was killed in his tent and his son Stauracius, who escaped, died of his wounds 6 months later.

AMORIUM 838

To revenge the destruction of his favourite town, Zapetra, by the Byzantines, Caliph Mu'tasim determined to destroy Amorium, the birthplace of the Emperor Theophilus. His army of 80–500,000 crossed the Taurus mountains by a number of passes, reuniting in larger forces in Byzantine territory.

Theophilus, having reached Dorylaeum, 3 days march from Amorium, was advised to evacuate the latter. Instead he strengthened the defences and sent in reinforcements under Aetius, the Anatolikon Strategos, remaining close by himself with the field army.

The Arabs split into 2 forces, one commencing the siege under Mu'tasim, the other raiding the surrounding countryside and acting as a covering force. The latter division, commanded by a certain Afsin, comprised at least 30,000 Persians and Arabs, 10,000 Turks, and a forced contingent of Armenians.

Early one morning while the cavalry of the covering force were away, the Byzantines attacked the infantry and were on the point of victory when the Arab cavalry returned at midday. The Byzantines withdrew in disorder, harassed particuarly by the Turkish horse-archers in Afsin's army – Mu'tasim's prototype slave-soldiers – until an evening shower rendered their bows useless.

The army dispersed, some Byzantines reaching their entrenched camp, others fleeing in various directions. Theophilus himself was rescued by the commander of his 30,000 Khurrami Persian mercenaries. He later succeeded in reorganising his army but found it too weak to interfere with the Arabs again.

The Arabs then made a 3 day assault on nearby Ancyra but were repulsed with loss. Amorium itself held out for 55 days before surrendering, the Arabs massacring 30,000 of the population and burning the town. Mu'tasim then withdrew, having heard rumours of revolt in his rear inspired by Byzantine gold.

FONTENOY 841

By attempting to destroy the forces of his rebel brothers Charles and Louis separately, the Frankish Emperor Lothair instead forced them into an alliance against him. As a result Lothair, short of troops, was obliged to hastily recognise his nephew Pepin II as independent ruler of Aquitaine, thus gathering a strong allied army before marching against his rebel brothers. The 2 armies met in the Yonne valley. The Neustrians under Charles drew up opposite Lothair, while on Charles' right Louis' Saxons and Bavarians faced the Aquitanians of Pepin.

The Aquitanians of the imperial left at first stood firm, until Lothair's right wing gave way in the face of an attack by Charles, reinforced by Burgundian troops under Count Warin, and was slaughtered in a downhill pursuit. The remainder of the army was then routed.

The total casualties of both sides amounted to 40,000 men, and losses were particularly severe amongst the nobility.

ASHDOWN 871

The Saxons, regrouping after a defeat by the Danes 4 days previously at Reading, faced the Great Army again at Ashdown.

The Danes drew up in 2 divisions on high ground, one division under Kings Halfdan and Bagsac, the other under 5 jarls. To counter this the Saxons also drew up in 2 divisions, that facing the kings under Ethelred, that facing the jarls under his brother Alfred, later to be known as Alfred the Great; however at the commencement of battle Ethelred was still saying mass in the Saxon camp and Alfred commanded both divisions, leading them in an uphill charge.

Fighting continued until nightfall and both Danish divisions were defeated with heavy losses, recorded as 'many thousands'. Of their leaders only Halfdan escaped alive.

BULGAROPHYGON 896

In 894 the Bulgars under Tsar Symeon invaded Byzantine territory, easily overcoming the small Byzantine army posted in the Balkans. Unable to transfer reinforcements from his eastern front, where the majority of the Byzantine forces were occupied in campaigns against the Arabs, the Emperor Leo VI appealed to the Magyars for help.

At Leo's instigation these launched an attack into the Bulgars' rear, laid waste a considerable portion of the northern Bulgar territories and inflicted a series of defeats on Symeon's army. The Byzantines themselves, under the Domestic of the Scholae, Nikephoros Phokas, occupied the southern Bulgar frontiers while their Danube fleet, under the Drungarius Eustathius, blockaded the mouth of the River Danube.

Symeon therefore opened negotiations with the Byzantines, stalling for time while he concluded an alliance with the Pechenegs. In 895 the combined Bulgar and Pecheneg forces crushed the Byzantines' Magyar allies, whose losses must have been immense since even the victors lost 20,000 men. The Magyars quit their lands as a result of this defeat and fled west into modern Hungary.

Having dispensed with their allies, in 896 Symeon turned his attentions to the Byzantines themselves. In the face of this new invasion the Byzantines planned a 2-pronged counter-attack; Leo Cataclon, the new Domestic of the Scholae (Nikephoros having been relieved), was to march north with the main army while Eustathius was to ferry the

Pechenegs (who had now abandoned the Bulgars and instead allied themselves to the Byzantines) across the Danube in the Bulgars' rear.

Unfortunately, as a result of either treachery or downright incompetence, Eustathius quarrelled with the Pechenegs, who therefore abandoned the fleet and returned to their homes. Unsupported by the expected diversionary attack in the Bulgars' rear Leo Cataclon was decisively defeated at Bulgarophygon, enabling Symeon to advance virtually unopposed to the very walls of Constantinople.

BRENTA 899

A force of 5,000 or more Magyars withdrew rapidly for several days in the face of 15,000 Lombards under Berengar I of Friuli. On reaching the River Brenta the Magyars pitched camp on the far bank and attempted to negotiate, but being refused safe conduct they suddenly attacked the Italian camp across the river.

The Lombards, exhausted after days of hard riding and many in the middle of a meal, were caught completely by surprise and routed. The Magyars, with the advantage of fresh spare horses, pursued closely and cut down a great number of the Lombards as they fled on their tired mounts. Lombard casualties are recorded as 20,000, the difference between this figure and the number of combatants possibly representing camp-followers and local civilians killed in the pursuit.

AUGSBURG 910

To bring Magyar raiders to battle King Ludwig divided his German army into 3 independent divisions. The Magyars defeated these piecemeal, the third and main division under Ludwig being defeated last.

After an indecisive battle lasting about 7 hours this division was finally drawn in disorganised pursuit of a feigned flight, and was ambushed by the Magyars in the rear and both flanks while the decoy body turned and poured volleys of arrows into them. Needless to say, the disorganised Germans failed to stand and suffered heavy casualties in the rout.

MERESBURG (RIADE) 933

After King Henry had refused to pay them tribute the Magyars invaded Germany in 2 armies. The smaller, of 50,000, was defeated by the Heerbann of Saxony and Thuringia at Sonderhausen, while Henry encountered the larger force at Meresburg. Henry arranged his army so that only his Thuringian infantry and a small body of ill-armed cavalry were visible to the large force of approaching Magyars, concealing in ambush his main body of Bavarian and Franconian heavy cavalry. These surprised the Magyars, who fled before the Germans could close with them.

The Magyars were pursued to the Unstrut, some being killed in the pursuit and more being drowned crossing the river.

BRUNANBURH 937

An allied force of Dublin Vikings under Olaf Guthfrithsson, Scots under Constantine III, and Strathclyde Welsh under Eugenius was faced by a Saxon army under King Athelstan and his brother Edmund. Simeon of Durham claims that there were 615 shiploads of Vikings, while another source mentions 4,000 Vikings and 30,000 Scots, plus others.

Both armies formed up in 2 divisions, the Saxon left, including 360 Norse mercenaries, facing the Scots and Welsh, and the right under Athelstan facing the Vikings.

The Scots were routed after a fierce struggle. The victorious Saxon left then swung onto the unshielded flank of the Viking division, which gave way under their attack and was routed by a frontal attack from Athelstan.

The pursuit lasted until nightfall and was close and bloody. Norse-Celtic losses were high, including 5 kings, one of whom may have been Eugenius, 7 Viking jarls, and Constantine's son.

LECHFIELD 955

100,000 Magyars besieging Augsburg under Karchas Bulcsu were approached along their line of retreat by a small force of Germans under Otto I, possibly including Slav auxiliaries.

Otto's force, consisting entirely of cavalry, was of 8 legiones, each of perhaps 1,000 men except for his own which was slightly larger. These advanced with 3 legiones of Bavarians leading, followed by Franconians, a mixed legio of Saxons and Thuringians (Otto's division), then 2 Swabian divisions, and finally the eighth division, of Bohemians, guarding the baggage.

The main part of the Magyar force made a frontal assault on the Bavarian divisions while a smaller body rode round behind the flank, routed the Bohemian baggage guard and then charged into the rear of the Swabians. They were only driven off by the Franconian division, which was ordered back to face them.

The frontal attack was then repulsed with heavy losses and the Germans made a general advance, probably in line, the Magyars fleeing before them under the cover of volleys of arrows.

Many Magyars were captured, many drowned in the River Lech, and others burnt in surrounding villages where they had taken refuge. Their line of retreat blocked, the survivors had to make a great detour to bypass the Germans and in a 3-day pursuit many more were killed, many being hounded down by peasants and others being killed trying to force guarded bridges and fords, one tradition recording that only 7 Magyars survived this battle. Bulcsu and several other Magyar commanders were captured and executed.

SILISTRIA 972

A mixed army of some 60,000 Rus and subject nations under Svyatoslav, including Pechenegs and Magyars, was defeated by a Byzantine force of 30,000 under John Tzimisces. Many of the Rus Turkish auxiliaries were encouraged to desert by Byzantine agents early in the campaign; by the time the main encounter took place around Peristhlaba and Silistria there were probably very few present.

Forced to take refuge in the fortified strongpoint they had established at Silistria on the Danube, and pursued there by Tzimisces, the Rus marched out from their entrenchments and formed up. In the ensuing battle their shield-wall was weakened and disorganised by Byzantine infantry archers but still managed to repulse 12 successive charges by the heavy cavalry. Only when a wind raised a cloud of dust and blew it in the Rus' faces were they defeated, Tzimisces seizing the opportunity to lead a final charge in person in which the Rus, half blinded and disordered, were ridden down. The Rus withdrew into their stronghold, where they were then surrounded by Tzimisces' land forces and a fleet of 300 Byzantine ships which had sailed up the Danube.

Eventually, after the failure of a number of sorties, the Rus surrendered after a 65-day siege. Svyatoslav and the 22,000 other survivors were released after agreeing to a number of Byzantine demands. In return the Byzantines promised to restrain the Pechenegs from attacking the Rus as they withdrew. However they were attacked and largely destroyed as they returned to Kiev when the Pechenegs, apparently forewarned of Svyatoslav's retreat by the Byzantines (who had shrewdly negotiated a separate peace with them), ambushed his boats as they were being dragged overland between 2 parts of the River Dneiper.

Svyatoslav's skull ended up as a silver-lined Pecheneg drinking cup, inscribed appropriately 'He who covets others' property often loses his own'!

COTRONE 982

40,000 North African Moslems under Abul Kasim fighting in Italy as allies of the Byzantines faced a German army under Otto II.

Having defeated and captured the Saracen advance guard in a village, the Ottonians advanced to meet the main Saracen body on the coast.

The Ottonian charge broke their centre and Abul Kasim was killed. However, while still engaged the Germans were attacked in the flank by a Saracen reserve which had been concealed in some hills and were rolled up, losing 4,000 dead and many more captured. Otto himself only got away by swimming his horse out to a Byzantine ship moored offshore. The crew, unaware who he was, landed him at Rossano, which his troops still held.

MALDON 991

93 shiploads of Viking raiders (390 ships in another source), encamped on the island of Northey on the River Blackwater, were prevented from crossing the narrow causeway to the mainland by the Essex Fyrd under Byrhtnoth; 3 of his men held them back when they attempted to cross at low tide.

Overconfident, Byrhtnoth eventually allowed them to cross to fight it out on the mainland. In the ensuing melee he was killed and some of the Saxons fled, one taking the earl's horse and thereby spreading panic amongst the Fyrd, who assumed their leader had deserted them. Thus weakened the Saxon shield-wall eventually collapsed.

Olaf Tryggvasson, shortly to become King of Norway, may have been amongst the Viking commanders.

SVOLDR 1000

Returning from Wendland with a fleet of 60 ships, Olaf Tryggvasson and his 11 largest vessels were tricked into an ambush off the island of Svoldr by their Jomsviking escort.

The ambushers, a combined fleet, formed up with Danes in the centre under Swein Forkbeard, Swedes on the right under King Olaf, and a small number of Norse ships on the left flank under Jarl Eric. The Jomsvikings own 11 ships lay to by the island and took no part in the battle. Olaf ordered his 11 ships to be bound together in a line with the famous 'Long Serpent' in the centre.

Both Danes and Swedes were repulsed with heavy losses in their attacks on the Norse centre. Eric then attacked the ships on the extreme flanks of Olaf's line and, clearing them one by one, cut them loose in turn until only the 'Long Serpent' remained, crowded with survivors of the flank ships as well as her own crew. Many were killed by missile fire from the surrounding ships and others went berserk, jumped overboard and drowned.

On the second attempt Eric's men succeeded in boarding the 'Long Serpent' where her defenders had been thinned. The crew were forced back into the stern of the ship, where they were cut down or leapt over the side to be killed in the water. Olaf Tryggvasson jumped overboard towards the end and drowned.

CLONTARF 1014

A mixed force of Leinstermen under King Maelmordha and Vikings under Jarls Sigurd of Orkney and Brodir of Man faced an Irish army under the High King Brian Boru. The Irish forces included a small contingent of Manx Vikings.

The Viking army was an international outfit with Scandinavians from Dublin, England and all of Western Europe, plus Gall-Gaels, Welsh, Flemings and allegedly even Normans; 2 sons of the King of France were even claimed to be amongst its commanders! They formed up in 5 or 7 divisions with their left flank on the River Liffey and their right on Dublin Bay, where the ships of the foreign mercenaries were moored. Another division remained within the fortress of Dublin under King Sigtrygg Silkybeard.

In the centre the Leinstermen routed the Irish and isolated their flanks. These drove back both Viking flanks while the Leinstermen, having advanced too far unsupported, became disorganised and suffered heavy losses. The Viking right flank rallied briefly and the Leinstermen fell back on it, but both they and the Vikings were soon scattered and routed, hundreds being pursued into the sea and drowned, others being cut down in the pursuit. This cut the Vikings' line of retreat to their ships – which were beyond reach anyway because of high tide.

On the left flank the hard-pressed Dublin Vikings, the nucleus of the army, withdrew towards a single bridge into Dublin, but so close was the pursuit that only 20 men, or perhaps even only 9, reached the fortress alive. Their collapse marked the end of organised resistance.

Both Sigurd and Brodir were killed, the latter only after he had himself slain Brian Boru, who was unarmed and took no active part in the battle. Brian's son Murchadh and grandson Tordelbach, who drowned in the pursuit, were also killed. Irish losses amounted to 4,000, Viking losses to 6,700 including 2,500 Dublin Vikings and over 1,000 foreign mercenaries.

BELASITSA 1014

The Bulgars under Tsar Samuel attempted to hold the Kleidon Pass in Macedonia against a Byzantine army under Basil II. They built a palisade across the entrance of the pass but were stormed from the front and simultaneously surprised from behind by a Byzantine force which had traversed the mountains.

Samuel succeeded in escaping, but the Byzantines took 14–15,000 prisoners, of whom they blinded 99 per cent (leaving one man in each hundred with one eye each to guide the others home) before they were released. Samuel is supposed to have died of grief because of this.

A Bulgar diversionary force sent to Doiran was defeated by Theophylact Botaniates.

BUG 1018

Allied with Svyatopolk of Kiev, Boleslav of Poland marched against the Novgorodian Russians under Yaroslav, whose army included Varangian mercenaries and Slavs. Boleslav's army also included auxiliaries; 1,000 Pechenegs, 500 Magyars and 300 Germans are recorded, all cavalry.

The armies met on the River Bug. Yaroslav's Varangians were unsuccessful in holding a ford, and the Novgorodians failed to make a stand against the Poles once they had crossed. They suffered heavy losses, including at least 800 captured by the Poles.

Yaroslav fled to Novgorod and raised a new army of Varangians. Boleslav in the meantime had returned to Poland, and on the approach of Yaroslav's new force Svyatopolk fled to the Pechenegs.

STIKLESTAD 1030

10,000–14,400 Norse rebels faced a largely Swedish force numbering about 3,600 or even less under Olaf II of Norway. The battle lasted only some 2–3 hours, during which time a total eclipse took place.

Olaf s army charged down from high ground, and his centre succeeded in pushing back the rebels when a misunderstanding on their flanks led to them fighting amongst themselves in the gloom. However, when Olaf was killed the royalist centre collapsed and the victorious rebel centre then turned on the king's right flank, which had arrived on the battlefield late, and drove it from the field.

Harald Hardrada, Olaf's step-brother, escaped wounded and fled to Russia.

MONTE MAGGIORE 1041

The Norman mercenaries of the Byzantine general Maniakes, feeling themselves to have been inadequately rewarded and poorly treated during his Sicilian campaign, revolted on their return to southern Italy.

At Monte Maggiore a Norman force of 2,000, including 700 heavy cavalry, faced a superior Byzantine army, including Thematic troops from the Opsikion and Thrakesion Themata as well as Varangian units, under Doceanus, the Katepan of Langobardia. The Byzantines drew up in 2 lines.

The Normans attacked in 'spearhead' formations. These broke the first Byzantine line, which reeled back in confusion and carried away the reserve line in its flight. Doceanus was captured in the ensuing rout.

This battle effectively ended Byzantine power in Italy.

CIVITATE 1053

An Apulian Norman force intercepted a Papal army under Leo IX before it could be joined by its Byzantine allies. The Norman army consisted of 3,000 cavalry commanded by Richard d'Aversa, Humphrey de Hauteville and Robert Guiscard. It also included a contingent of Calabrian infantry, but these appear to have taken no part in the main battle. The slightly larger Papal army consisted of Italo-Lombard cavalry and infantry and 700 mercenary Swabian infantry.

The Italo-Lombards, drawn up in a disorderly mass, were driven from the field by the first Norman charge and fled with Richard at their heels. The Swabians, however, fighting in close order and wielding their swords 2-handed, withstood both Humphrey's division and Robert Guiscard's reserve until, attacked also by Richard's rallied cavalry, they were forced into defensive squares and wiped out after a fierce fight.

Pope Leo, who had watched the struggle from Civitate, was handed over to the Normans by the citizens after the battle.

MORTEMER 1054

The French, invading Normandy, advanced in 2 divisions to east and west of the Seine.

Scattered to loot and pillage, the western force was caught in a surprise attack by a Norman army under Robert d'Eu. Although the fight lasted several hours the element of surprise secured the victory, since the scattered French were unable to rally.

The second division, under King Henry, withdrew on hearing of this defeat.

VARAVILLE 1057

A French army, crossing the River Dives at the Varaville ford, was cut in half by the incoming tide. The Normans under Duke William, made aware of this by reconnaissance parties, massacred those who had not managed to cross.

NISSA 1062

In an attempt to decide the mastery of Denmark a Danish fleet of 300 ships under Svein Ulfsson faced a Norse fleet of 150 ships under Harald Hardrada. Both fleets roped their central ships together.

Jarl Hakon, commanding one of the Norse flanks, drove back the opposite flank, then rowed back and forth with his ships harassing wherever the need seemed greatest.

The battle continued after nightfall, though towards the end of the night Svein's ship was attacked and cleared and his standard cut down. All the Danish ships not roped together fled at this, the Norse pursuit being partially hampered by unmanned derelicts clogging the fjord. The Danes lost over 70 ships, mostly in the central platform which had been abandoned in the rout. Svein himself had escaped in a small boat.

GATE FULFORD 1066

A large Norse army under Harald Hardrada invaded northern England, intending to press the Norwegian claim to the English crown. They were aided by King Harold of England's outlaw brother Earl Tostig commanding a Flemish contingent.

Marching on York they were confronted by Earls Edwin of Mercia and Morkere of Northumbria with a similar sized force described as a'vast army', one third of the Norse army having been left to guard their ships at Riccall.

The Norse drew up along a waterlogged ditch with their strongest flank on the banks of the River Ouse and the least reliable flank protected by a marsh. The Saxons attacked at an angle and drove back those in the marsh. Hardrada then extended his line and charged with the remainder of the Vikings, catching the Saxons in the flank and driving most of them into the marsh where so many were slaughtered or drowned that the Norse allegedly pursued dryshod.

STAMFORD BRIDGE 1066

4 days after their victory at Gate Fulford, the Norse under Hardrada were encamped on both sides of the River Derwent outside York awaiting hostages, and being a hot day many of them had left their armour with the ships.

A second Saxon army under King Harold, having force-marched from the south, caught them completely by surprise and destroyed those Vikings on the west bank almost immediately, though the bridge to the east bank was held against them for a while by one champion; the bulk of the army, however, appear to have crossed by a ford which the Norse failed to hold. The surviving Norse formed a circular shield-wall on high ground on the east bank and were gradually wiped out by repeated charges (by Saxon cavalry according to Snorri Sturlusson) and volleys of arrows, Hardrada being killed by an arrow in the throat.

Summoned by messengers the Viking reinforcements from the boats at Riccall now arrived, having run to the battlefield; they were therefore exhausted even before they began to fight, many dying of exhaustion and the rest being decimated.

Out of the original invasion force of 240–500 ships only 20–24 were needed for the survivors to return home. It was recorded in 1130 that piles of bones still marked the site of this battle.

HASTINGS 1066

Having defeated Hardrada, Harold had to force-march back south again to oppose the Norman invasion of Duke William, whose army had crossed the channel with a large fleet. Harold failed to wait in London for a full muster of the Fyrd, instead marching towards Hastings with those who had managed to keep up in the retreat from the North plus any Great Fyrd troops he could gather en route.

Only one-third of the Saxon army had formed up and the majority were still deploying when the Normans arrived on the battlefield at about 9 o'clock, and many of the Fyrd deserted, thinking the situation unfavourable. The Saxon shield-wall was formed along a ridge with the Huscarls in front and the Fyrd levies crowded behind them.

The Norman army attacked in 3 lines, archers first, then heavy infantry, and lastly cavalry, with Bretons on the left flank, Normans in the centre, and French on the right. Their infantry assaults failed, arid the cavalry were repulsed by the Huscarls, the Saxons being crowded so tightly that 'the men who were killed could scarcely fall to the ground'. Some 'thousands' of the Saxon Fyrd then broke formation to pursue the Bretons, only to be cut off by the rallied Norman cavalry and massacred, the Breton flight having apparently been a deliberate feigned retreat. Following this, the Normans resorted to a second feigned retreat, drawing 'a thousand or more' Saxons in pursuit and destroying them, thus weakening the shield-wall further.

The final attack was at dusk, a direct charge by the cavalry which broke the shield-wall. Harold was killed, and the Saxon army disintegrated, though some Huscarls rallied on a ditch-covered slope and inflicted heavy losses on the pursuing knights before withdrawing.

Casualties were heavy on both sides, and one source records Norman losses as 12,000. However, none of the authorities for this battle quote reliable figures – Wace gives an impossible 400,000 for the Saxon army, and even William of Poitiers, who wrote within a decade, records 60,000 for the Normans. Wace also gives 696 ships for the invasion fleet, while a late list of quotas of ships to be supplied by feudal vassals for the invasion totals some 777, or perhaps 1,000 vessels. William of Jumieges records the unlikely figure of 3,000 ships.

DRESS AND EQUIPMENT

1. LAMELLAR ARMOUR

Lamellar was a type of body-armour which originated in Central Asia some time before this period and remained popular throughout, surviving in the Far East until the 20th century. It consisted of basically rectangular lamellae punched with a number of holes and laced together in rows by leather thongs, usually overlapping from left to right or right to left, the rows then being laced to each other overlapping upwards. Lamellar gave greater freedom of movement than scale and was lighter, cheaper and easier to produce than mail.

Splint-armour is an alternative name sometimes applied to lamellar though that term has been reserved here for non-body armour of similar laced or rivetted lamellae construction.

The oldest practically intact non-Asiatic lamellar corselet, excavated on the site of the Battle of Visby of 1361 but of somewhat earlier date, consists of over 600 lamellae averaging 9.5cm by 2cm, arranged in 8 rows at the back and 6 rows plus 3 short vertical rows at the front, joined at the shoulders by 2 more vertical rows and buckled at the sides. Asiatic corselets seem generally to have had only one opening, at back or front.

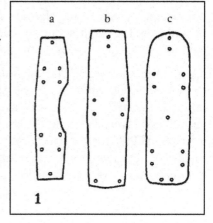

Three examples of lamellae are shown here. la is 5th century Hunnic or Turkic, lb is 7th century Lombard, and lc 10th century Swedish; some of the lace holes have been reconstructed.

Archaeological and literary sources point to iron, leather and bronze (probably sometimes really brass) being the most common materials. Bone, horn and wood were also used, and gold lamellae, such as would have been worn by Byzantine guardsmen, have also been excavated. Metal lamellae were rarest amongst Asiatic peoples.

2. 7TH–8TH CENTURY BYZANTINE SKUTATOS

This is based on sources dating to the reign of Heraclius (610–641). Equipment consists of lamellar corselet with pteruges at shoulder and waist, 3 by 4 foot oval shield called a skuta (hence skutatos), a 12–14

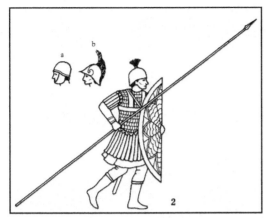

foot spear called a kontarion that had a socketed 18-inch blade, a sword suspended from a baldric, and a plumed helmet. The kontarion could be thrown in battle. Javelins were also carried, apparently by ranks 5 back.

The skuta was constructed of leather-covered wood. It was slightly curved but not convex, as can be seen from its profile view here. An anonymous 6th century military manual describes those of front-rank men having a circular metal reinforcement with a 3-inch spike at centre.

Main differences from late Roman dress are the substitution of trousers and boots for breeches and sandals, and the addition of leather shoulder reinforcements, secured by a breast-strap rather than tied down Greek style. This leather harness is not mentioned in any of the manuals of the period but is to be found in practically all contemporary illustrations. It was probably buckled at the centre of the back.

The late-6th or early-7th century Strategicon substitutes a mail corselet for the lamellar and lists heavy javelins or martiobarbuli (see 15a) in addition to the kontarion. Short mail corselets and cloaks are shown in some pictorial sources, as are plain leather cuirasses.

2a and b show alternative helmets of c. 600 and c. 630. The latter is that of an officer, those of ordinary soldiers having only the central plume.

3 & 4. 9TH–10TH CENTURY BYZANTINE SKUTATOI

These heavy infantrymen wear iron helmet, characteristic short lamellar corselet buckled down front or back (horn or iron scales or mail could also be worn), leather gauntlets, splint-armour vambraces called cheiropsella or manikelia (never, to my knowledge, shown in a contemporary Byzantine illustration) and square-toed boots. The ring on top of the helmet would take a crest like that of 13 on parade and sometimes in battle, but such crests appear only rarely in the sources.

The Tactica of Leo VI records that body-armour of this kind was often worn only by the front 2 ranks, others wearing instead a padded and

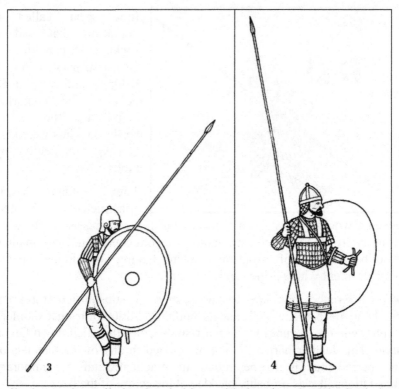

3

4

quilted corselet called a bambakion with hood and 18-inch sleeves. The name 'bambakion' derives from the Arabic 'pambuck', cotton, in the same way that the mediaeval aketon was later derived from the Arabic 'al-qutun'. As early as the 6th century such padded tunics were being worn under the body-armour. They are described as being ¾-inch thick.

A certain proportion of men in each unit carried a heavy javelin of cornel, oak, or other non-splintering wood called a menaulion in place of the kontarion. Secondary weapons for all skutatoi were a light hand-axe called a tzikourion (the Roman securis), or sword (spathion) or paramerion, the latter a sabre-hilted one-edged weapon which first appeared in the late-9th century. The mid-10th century Praecepta Nikephori suggests that the axe might be replaced by a mace, while both the Praecepta and Leo mention that some skutatoi might be armed in addition with slings, though Leo's seems to be no more than a suggestion, and I have found one 10th–11th century casket which shows a heavy infantryman using a sling and holding his skuta before him. Leo also mentions another one-edged sword called a machaira, possibly an alternative name for the rhomphaia. While the sword was invariably suspended from a baldric during this era, the paramerion was usually girded at the waist.

Note the beards, rare before the 9th century but by the 10th century essential to the dignity and masculinity of every Byzantine male. They were usually neatly trimmed.

5. 10TH CENTURY BYZANTINE FRONT-RANK SKUTATOS

The military manuals claim that front and rear ranks were more completely armoured than other skutatoi. According to Leo they wore splint greaves called podopsella, while the Strategicon says that a mail hood was worn by the front rank and flankers and wooden greaves and knee-guards by the front 2 ranks. However the late-10th century Sylloge Tacticorum lists greaves and mail hood as standard skutatoi equipment, and iron, felt or leather greaves are elsewhere recorded worn by skutatoi in general as early as the 6th century.

Leo mentions a type of padded body-armour to be worn, when available, over the corselet – hence its name epilorikia – though it could also be worn on its own. This was a hooded, quilted or felt corselet reaching to the knees or lower, with thick, wide sleeves, and must have been basically very similar to the bambakion described above. It seems to have been worn chiefly by cavalrymen.

6. 9TH–10TH CENTURY BYZANTINE INFANTRY OFFICER

This figure is based on the Joshua Roll of c. 925. He differs little from 3 except that he sports an impressive helmet crest and has a sash or cloak wrapped round his torso and tied at the front. Such 'sashes' appear in a number of contemporary illustrations, often wrapped horizontally round the chest as in figure 20, and quite clearly they served to denote rank. They are shown in the sources being worn by both infantrymen and cavalrymen whose equipment is otherwise virtually indistinguishable from that of the rank and file that they led except in being often more ornate. Standard-bearers (bandophoroi) may have also worn the sash.

Byzantine officers appear to have favoured the mace (see note 13) but many probably carried a kontarion like their men. Clothing was decorative and elaborately embroidered and equipment was often engraved and inlaid.

6a shows an officer's crest of the 11th century. An earlier one is shown in 2b.

7. 10TH–11TH CENTURY BYZANTINE PELTASTOS

These appeared in the second half of the 10th century and though they are still recorded under the years 1081 and 1084 in the Alexiad of Anna Comnena there were probably never many of them. Their equipment, described in the Sylloge, was lighter than that of the skutatoi and they probably evolved as a result of cutbacks in military expenditure, the expensive armour of the skutatoi probably having become less widely available. They were to wear mail or lamellar corselets when they could be got, but otherwise had to make do with thickly-quilted cotton bambakia (also called kabadia) or horn or leather epilorikia. 'Peltastoi' therefore probably describes their equipment rather than their military function.

Weapons were kontarion, javelins and paramerion. They carried a 3-foot diameter shield which Leo earlier calls a thureos, also carried by some skutatoi.

8, 9, 10 & 11. BYZANTINE PSILOI

According to the military manuals psiloi (light infantry) wore neither body-armour nor helmet, carrying only a 12-inch diameter shield for protection, and even this was sometimes discarded in battle as too heavy according to the Strategicon while Leo actually forbids its use. However, pictorial sources – and a few written ones – indicate that most in fact wore light helmets and that shields were rather larger, as shown here. In addition light mail or lamellar corselets were supplied to as many archers as possible when available, but these were undoubtedly restricted to heavy units. Some sources show such armoured archers with not only waist-length corselets but helmets and fairly large circular shields too, usually slung at the back when the bow is in use. 8 shows such an armoured archer.

Although the principal weapon of the psilos-proper was also the composite bow drawn to the chest, some psiloi were armed with light or heavy javelins, staff-sling (spendobolon), or marzobaboula (often translated mace but really martiobarbuli, for which see note 15). Archers were often issued in addition with a sling as a reserve missile weapon. The crossbow (called a solenarion) was also used but dropped out of use after the mid-10th century to be reintroduced by the Normans in the late-11th, when Anna Comnena calls it by the name tzangra. The use of the bow itself seems to have undergone a decline during the 9th century which Leo VI was only partly successful in checking; he proposed the reintroduction of enforced archery practice (even for those exempt from military service) and instructed his generals to ensure that every household possessed a bow and 40 arrows, but apparently without effect. 40 was the usual number of arrows held in a quiver, though it occasionally held as many as 60. Psilos' secondary armament consisted of paramerion or tzikourion, carried by 9 and 10 respectively.

Nikephoros II Phokas (963–969) lists complete psiloi equipment as 2 bows, 4 bowstrings, 2 quivers containing 40 and 60 arrows, small shield, sword, tzikourion and sling. Psiloi were expected to keep their hair short.

Servants, armed with slings, probably dressed similarly but less uniformly and would have been sans shield and helmet.

12. BYZANTINE SAILOR

This man represents a lower bank oarsman. He wears a lamellar corselet over 2 thicknesses of leather (probably a bambakion) and is armed with a bow and sword. Upper bank oarsmen, marines and other deck fighters were equipped more like skutatoi with helmet, mail or lamellar corselet, vambraces, greaves, long spear, javelins and sword. Heavy cloth surcoats,

12

probably quilted epilorikia, were sometimes worn as additional armour. Leather and wood shields of a type called dorkai were carried by both sailors and marines, sometimes with polished iron plates stitched on.

13 & 14. 10TH CENTURY BYZANTINE TAGMATIC KATAPHRAKTOI

These figures and the next 2 are based on descriptions given in the 10th century military manuals; cavalrymen depicted in contemporary manuscripts are equipped more like 18, 20 and 21. An earlier Byzantine heavy cavalryman is described in *The Armies and Enemies of Imperial Rome.*

13

By the 10th century kataphraktoi no longer carried both lance and bow as they had in the earlier period, in a 5-rank formation ranks 1, 2 and 5 being lancers (figure 13) while 3 and 4 were archers (figure 14). The former were armed with kontarion (the cavalry version being a slender 12 foot lance originally, and occasionally still, called a kontos, 'barge-pole', in recognition of its length), plus a dagger, and a sword carried from a baldric. The sword could apparently be as long as 3 feet, including the hilt. The shield carried was larger than that recorded in the Strategicon, probably because the bow was no longer a handicap to its use. In an appendix to Leo shields are described as a maximum of 40.5 inches, which is also the basic length of the average 11th century kite-shield. The Sylloge describes '3-cornered' infantry shields, clearly kite-shields, as 54 inches in length, though the cavalry version appears to have been smaller, only 36–40 inches long, which tallies with Leo. Kite-shields of the type shown here began to appear in Byzantine mss. illuminations in the mid-10th century and it was probably from this type that the European version developed (see note 61). Judging from pictorial sources it appears to have been about 2 feet broad at its widest point. In his main text Leo actually specifies that the small 12-inch shield was to be carried, but larger 24–30-inch circular shields appear in most sources of the 8th–10th centuries.

Early sources record that the cavalry kontarion could be slung behind the back by a strap in its middle (a feature of Avar origin), and a spare was carried in the baggage. It was thrust overarm, often 2-handed but more commonly in one hand, until the late-10th century when it began to be couched. Officers carried in addition a flanged mace called a bardoukion, meaning 'sledgehammer', in a case right of the saddle bow. This had become fairly standard equipment by the late-10th century.

14

Body armour consisted of a mail lorikion, thorax or zaba (from which the Arabic 'zardfaa', long mail coat, derived) to knees and elbows, or horn or iron scale armour if mail was unavailable. A lamellar corselet called a klibanion could also be substituted; technically this was a short sleeveless defence of the type worn by 2 and 4, but it was also a blanket term for lamellar armour in general. It was sometimes worn over the mail lorikion for extra protection, as here. Most men wore mail hoods or aventails, those without wearing a padded wool or linen gorget instead. Additional armour consisted of vambraces and greaves of iron, wood or ox-hide. Dyed horsehair tufts were worn on each shoulder and also as helmet crests.

Archer ranks were usually less-heavily armoured, and although they officially carried no shield the 12-inch diameter one was probably still in use by many, strapped to the left forearm. Their composite bow was 45–48 inches long and more powerful than those of the Turks and Persians but 'slower firing', probably because it was fired by volley. When not in use it was kept in a waterproof case which hung from the saddle at the left. The quiver, containing a spare bowstring and 30–40 27-inch arrows, was suspended from the belt at the right hip. Bad archers could substitute 2 javelins for the bow and by the reign of Nikephoros II 2 javelins and a spear might also be substituted for the kontarion.

Clothing consisted of bleached linen tunic embroidered with coloured thread, loose linen trousers, and yellowish leather boots; in winter goatskin dyed in solid colours and with the hair left on was substituted for linen clothing. A long, sandy-brown cloak was rolled up and strapped behind the saddle, sometimes being worn to conceal the gleam of armour. Such is the description of dress given in the manuals. The pictorial sources, on the other hand, tell a different story. Uniforms were dyed throughout this period, predominantly in red, also in all shades of blue and sometimes green and purple; trousers are most often shown as white or grey so were presumably bleached or left undyed. Tunic embroidery at hems and cuffs appears to have been generally gold. Boots were black, brown or sometimes dyed, usually red or white; they were invariably decorated with dark bands as shown in the drawings. The army-issue cloak would appear to have been replaced on active service by non-regulation, brightly-coloured civilian types with embroidered hems and panels, particularly amongst the officers. Either way the cloak was not normally worn in battle. The military manuals specify that each bandon had lance-pennons, plumes, shields and standards in a particular distinctive colour.

Probably all lancers rode armoured or half-armoured horses, though it is less likely that archers did so. Note that the Byzantines do not appear to have used spurs.

15. 10TH CENTURY BYZANTINE KLIBANOPHOROS

These were a revival by Nikephoros II of the late Roman true cataphract and they were probably limited to the Tagmata. Manzikert in 1071 probably saw the end of them.

Their equipment consisted of klibanion or mail zaba with pteruges and elbow-length sleeves, vambraces, and mail-strengthened gauntlets, all joined by pieces of mail. A hooded bambakion or epilorikion of quilted cotton was worn over this, probably dyed in uniform colour. Legs were protected by greaves called chalkotouba, and it seems likely that the feet too were protected, probably with the metal overshoe covering toe and heel but not sole listed by Leo as general cavalry equipment. The face was covered with 2 or 3 layers of mail so that only the eyes were visible. In addition a shield appears to have been carried, but whether it was kite-shaped or round is a matter of opinion; because klibanophoroi were so heavily armoured the author personally favours the small round shield.

The first 4 ranks were armed with marzobandoula, once again the Roman martio-barbuli, in addition to the usual kontarion, sword and dagger. 15a shows a martiobarbulus; it was 12 inches long with a feathered wooden shaft, lead weight and barbed head.

Klibanophoroi sometimes included archers, but these were less heavily armoured and would resemble 14. However, like the lancers they rode fully-armoured horses as described under 144.

16. 7TH–10TH CENTURY BYZANTINE TRAPEZITOS

Light cavalry were usually barbarian auxiliaries as described under 17. There were a few Byzantine horse-archers (non-existent by the end of this period), but most of the native light cavalry were of the sort called monozonai or trapezitae, whose trick riding gave us our modern circus term. Their equipment marks them as a close relation to, or more accurately a direct descendant of, the late Roman scutarii.

Except for a crested iron helmet and occasionally a hood of horn scales they usually wore no armour, though officers may have worn light mail corselets. Tunic would be red or blue, the standard Byzantine uniform colours during this era. They were armed with kontarion, sword and 2 or 3 javelins. Although one would have assumed the latter to be small and light Leo specifies that they should not exceed 9

feet in length! They must therefore have been relatively close-range missiles.

The shield could be either the circular 3-foot thureos or the oval infantry skuta. However it may have sometimes been much smaller, the 12-inch type apparently also being used while the Sylloge describes light cavalry shields of 27 inches diameter. Circular shields continued to predominate amongst Byzantine light cavalry even after the kite-shield was in widespread use.

This type of cavalryman does not appear in the Strategicon but does in Leo. However, it seems reasonable to assume that such troops were in use from the beginning of this period.

17. BYZANTINE AUXILIARY LIGHT CAVALRYMAN

The Byzantines employed large numbers of auxiliary light cavalry throughout this period until by the reign of Nikephoros II and thereafter light cavalry consisted entirely of allied horse-archers.

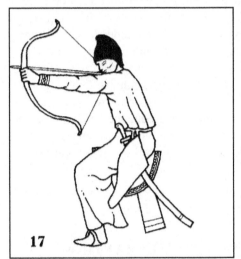

This figure is based on a source dating to the 10th–12th centuries and is practically identical to the figure described under 82 and despite his clean-shaven appearance he is almost certainly a Pecheneg, called Patzinaks by the Byzantines and one of the principal mercenary elements in the Byzantine army by the 11th century. Other figures of the same type in a variety of sources carry shields of about 20 inches diameter and shortish, fairly broad-bladed swords, both probably Byzantine issue.

18. 10TH–11TH CENTURY BYZANTINE THEMATIC KATAPHRAKTOS

Thematic troops supplied their own equipment, which could therefore be better than that of their Tagmatic equivalents but was usually worse, especially during the provincial decline of the 11th century. A Thematic muster in the Anatolikon Thema in 1067 saw infantry armed only with hunting spears and scythes and equally ill-equipped cavalry with no horses and a dearth of other arms. Even in the mid-10th century equipment may have often been lacking; in a largely Thematic army led by Nikephoros II, described as 200,000 men by an Arab chronicler, only 30,000 apparently wore armour, and though the figures are improbable the proportions – even allowing for light troops and auxiliaries – indicate a generally low standard of equipment.

This figure, based on a source of c. 1000, is typical of Thematic types, with only helmet and short mail corselet; the breast-strap, frequently depicted being worn by cavalrymen, has no shoulder-pieces. Others would have worn longer corselets, scale or lamellar or carried kite-shields, and there would have been little or no uniformity except, presumably, in shield-devices, crests and lance-pennons. Clothing may have often followed uniform colouration but was otherwise probably a mixture of black, grey, white, brown and green, the other principal clothing colours favoured in the Empire. Bow-armed Thematic kataphraktoi would have been similarly equipped in a wide variety of styles.

The officers and at least the front rank of Thematic units would have ridden partly or, where available, fully armoured horses.

19. LATE–10TH OR 11TH CENTURY BYZANTINE SKUTATOS

This figure, from a ms. of 1017, differs very little from figures 2–4 except for his helmet, which is of a new variety that became standard and occurs in most 12th–13th century sources. 8–10-foot spears may now have been becoming more common than the 12-foot kontarion, which probably largely disappeared in the course of the 11th century. The oval skuta too, though it remained in use for much of the 11th century, had by c. 1080 at the latest been generally replaced by the kite-shield.

20, 21 & 22. 11TH CENTURY BYZANTINE KATAPHRAKTOI

20 dates to c. 1050 though his equipment is equally characteristic of 10th century pictorial sources. Note the lamellar corselet with pteruges at shoulder but not waist (a common practice) and his circular shield, which appears to be 30–36 inches in diameter; a shoulder-strap, called a guige in the West, was adopted during the 10th century. He wears the sash of an officer (see note 6). His tunic is red, cloak dark blue with a heavily embroidered gold and black tablion (decorated panel) and

20

trousers are brown or tan brocade. The lamellae of his corselet are shown in the original as blue and yellow in alternate horizontal rows, such decoration of lamellar being not uncommon.

21 is from a ms. of 1066. He carries a tapering kite-shield, the predominant type amongst Byzantine heavies by the mid-11th century, though as we have seen the circular shield also remained in service. The Byzantines may have developed this modified version of the kite-shield themselves from the indigenous type described in note 13, or it may have been adopted as the result of Western influence, possibly being introduced by Norman mercenaries who were first employed in 1038. It should be noted, however, that this modified Byzantine type was somewhat broader than that in use in the West, being of an 'almond'

21

shape that prevailed in Eastern Europe for as long as the kite-shield did. The type of grip most commonly employed by the Byzantines on their kite-shields can be seen in figure 22.

He wears a scale corselet, tubular upper-arm defences, and a helmet which in the original is depicted blue or red, possibly indicating it to be cloth-covered or dyed leather. His shield could be red, blue or green with a gold pattern. The source shows tunics and trousers in the same three colours. Boots are black.

22 is from the Scylitzes ms. of c. 1200 which contains a vast number of illuminations largely copied from earlier originals. This figure, judging by his complete armour, is possibly a late klibanophoros, even though the original shows such figures mounted on unarmoured horses. Note that he too carries a kite-shield.

Cavalry lances appear to have become generally shorter judging from the illustrative sources, probably under the influence of mercenaries from Western Europe. However, the 12-foot kontos or kontarion remained in use until at least the mid-11th century, and the word 'kontos' itself was still in use when Anna Comnena wrote c. 1140. By the late-10th century the lance was usually couched underarm, though the source from which 21 is taken shows lances being used both over and under arm.

23, 24 & 25. VARANGIAN GUARDSMEN

The rhomphaia, a falx-like weapon with a curved blade of about the same length as its handle, was the principal weapon of Byzantine guardsmen, replacing the kontarion. Clearly, however, not many Varangians were ever equipped with it, instead retaining their native Scandinavian weapon, the axe; there are constant references to them as 'axe-

24

bearing barbarians' in the Byzantine sources, and an illumination in Scylitzes depicts a group of Varangian guardsmen in which 18 axes can be counted. Gaufredus Malaterrae, a Norman chronicler, records the Varangians using axes at the Battle of Durazzo in 1081 which he describes as plumed and wielded in both hands.

During the 11th century at least 2 Varangians were certainly armed with rhomphaiai on campaign, accompanying the Emperor on foot and guarding his spare horse in battle. Psellus even claims that 'without exception' the Varangians were armed with rhomphaiai 'which they carry suspended from the right shoulder' and confirms that they carried in addition a shield. (Shields are also mentioned by Anna Comnena; neither source specifies size or shape, though it seems reasonable to assume they were of Scandinavian design, i.e. circular and 30–36 inches in diameter.) Conceivably the Varangians carried rhomphaiai for palace duty and axes in action, though this theory is somewhat negated by the presence of troops armed with rhomphaiai in the rebel field army of Isaac Comnenus in 1056. Either way the shield must have been laid aside or slung at the back in close combat so that both hands were free to wield the weapon. 23a depicts what is probably a rhomphaia from a Byzantine ms. of c.900.

Spears and swords are also recorded in the sources, the sagas making it clear that many Scandinavians retained their own swords when they entered the Guard, in which case one is justified in questioning just how much of their equipment was actually Byzantine. Probably a mixture of both Scandinavian and Byzantine gear was in use, the latter becoming more predominant as the former was damaged or lost. The Varangians were generally heavily armoured.

25

24 and 25 are typical of many figures which appear in Byzantine art from the late-10th century. The date of their initial appearance and the general richness of their equipment lends support to the belief that their costume, with the probable exception of the head-

dress, may be based on that of the Varangians. 24 dates to c. 1040; his tunic is red, cloak purple, scabbard and trousers mauve, all with gold and red decoration, boots and head-dress being white with black markings. 25 is little different except for the addition of a lamellar corselet with short pteruges. His shield appears to carry a Black Raven design (see 72), and I have since found a second such figure that carries a similar shield device.

Laxdaela Saga, recording the return to Iceland of several ex-Varangian guardsmen in 1030, describes their dress being of scarlet and gold-embroidered silk. One also wore a scarlet cloak. A gilt helmet and gold-inlaid weapons and saddles are also mentioned, in addition to a red shield with a gold warrior on it. At least some, if not all, of this equipment was Byzantine-issue, though scarlet or red tunics do not tally with the 'sky-coloured' ones recorded by Haroun ibn Yahya to be worn by axe-armed guardsmen that he saw in Constantinople c. 900, though the date makes it unlikely that these were Varangians even though they may have been Rus mercenaries.

A Byzantine source tells us that the Varangians had fair or reddish hair worn long on either side of the face, with beard and bushy moustache.

It seems clear from Anna's account of Durazzo that the Varangians used horses as transport to, from and even on the battlefield, but they clearly dismounted to fight.

26. BYZANTINE EMPEROR IN PARADE ARMOUR

This figure is based mainly on a portrait of Basil II Bulgaroktonos (976–1025). He wears a hip-length klibanion and tubular upper-arm defences, both either gold or gilt. Tunic is purple with gold embroidery, while cloak, trousers and fringe on corselet are light blue. Boots are red leather decorated with small white dots, probably pearls, the scabbard being likewise red but decorated in gold. The helmet, with officer's crest of peacock feathers, is from a mid-11th century textile.

Contemporary illustrations often show Emperors wearing such armour in battle scenes, but this is undoubtedly artistic licence. Other sources speak more credibly

26

of Emperors wearing the same armour as ordinary cavalrymen but far more ornate – bejewelled helmet, gilded corselet and so on.

The Emperor's horse-trappings and saddle-cloth were purple, the harness including gold decoration and sometimes jewels. It would appear that imperial horses sometimes also wore silk housings.

27. BYZANTINE STANDARDS

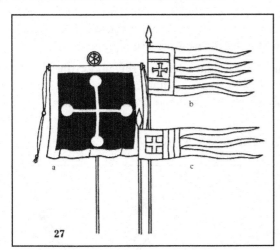

The old-style bandon (the same as the older vexillum) had now become the Imperial standard, 27a showing an example of c. 856. Many variants of the crucifix or cruciform pattern are to be found in contemporary art.

The other principal standard which accompanied the Emperor was an ikon which instead of a crucifix bore an image of the Blessed Virgin. This was the famous 'Lady of Blachernae', still recorded as late as 1204 when together with the Imperial standard it was captured by the crusaders from Alexius V; at that time it was described as 'all of gold'. Draco standards similar to those described under 63a and 122a remained in use with infantry units at least during the 7th and 8th centuries, but had largely disappeared by the time Leo's Tactica was written c. 900; however, certain Excubiti standard-bearers were called draconarii, which implies that they at least continued to use draco standards. Leo records instead that a new type of swallow-tailed bandon had become the principal standard of both infantry and cavalry units. Its size appears to have varied with the size of the unit, those of dhoungoi and turmai apparently being similar to but longer than those of banda. 27b and c show such standards; they postdate this period, being from the Scylitzes ms., but were probably copied from 11th century originals. In this source the number of tails varies between 3 and 8, the standards often being grouped in such a way as to suggest that the greater the number of tails, the larger the unit. This would perhaps give us 3 tails for an allaghion, 4 for a hekatontarchion, 5 for a bandon, 6 for a moira, 7 for a meros or turma, and 8 for a stratos or thema.

Standards are normally shown in contemporary sources in shades of red, blue or purple, sometimes green, and often gold-decorated. In Scylitzes they are usually red with a white cross and alternating white and red tails, though tails are sometimes red, blue and white. Leo says that the standards of each of the banda should be a different colour, but it is hard to conceive that there could be enough colours in the spectrum for this regulation to be strictly adhered to; perhaps it was only the tail colours that differed. The cross appears to have been the most common (perhaps even regulation) standard device, often embroidered in gold or silver. Even the navy's standards had crosses on them, though surrounded in their case by 4 fire-siphons.

Auxiliary and mercenary units generally fought under their own standards, though Sigfus Blondal suggests that the Varangians, having replaced the Excubiti, may like them have had draco standards.

28. SUB-ROMAN BRITISH CAVALRYMAN

He wears a mail corselet called a lluric (cf. Latin lorica) and a late Roman iron helmet, similar to the modified one found at Sutton Hoo (see 112c). One poem of c. 660 mentions golden plumes, which is supported by Arrian's statement that all Roman cavalry wore yellow crests. Helmets were not always worn and possibly only those of chieftains or officers would have been crested.

28

His shield is shown here as a Roman-style 2 by 3 foot oval, though it may equally well have been circular. It was of hide-covered alder wood, white-washed and with a central boss which was used offensively. Some shields may have been decorated with studs or gilt ornaments. He is armed with spear, javelins, sword and dagger, spear-shafts being of ash or less commonly holly wood. His cloak might be purple or scarlet if he were a chieftain, red and crimson also being recorded. In addition he wears a gold torque, as worn by some late Roman soldiers. In fact his overall appearance is still quite Roman, and this is not exactly coincidental, for Gildas, who wrote c. 540, tells us that when the Romans returned to Britain for the final time in the early-5th century they not only gave 'energetic counsel to the timorous natives' but also left them 'patterns to manufacture arms.'

The saddle is of yellow-brown leather, and horse-trappings could be decorated with silver. Taliesin contains a possible reference to horse-armour, which is recorded in use by the related Bretons in the 9th century, so it is possible that this was a continuation of late Roman practice. Some sources mention spurs.

29. SUB-ROMAN BRITISH INFANTRYMAN

This figure wears a leather corselet with pteruges called a caenet and

29

his clothing is of checkered wool, though upper classes could wear silk; checkered, striped and spotted clothing is mentioned in a number of sources. He is armed with a spear and a circular shield, though the large, nearly round shield of the late Roman legionarius may still have been carried by some. The cross it carries is implied by an entry in the 10th century Annales Cambriae for the Battle of Mons Badonicus. Likewise a passage in the 8th century chronicle of Nennius implies a shield with an image of the Virgin Mary. His secondary armament would have been a hand-axe (possibly a securis), mentioned in the Gododdin, or a long knife. Some substituted a bow for the spear and shield, but archery was not popular.

Hair ranged from yellow to light brown and was always long, the British being inordinately fond of their tresses. Most men wore moustaches and some had beards.

The sub-Roman Britons continued to use Roman-style draco standards. According to old traditions Arthur's father, Utha Pendragon, had a golden dragon standard, while Cadwaldr, a mid-7th century king of Gwynedd, seems to have used such a standard as late as 678. In old Celtic sources 'dragon' is even used as a word for a chieftain, undoubtedly because of the standards they carried. It is probably no coincidence that the dragon is the present-day emblem of Wales, and it is claimed that even this was originally red-gold rather than red.

30. SUB-ROMAN GALLIC INFANTRYMAN

Although taken from a Merovingian source of c. 600 this figure is probably typical of those late Roman units which Procopius records still surviving in Gaul in the mid-6th century, wearing Roman uniforms and serving under Roman standards. These sub-Roman soldiers were of 2 kinds – the Laeti, descendants of the old military settlers, and the Milites, the descendants of the regular army units. Most were Germanic.

30a shows a similar helmet of c. 550 found at Isere.

31 & 32. PICTISH CAVALRYMEN

Many illustrations of Picts from this period are shown in *Armies and Enemies of Imperial Rome*. These 2 are armed with lance or javelins and circular, convex shields averaging about 18 inches in diameter with prominent spiked bosses.

The pattern on that of 31, who is undoubtedly a chieftain, probably represents the heads of rivets securing the grip extension. He carries a short sword in a scabbard with a typical U-shaped silver chape, and wears a long-sleeved mail corselet and a helmet with nape-guard and nasal, similar to those of 52 and 64. Both men are barelegged but wear shoes. Long hair and trucculent beards were characteristic.

The last mention of Picts painting themselves appears to be an early-5th century Roman panegyric, and by the time Picts appear in the early Saxon chronicles there is no indication that the practice was still current, despite somewhat later Welsh sources describing the lands north of Hadrian's Wall as Prydein, the Land of the Painted Men. Probably woad went out of widespread use some time around the beginning of this era but could still be found in isolated areas for the next century or more.

33. PICTISH CHIEFTAIN

This is based on the Birsay grave slab from Orkney which depicts 3 chieftains of c. 700 of which this one is pre-eminent. He wears a long tunic with patterned hem, belted at the waist, and is armed with sword and thrusting spear. His shield, consisting of leather stretched over a frame of 2 sticks, is elaborately painted.

34 & 35. PICTISH INFANTRYMEN

34 is taken from the Aberlemno stones of c. 750, as are 31 and 32. He is armed with the usual longish thrusting spear, a short sword and a circular shield suspended at his back from a shoulder strap. Others would substitute a bow for the spear.

35 dates to the mid-10th century so is more accurately a 'Scot', though the inhabitants of Scotland were now a confusing mixture of Picts, Scotti, Strathclyde Welsh, Northumbrian Saxons and Scandinavians. He is armed with javelins and carries an unusual shield which, since it has a central boss, is probably of leather-covered wood rather than stretched hide; an identical shield is to be seen held by a foot-soldier

34   35

on the Ardchattan Stone, which has been assigned to the 11th century. His rough woollen cloak is checkered in Pictish fashion. Tartan as we know it did not develop until much later than the period we are here concerned with, the word itself evolving from 'tiretain', of Anglo-French origin, meaning simply a brightly coloured woollen material. Other clothing appears to have been of the same coloration as that of the Irish described below, tunics usually being described as light or bright, occasionally with coloured borders or red embroidery.

Trews such as those of 39 could be worn in addition to the tunic, though Scots soldiers normally went barelegged. Others wore only a sleeveless shirt which could be buttoned or tied between the legs. Certainly in the mid-6th century Gildas laments the Picts' and Scots' lack of decent clothing, many Scots remaining ill-clad until centuries beyond the end of this era.

36. PICTISH CROSSBOWMAN

This figure is from the 9th century Drosten Stone, close examination of which proves beyond doubt that the weapon carried is a variety of crossbow. 2 other stones, at Glenferness and Shandwick, show similar weapons but they are more weathered and their details are consequently far less clear. All 3 stones show such crossbows being used in hunting scenes by kneeling hooded men, but there is no reason to suppose they were not also used in war. The way they are held in the sources is a little obscure and has led one historian to the conclusion that they may have been fired by manually releasing the bowstring rather than by the use of a trigger-mechanism (see note 130). However excavations at the 6th–7th century Strathclyde British site of Buston Crannog in Ayrshire in the late-19th century yielded a crossbow trigger-nut made of horn as well as 2 arrows with pyramidal heads that have all the characteristics of crossbow bolts. These finds would seem to indicate that the crossbow was possibly in limited use in Scotland throughout this era.

36

37. IRISH CHIEFTAIN

This figure is based mainly on carvings from the Cross of the Two Scriptures at Clonmacnois, dating to the 10th century.

37

He wears a leine, a long tunic usually of linen (hence its name) but sometimes of wool or silk, which in battle would normally be shortened by being drawn up through the belt. Over it he wears a dyed 'shaggy mantle', a cloak made to look like fur by the incorporation of tufts of unspun wool between the threads whilst weaving. Normally a semi-circular woollen cloak, the brat, would be worn instead; this often had a fringe, and those of chieftains could be of satin or silk.

The brat was most often purple, crimson or green but could also be black, blue, yellow, speckled, grey, dun, variegated or striped. The leine, usually described as 'bright' or 'light-coloured', was generally bleached, often with a coloured border, but was sometimes striped or embroidered. It is not known when the characteristic saffron tunic of the mediaeval era came to be adopted, but the earliest evidence dates to the mid-14th century.

Helmets are often mentioned in Irish poetry but appear to be a literary convention, while mail was unknown in Ireland until the Viking invasions and even then was apparently not adopted by the Irish until after the close of this period, though the 12th century 'War of the Gaedhil with the Gaill' credits Irish chieftains at Clontarf in 1014 with mail corselets as well as helmets.

Irish swords were short and inflexible, averaging 20–24 inches in length. That the scabbard was suspended from a waist-belt is shown quite clearly in one of the Clonmacnois carvings.

38 & 39. IRISH WARRIORS

These represent lower-class warriors whose costume traditionally consisted of trews and jacket. The tight-fitting trews were either knee-length or ankle-length with a strap under the instep. Leather or cloth gaiters of some description were sometimes worn but shoes, although known in Ireland, rarely were and then only by chieftains. The jacket, called an inar, was waist-length with either full or three-quarter length sleeves or none at all. It could be open-fronted or closed with a brooch or pin or, by the 11th century, with buttons. Cloaks were also worn, that of 39 being a shorter campaigning variety of the brat. One mid-10th century king equipped his 1,000 followers with cloaks of leather, perhaps as a form of armour.

An 8th century law states that lower classes should wear yellow, white and black, though the Book of Kells shows a lower-class warrior in blue and green, and red is known to have been worn. Otherwise clothing was of natural or bleached wool and linen.

Arms consisted of small javelins or darts, usually 2 or 3, and the short, broad sword, the claideb. Sometimes a thrusting spear (gae, sleg or manais) or a light throwing spear (bir or foga) was carried in addition, the thrusting spear often with a pointed iron ferrule; shafts appear to have been of hazel and could be decorated with rivets or nails. The small shield was of wood and leather or plain hide. Bosses were often of brass or bronze but were otherwise of iron.

40. IRISH AXEMAN

From the late-9th century onwards the Irish began to adopt characteristically Viking weapons. The 'War of the Gaedhil with the Gaill', listing the equipment of the Irish army at Clontarf, tells us that the kings, chiefs and leading warriors had broad-bladed 'Lochlann' (i.e. Viking) axes 'for cutting and maiming the close, well-fastened coats of mail' that their Viking opponents wore. The same source also seems to indicate that longer swords were now in use (in which it is backed up by archaeology), and that larger shields had been adopted, these latter having brass bosses and bronze decoration and being painted in variegated patterns as described under 66.

This particular figure is based on carvings on a shrine of a slightly later date (c. 1130). His hair is plaited with the end of each plait secured by a small golden ball, while his beard is forked Viking-fashion. The Irish generally wore their hair long and thick.

41. 7TH CENTURY VISIGOTHIC INFANTRYMAN

This man's costume is based on the 7th century Ashburnham Pentateuch ms. It consists of close-fitting wool or linen breeches and tunic, boots, short cloak, and tall felt hat, possibly only worn by freemen and royal slaves. Traditional Gothic dress had died out in the late-6th century and influences in clothing were principally Byzantine. In this source tunics are mainly white, red or a buff colour and breeches mainly red or dark blue.

He is armed in accordance with the army laws of Wamba (673) and Erwig (681), by which most men were expected to appear for service

41

with spear, shield, sword and scrama or bow and arrows. Some had to wear in addition mail or scale zabae or loricae. Yet others had to be slingers with whatever equipment their masters had given them (armies being comprised largely of conscripted slaves by this date). Isidore of Seville's Etymologicon of c. 615 gives a general list of Visigothic arms which includes all of those so far mentioned plus semispathae, franciscas (which the Visigoths called cateia or teutona) adopted from the Franks, cavalry lances, and crested helmets.

42. 7TH CENTURY VISIGOTHIC CAVALRYMAN

Visigothic cavalrymen were armed with lance and javelins; Isidore says 'they fight on horseback not only with lances but also with darts. They enter battle both on horseback and on foot; nevertheless, they prefer the swift course of cavalry, wherefore the poet says "There goes the Goth, flying on his horse".'

The heavy element probably consisted of the nobles' warbands and later the better-equipped slaves. Basic equipment consisted of corselet, helmet, shield, sword, lance and javelins. The corselet, as we have seen, could be lamellar or mail, while contemporary coins show 2 principal helmet-types in use, these being hemispherical, possibly with a faceguard, and conical with cheekguards as here. Nobles usually wore decorated armour, loot taken by the Arabs at Toledo in 711 including gilt corselets and richly mounted swords and daggers. King Roderick's horse at the battle of that same year had a saddle encrusted with rubies and emeralds.

42

Some horsemen may have been 'extra-heavy', Isidore mentioning that horse-armour was in use among the Alans of neighbouring Armorica, which suggests that it was probably also known to the Visigoths.

Unarmoured cavalry would have resembled 54 sans stirrups.

43. 7TH–8TH CENTURY LOMBARD CAVALRYMAN

This figure dates to c. 615. He is armed with sword, dagger, and a long lance wielded in both hands called a contus (the Byzantine kontos), stout enough to lift a small man from his saddle and hold him aloft according to Paul the Deacon. A shorter spear capable of being thrown could be substituted, and axes and javelins are also recorded. Of their swords, Cassidorus wrote c.520 that they were capable of cutting through armour; they averaged about 33 inches and were parallel-edged with a rounded point.

Armour was rare in their early period and even after the establishment of their Italian kingdom only the wealthier cavalrymen were expected to serve with body-armour, the majority again probably resembling 54. This man wears a lamellar corselet, greaves called by their Roman name of ocrea, and an Avar-style helmet with cheek-guards, aventail and plume. 43a shows an alternative of spangenhelm construction. Lombard helmets often had a small cross instead of the plume. The shield was of lime-wood.

The Lombards certainly wore spurs and it seems probable that stirrups were introduced in the 7th century.

44. 7–8TH CENTURY LOMBARD INFANTRYMAN

Though the Lombards were principally cavalry their lower classes served as bow-armed infantry.

Typical Lombard costume can be seen here. Their early dress apparently resembled that of the Saxons, except that their linen tunics were dyed in broad bands, either stripes or wide hem-bands. They customarily wore wrappings of white cloth round the lower leg, as a result of which their Gepid enemies ridiculed them as 'white-legged hacks'; proper trousers apparently only being adopted in the early-7th century, horsemen wearing shaggy woollen leggings over these. Boots were also in common use by the 7th century.

The Lombards wore their beards extremely long (the derivation of the name Langobard or Lombard) while their hair was cropped short at the back but hung long at front and sides, parted at the centre.

44

45. 6TH–7TH CENTURY MEROVINGIAN FRANK

This figure, based on late Roman and Byzantine descriptions, depicts a Frank as they probably appeared at the very beginning of this period. He carries an iron-rimmed shield with a prominent boss, sword, angon (a barbed thrusting or throwing spear with an iron-covered shaft) and francisca, a throwing-axe with a short wooden handle. The latter seems to have actually dropped from use by the 7th century, Gregory of Tours only once mentioning an axe in a throwing context and only mentioning axes 5 times at all. Bows are not recorded in the classical sources, though Gregory records the bow to have been introduced in the 4th century.

Likewise, although Gregory mentions both helmets and mail corselets the other sources record the absence of body-armour and rarity of helmets. Probably only chieftains and their retinues were thus equipped anyway.

Procopius records in the mid-6th century that even at that early date the Franks had a few spear-armed cavalry, though Agathias of Myrna says c. 570 that they only appeared on rare occasions.

Sidonius Apollinaris, writing c. 470, describes Franks wearing

45

'many-coloured', probably striped, short-sleeved and close-fitting tunics, and red-embroidered green cloaks. Legs at that date were apparently bare, though Agathias speaks of linen or leather trousers. Agathias, incidentally, says that the shield was hung at the left hip, which could mean it was slung from a shoulder-strap or alternatively implies that it was small.

46 & 47. 8–10TH CENTURY CAROLINGIAN INFANTRYMEN

By the end of the 8th century the traditional costume of the Franks consisted of a long-sleeved woollen or linen tunic called a gonelle, with linen trousers, wrappings round the lower leg, which could be cross-gartered, and a long cloak reaching almost to the ankles in front and behind. Short cloaks were adopted from the Gallic population as more practical for fighting. These were often striped. There were, however, regional variations in costume; Gascons, for instance, wore a round-edged coat, puffed trousers and boots.

Tunics were predominantly white or blue. Other colours included bright red, dark red, violet, brown, ochre, yellow, grey, and sometimes green, often with contrasting hem, cuffs and collar. Purple was reserved for the nobility and royalty. Cloak colours included white, grey, sapphire blue, blue, crimson, red and brown. Leggings were most commonly scarlet.

The spear and shield were the standard arms of the general levy, though 2 or 3 javelins might be substituted for the spear. Secondary armament if carried at all would have been a knife or scramaseax, though a club or cudgel of knotted apple-wood was carried in addition to the spear by some. 46a shows the characteristic shape of the Frankish scramaseax, which had an average blade length of 10 inches. The winged spearhead is often mistakenly referred to as a 'Carolingian' feature though it had been in use much earlier; the function of the wings was to prevent the head from penetrating too far.

47 is better equipped, with a sword and helmet. His helmet is of a shape that is characteristically Carolingian, similar to a late Roman design from which it was probably evolved; identical warriors appear in mss. as late as 1000. 47a and b show types of crest that sometimes appear in ms. illustrations.

48 & 49. 9TH CENTURY CAROLINGIAN HEAVY INFANTRYMEN

Both these figures date to c. 850 and are armed with spear and sword.

Frankish swords were the best in Europe at this time, pattern-welded and well-balanced with a broad fuller down the centre. This groove is often referred to in Scandinavian sagas as a 'blood-channel', but its real purpose was to lighten the blade without weakening it. These swords were principally intended as cutting weapons, sword fighting being a matter of heavy blows with the edge of the blade, which had to be parried with the flat if a dented cutting edge or shattered blade was to be avoided. Scabbards are recorded as covered with white linen hardened with shining wax. They were usually wooden throughout this period and lined with wool or fur. Other cover materials included leather and parchment. The scabbard could be suspended from either the waist-belt or a baldric.

49 has a slightly Roman look, possibly as a result of artistic licence on the part of the illuminator, though the source adheres mainly to Carolingian styles for shields, weapons and general clothing, with the exception on many figures of knee-breeches and Roman-style sandals (which we know were still being worn in Carolingian times – Charlemagne himself wore short breeches and sandals). He wears a sleeveless scale corselet over a pattern-edged leather jerkin. The aventail of his helmet, the halsberge or 'neck-protection' of written sources, is of mail. The same source shows scale and leather aventails and coifs, and helmets similar to that of 50.

50. CAROLINGIAN HEAVY ARCHER

This man, from a ms. of c. 924, wears a short mail or scale corselet and a helmet with a nape-guard. Other sources show archers dressed identically to 48. It has often been suggested that such figures as this represent dismounted horsemen which, in view of the fact that horsemen had to provide a bow and one or more quivers of arrows as part of their equipment (see notes 52 and 55), is not impossible.

As we have seen, the bow was first adopted by the Franks in the 4th century, but it only became regulation equipment c. 802 when it was substituted for the apple-wood club described under 46. However it remained unpopular and archery was never a major element in Carolingian warfare.

50

The quiver could either hang at the right hip or across the back. Other mss. sometimes show archers with no quiver at all, the arrows being stuffed through their belts or held in the left hand with the bow. The majority of what few Carolingian archers there were would be identical to the Saxon described under 115.

51. CAROLINGIAN MUSICIAN

Horns were used throughout Europe to transmit simple pre-arranged commands on the battlefield. They were either curved as shown here or straight-sided and of assorted lengths. They remained in use by most nations throughout this period, being recorded on both sides at Hastings in 1066 by William of Poitiers.

52 & 53. 7–8TH CENTURY MEROVINGIAN CAVALRYMEN

51

Although their occasional use is recorded from the mid-6th century, the first decisive use of cavalry by the Franks was against the Old Saxons in 626.

52 is based on a funerary stele of c. 700. The helmet is similar to that described under 64c. A late-7th century source lists the equipment of a member of a warband as mail corselet, helmet, shield, lance, sword, and bow and arrows. Gregory of Tours mentions that the quiver was suspended from the waist-belt. However, there is no evidence that Frankish cavalry were ever intended to fight as horse-archers or ever did, though on very rare occasions continental mss. shows bows used by horsemen (one even appears towards the end of the later Bayeux Tapestry, though this is fairly certainly a mistake introduced during its 19th century restoration); as mentioned above, perhaps figures such as those described under 50 represent dismounted cavalrymen. An alternative solution that has been occasionally put forward is that the bow was given to a foot-slogging retainer. Interestingly a source of 792

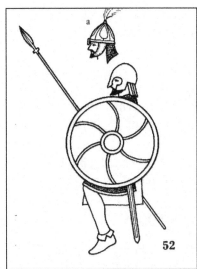

52

53

lists arms as comprising only lance, shield, sword and semispathum anyway and makes no mention of bows.

52a shows a spangenhelm of c. 600, typical of early Frankish helmets. It has plume, mail aventail and short nasal. Cheek-guards were of iron or sometimes horn.

53, dating to the 8th century, also wears a mail corselet, though scale could be substituted for either (see note 55). He wears spurs but stirrups had not yet been adopted.

54. 8–10TH CENTURY CAROLINGIAN MEDIUM CAVALRYMAN

Stirrups now appear, introduced in the second half of the 8th century through contact with the Avars and Lombards. However, early 9th century sources still often show figures riding with no stirrups, though wearing spurs.

Because of its cost (see next note) armour was uncommon amongst the general levy of cavalrymen, lesser vassals often being equipped only with lance, javelins, shield and scramaseax or sword,

54

though some also wore a helmet. Warriors of this type often appear in contemporary sources, where they frequently outnumber those wearing armour.

In addition similar lightly equipped cavalry were supplied by Gascon and Breton contingents, armed chiefly with javelins, and by Old Saxons and to a lesser degree by East Franks. They were generally used as skirmishers or simply to swell the numbers of the heavier-armed contingents of the nobility.

Except for the stirrups the majority of the mounted city levies of Merovingian armies would have been little different.

55. 9TH CENTURY CAROLINGIAN HEAVY CAVALRYMAN

This man represents an upper-class warrior. He wears a corselet called a brunia or broigne about the construction of which there has been some debate; it was probably often mail (the term lorica being sometimes used instead), but in contemporary illustrations corselets certainly look rather more like scales attached to a leather foundation, as depicted here. Either way the corselet was an  expensive piece of equipment which few could afford, and for a long time corselets were obligatory only for men with estates of 12 mansi, while one capitulary (c. 802) made it obligatory for counts to have spare bruniae and helmets to equip their retainers. In addition splint-armour greaves called bagnbergae or bauga, of iron or less commonly leather, were in use at least as early as the late-8th century, while a single vambrace (manica) could be worn on the right arm, the left arm being protected by the shield, and a passage in Notker implies mail-strengthened gauntlets. Obviously, however, such additional armour would have been even rarer than the corselet.

Some idea of the cost of such full equipment as is illustrated here can be got from the following assessment of 9th century arms in cows: the helmet was worth 6 cows; the brunia, 12 cows; sword and scabbard, 7 cows; greaves, 6 cows; spear and shield, 2 cows; and the horse, 12 cows. The total of 45 cows (which, admittedly, can be reduced to 15 by assessing in terms of the dearest cows) should then be compared to the bovine population of some of the richer individual royal estates, which had at the most only about 50 cows (excluding oxen, heifers and bullocks). Men as well-equipped as this were therefore probably in extremely short supply. This makes it very likely in turn that until about the mid-9th century figures such as 48 and 49 must have been provided by dismounted horsemen.

Leather or padded tunics similar to the bambakion (see note 3) or the quilted garment described under 68 were probably worn under the corselet from the beginning of this period as some protection against heavy blows which though unable to pierce the armour were still capable of breaking or fracturing bones or causing serious bruising. Such quilted tunics also prevented the armour itself from being driven into the flesh.

55a shows an alternative 9th century corselet with a strengthened leather breastplate worn over it. The thighs are also protected by scale armour, though this was not favoured by the Franks, who claimed it hindered their riding. Lamellar may also have been sometimes worn.

The lance, which varied in length between about 7 and 10 feet, was usually thrust overarm or hurled at this date (Charlemagne himself is described in one source as habitually carrying a throwing spear), though by the middle of the 9th century it is already sometimes shown couched as a lance. Sword, dagger and shield were also carried; the inner face of the shield is shown here, revealing the metal frame on which the orb was constructed. Carolingian shield bosses were prominent, protruding up to 8 inches.

One capitulary also includes in its inventory of arms a bow, 2 bowstrings and 12 arrows, while another demands more than one quiver of arrows. See comments under notes 50 and 52.

56. CAROLINGIAN GUARDSMAN

This figure, based on illustrations in the Bible of Count Vivian (846) and the Gospels of Emperor Lothair (849–851), probably represents a guardsman of the Imperial household. As with figure 49 his Roman appearance may be artistic licence, but the Carolingians took their title of Emperor very seriously indeed and deliberately copied many Roman practices, including – as we have seen – some elements of their dress.

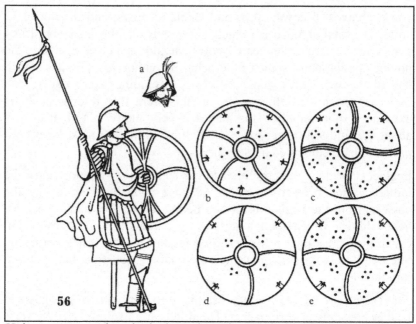

56

Helmet-crest, tunic, cloak, knee-breeches and shield-face are all red. The sources also show cloaks of salmon pink and rust (probably the result of discoloration) and light grey-green, as well as crests of feathers as shown in 56a. The lance pennon is red or gold/ochre. Knee laces and tunic hem-band are gold, as is shield decoration and boss. Shield patterns of such figures are shown in 56b–e. The muscled cuirass with pteruges at shoulder and waist would probably have been of leather, though coloration in the originals implies iron.

Interestingly a similar figure appears in the somewhat earlier Utrecht Psalter of c. 825.

57. 10TH CENTURY CAROLINGIAN CAVALRYMAN

Although he is described as Carolingian, France had alternated between Carolingian and Capetian dynasties since the late-9th century, and this figure and 50 are both from a ms. that is in fact Capetian. The last Carolingian king, Louis V, died in 987.

The same source and others also show cavalry in shorter hip-length corselets or

57

152

equipped like 54 with or without helmets. Written sources and a few illustrations indicate that yet others were identical to 59.

58. CAROLINGIAN SHIELD PATTERNS

58a and b show typical designs. The radial lines probably represent

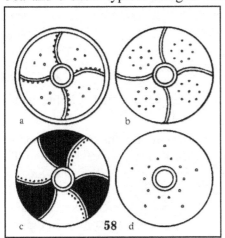

strengtheners attached to the framework shown in figure 55. The number of radials varied, 5 or 6 being most common, 3 least common. 58c is interesting in being painted with variegated dark and light panels Viking-fashion, Frankish mss. more usually showing shields painted in a single basic colour or left plain, with just rivets and radials for decoration.

Similar shield patterns to these are also to be found in Saxon sources.

59 & 60. OTTONIAN HEAVY CAVALRYMEN

These figures, dating to the mid-10th century and c. 1000 respectively, wear mail corselets with short baggy sleeves and loose coifs. The coif ultimately gave its name to the complete mail body-armour, having

evolved from the halsberge (see note 49), a word which became in time 'hauberk'. It was sometimes worn without a helmet. Similar figures are to be found illustrated and described in late Carolingian sources.

The oval shield of 60 is unusual, others in the same source having no boss.

The greater number of horsemen would still have been of the less well-equipped type described under 54. Under the Ottonians these were supplied by Old Saxons, Thuringians and Wends

60

and other Slav auxiliaries. Except for their nobility none of these wore armour, and even helmets were uncommon; Old Saxon troops described on campaign in 946 wore only straw hats. The spear was their principal weapon, both for thrusting and throwing, while their shields were often only of leather and were easily pierced. In the 9th and early-10th centuries Old Saxons were frequently placed before the main battle-line to act as skirmishers.

In fact despite a number of attempts to encourage their use of cavalry from the 9th century onwards the Old Saxons and Thuringians continued to often fight on foot, freemen and chieftains alike. Cavalry were principally Franconians and Bavarians, though by the mid to late-10th century even the Old Saxon nobility had acquired a reputation as excellent cavalrymen.

61. OTTONIAN HEAVY INFANTRYMAN

This figure is from a Codex Aureus ms. of c. 983–991, showing the kite-shaped shield in Europe for the first time. It is convex, of wood and leather with a boss that no longer covers a handgrip. In shape it is not yet as long or tapering as those of the Bayeux Tapestry, and it may represent a transitional type between those and the earlier type described under note 13 (some of which also appear in late-10th and early-11th century Western art). There is no evidence in the Aureus ms. that it was developed for cavalry as is so often claimed, being shown there in use only by infantry. It was probably adopted from the Byzantines during clashes with them in Italy in the last decades of the 10th century.

It was also at about this time, c. 1000, that a new type of sword began to

61

appear, with a more tapering blade and better balance. The mace, sometimes wielded in both hands, also begins to appear in Western sources in the second half of the 10th century.

62. OTTONIAN MEDIUM INFANTRYMAN

Also from the Codex Aureus ms., he has no obvious secondary armament though a knife or scramaseax would probably have been carried, or even a sword. Others would have been like those described under 46, 115, 130 and 131, armed with bow, crossbow or javelins.

63. CAROLINGIAN AND OTTONIAN STANDARDS

63a shows a Carolingian draco standard of windsock design, another inheritance from the late Romans, from a ms. dating between 841 and

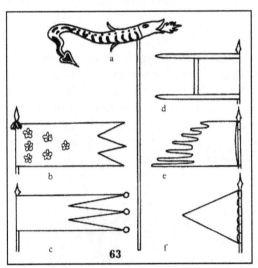

872. It would probably have been red, heavily embroidered, with a silver or metal head.

63b is from an 18th century sketch of an early-9th century mosaic in the Lateran which has since been altered beyond recognition. It is green with red flowers that have blue edges and yellow centres, the tassel being white, blue and red. In the original it is shown being presented to Charlemagne

by St. Peter and therefore possibly represents the Emperor's personal standard.

63c is a typical 9th century banner, each of the 3 tails here ending in a cotton or wool bobble. 63d and e are from coins of Conrad I (911–918) and Otto III (994–1002) respectively. 63f is a simple lance pennon, others being like those described under 126a–h.

Notker records the Cope of St. Martin being carried as a battle standard by the Carolingian kings and other religious banners are recorded in various sources. A banner of St. Denis was adopted by the Merovingians as early as c. 630, which may have been rectangular and flaming red like the Oriflamme recorded in later sources (see note 43 in 'Armies of Feudal Europe'), while the early Ottonians carried a standard depicting St. Michael, recorded at both Meresburg and Lechfield.

64. 7TH CENTURY SCANDINAVIAN CHIEFTAIN

He wears an unusual cross-over mail coat with richly decorated edging, metal greaves, vambrace on swordarm only, and decorated, boar-crested helmet. He is armed with 2 long javelins and a sword, the scabbard for which hangs from a baldric. His white-washed shield is relatively small, about 24 inches in diameter, with a prominent iron boss.

64a, b and c show alternative helmets from the graves at Vendel and Valsgarde in Sweden. 64a is very eastern in style and has a mail aventail hanging all round, while 64c has a neck-guard of hinged metal strips. The cheek-guards of b and c join in front of the chin. 64d, from a decorated plaque, has a stylised eagle crest. Skullcaps, cheek-guards and neck-guards are iron, all decorated with plates of patterned bronze and gold inlaid in copper and silver.

65. 7TH CENTURY SCANDINAVIAN WARRIOR

This figure's leather or padded topcoat, worn over a woollen or linen tunic, is of the same cross-over pattern as the mail coat worn by 64. It could cross over either way and has heavily embroidered edges. His arms consist only of spear and shield; the cord binding about halfway down the spear shaft marks

the centre of balance to facilitate throwing.

Others carried a sword as well, suspended from a baldric, or a scramaseax of about 18–21 inches, and might wear helmets.

66. VIKING CHIEFTAIN

He wears a cloak, which would be richly embroidered, and a long mail corselet (the hringserkr or hringskyrta, 'ring-shirt'). Dagger, sword, helmet and shield-face could all be decorated with gold and silver. His main weapon is a double-handed axe which might also be decorated, the blade becoming more crescentic, like that of 120, after the 9th century. The axe is the characteristic weapon of the Vikings in contemporary sources and they excelled in its use; a single axe-armed champion at Stamford Bridge in 1066 is reputed to have killed as many as 40 Saxons!

66

The helmet he wears dates to the 10th century and echoes the earlier Vendel types, some of which were probably still in use. Despite the misleading and too frequent confusion with Celtic British helmets, NO Viking fighting helmets had horns or wings, though it is possible that horned helmets such as 66a (from the 9th century Oseberg Tapestry) were worn in religious ceremonies since according to Scandinavian myth Odin's most valued champions, the Einherjar, wore helmets with beaks like eagles and horns like bulls. In battle Viking helmets often had a 'herkumbl' ('war-mark') painted on the front, presumably for identification on the battlefield. Oxenstierna even suggests that a boar-crest like that of 64 might be considered a herkumbl.

Viking shields varied between 24 and 36 inches in width. They were light, made of lime-wood with rims of iron, leather or even bronze, and could be used offensively. Colours were red (by far the most popular), yellow, black, white, and to a lesser extent blue and green; the 64 shields of the 9th century Gokstad ship were painted alternately yellow and black. The leather face could apparently also be divided into halves or quarters and painted in alternate colours, while other sources record shields being painted with mythical scenes, dragons and other creatures. At Nessie in 1015 many of King Olaf's men had gilt, red or blue crosses on their white shields, though these were Christians. The Gotland picture stones show many shields patterned like that of 59.

67. VIKING HIRDMAN OR HUSCARL

He wears a short mail corselet and a helmet of the most common variety, conical with or without nasal. 67a shows a variant from a picture stone with a chin-strap and sides extended into ear-guards, and 67b another variant with eyebrow ridges as well as nasal. Mail aventails and, later, coifs, were also worn. Archaeological evidence indicates that lamellar was sometimes worn in Sweden at least.

He is armed with sword, knife, characteristic one-handed bearded axe

67

(in use by the 8th century) and 2 light javelins which are little longer than arrows. Swords were generally of Frankish origin since their own lacked flexibility and tended to break in use. The scabbard was often suspended from a baldric.

The baggy trousers shown here can be seen quite distinctly in tapestries and picture stones and were of steppe origin. Clothing colours popular amongst the Vikings included red, scarlet, red-brown, brown, blue, green, white, black and grey, the last particularly for cloaks; red, leaf-green and blue were favourites, the Dublin Vikings having a particular preference for red. Trousers were sometimes striped vertically, and one anecdote records that leggings should be brown or any other colour except scarlet. Cowhide or sealskin boots might also be worn, hairy side out.

The Vikings were vain about their appearance, bathed and changed clothes regularly, and may have even worn eye make-up! All Vikings wore beards, which were looked upon as proof of their masculinity; this man has his plaited. Hair was likewise often plaited and, though it seems to have often been worn short, might also be grown to considerable length – that of Brodir, one of the commanders at Clontarf, is supposed to have been so long that he tucked it into his belt. Hair colours ranged from blonde and red to black, darker hair being more common amongst the Danes.

11th century Viking huscarls would have closely resembled the Anglo-Danish Huscarl described under 120 (though substituting a round shield, the kite-shield apparently not being generally adopted in Scandinavia until the 12th century); such longer mail corselets were clearly in use by the 11th century at the latest, Harald Hardrada's being described in 1066 as 'so long that it reached below the knee, and so strong that no weapon could pierce it.'

68. VIKING BONDI

The Gulathinglaw and Frostathinglaw (which Snorri Sturlusson says date to the reign of Hakon the Good, 935–961, but are probably earlier)

record that each ordinary freeman serving in the levy is to have an axe or sword, ash thrusting spear (spjot), and a wooden shield of 2 boards thickness with at least 3 iron strengtheners 'laid across it.' These were the obligatory folkvopn (folk-weapons), which in Denmark and Sweden also included an iron helmet (stalhufa). Men of more substance were also expected to provide themselves with a mail corselet or quilted jerkin (for which see below), ordinary men also sometimes having to supply either one such corselet per rowing bench or even on occasion per man.

This man wears cloak, loose trousers, and for protection a quilted and padded leather jerkin, a common substitute for mail, capable of turning or at least slowing any blow except a direct thrust. Saint Olaf's Saga records some huscarls wearing such jerkins at the Battle of Stiklestad in 1030; these were made of reindeer hide and we are told 'that no weapon could cut or pierce them any more than if they were armour of ring-mail, nor even so much.' What appear to be such jerkins are shown on a number of Gotland picture stones. In fact the sagas make it quite clear that mail was not as common amongst the Vikings as is so often suggested. Irish chroniclers record that of all the Vikings at the Battle of Clontarf only 1–2,000 had mail coats.

He also wears a round-topped cap, possibly of leather. Other hats were pointed or had broad brims.

69. VIKING ARCHER

The Vikings made considerable use of the bow both on land and at sea, Not only was it used to a considerable extent by the bondi (particularly in Norway, and in Sweden where the word 'bow' could even be used to mean a warrior) but also by nobles and kings, who took great pride in their personal accuracy.

Viking bows were mainly of elm, though yew was also used. They were almost longbows in their proportions but the length of excavated arrows confirms that they were only drawn to the chest. In the Leidang bows were provided as part of the ship's equipment; the Gulathinglaw and Frostathinglaw say a bow and 24 arrows per thwart, to be supplied by the 2 oarsmen. This implies that up to 50 per cent of a Viking national army might in fact be bow-armed.

This man's hair is held back by a decorated headband; these were highly popular and brightly coloured. A cylindrical quiver holding on average 2 or 3 dozen 24-inch arrows hangs at his right hip, some quivers containing up to 45 or 48 arrows. His sword is a one-edged sax, particularly popular amongst the Norwegians. The word sax, or seax, seems to have been applied generally to the longer types of scramaseax.

Some use was also made of the sling, and a chronicle of the siege of Paris in 885 mentions lead-cast slingshot.

70. VIKING BERSERKR

Berserkr means 'bear-shirt' rather than 'bare-shirt', and originated in the ritualistic donning of animal skins in the hope of thereby attaining the beast's strength. Bear-pelts continued to be worn by Berserkir throughout the Viking era and are often mentioned in Scandinavian poetry of the period.

The Berserkir were probably a mixture of psychopaths and sufferers from paranoia, lycanthropy and epilepsy. In battle they fell, or worked themselves up, into a wild frenzy, of which the commonest signs were gnawing at the shield-rim and throwing off their armour and clothing – hence the confusion 'bare-shirt'. When in such a frenzy they had the proverbial strength of madmen and were impervious to pain and wounds. Ynglinga Saga records how they 'went into battle without armour, like mad dogs or wolves, biting their shields, strong like bears or bulls, mowing down everything in their path, immune to fire and iron.'

Berserkir formed the bodyguards of the pagan Scandinavian kings, being highly prized as a result of their 'supernatural' powers. Later, when the Vikings had become Christians, the Berserkr was frowned upon as some sort of ungodly fiend, and in Iceland at least he could be fined or outlawed for going into a berserk rage.

71. VIKING ULFHEDNAR

These were a variation of the Berserkir, Ulfhednar meaning 'the wolfskin-clad ones' or 'wolf-coats'. They added to their attributes the howl of the wolf. Volsunga Saga records Ulfhednar who each undertook to fight up to 7 foes at once! This particular figure actually predates the Viking age, being taken from a 7th century helmet plaque which clearly represents a warrior dressed in the pelt of a wolf. A similar warrior, dressed in a (bear?) skin, can be found in the Oseberg Tapestry.

71

72. VIKING STANDARDS

Scandinavian standards were called gunnefanes or 'war-flags' (French gonfanons). Asser records a Viking standard captured in 878 to have been called 'Reafan' (Raven), and various other sources also record Black Raven standards. For example the eleventh century Encomium Emmae records a raven standard of white silk, and Earl Sigurd of Orkney's standard at Clontarf was so shaped that when the wind caught it it looked like a raven in flight. Saxon sources also record that if the raven fluttered it meant a Viking victory, but if it drooped it meant a defeat. It is also reasonable to suppose that Harald Hardrada's famous 'Landeythan' (Landwaster) bore a raven device. Other devices were also in use, Olaf Tryggvasson having a white standard with a serpent on it, and it was probably such fanged and winged monsters

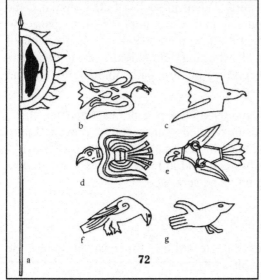

72

that were intended by the Annales Fuldensis' description of Viking standards as 'signia horibilia'.

72a shows the only Norman banner in the Bayeux Tapestry that is not merely a geometric pattern. Bearing in mind the Normans' Viking ancestry it seems a reasonable assumption that this is a late example of a Black Raven standard.

72b–g are from contemporary Scandinavian art. 72b and c are from Gotland picture stones, 72d is from a 10th century Viking coin from Dublin, 72e from a Norwegian picture stone, 72f from Thorvald's Cross on the Isle of Man, and 72g from the Oseberg Tapestry. Some portray eagles rather than ravens but they are characteristic of the execution of birds in Viking art.

73. 10TH CENTURY RUS CHIEFTAIN

The Rus were Scandinavians, mainly Swedes, who established themselves among the Slavs of modern Russia (to which they gave their name) and were by the end of the 10th century largely absorbed by them. Rus princes and their retinues sometimes fought on horseback by the late-10th century but only took to mounted combat on a large scale from the middle years of the 11th century.

73

This figure wears lamellar corselet, gold armbands, and a decorated Persian-style Slavic helmet with mail aventail. He carries a sword of Frankish origin rather than the sabre more common in Central Asia at this time (see 81 and 82). The decorated scabbard is of gold.

The Rus were largely blonde or red-haired. Most shaved the beard but grew moustaches. 73a shows the hairstyle of a 10th century chieftain, the scalp being shaved except for 2 braids signifying his rank. This was a custom adopted from the Turks, as was the recorded tattooing of green zoomorphic patterns from finger-tip to shoulder.

74. RUS WARRIOR

Rus costume consisted of boots, white linen tunic, baggy trousers, and a cloak secured at the shoulder. Furs were also worn, particularly for their cloaks and tall hats; sable was predominant but ermine, squirrel, fox, marten and beaver are also recorded. Upper-classes might wear brocade.

Ibn Miskawaih, an early-11th century Arab author, records main Rus weapons as spear and shield; they carried in addition sword or axe, knife and a javelin slung at the back. Leo the Deacon records that a great many wore mail corselets; he also says that they fought with swords, bows, spears and javelins and carried long shields 'the height of a man', clearly the tall rectangular shields of Slav origin described under 103 in 'Armies of Feudal Europe'.

75. SLAV WARRIOR

This man is dressed and armed in accordance with 6th–10th century Arab and Byzantine sources. He wears a linen tunic, loose linen trousers, cloak and boots. Others would substitute leather or bast shoes, the latter made from willow, birch or oak bark fibres and common amongst the forest-dwelling Slavs. Furs, sheepskins and woollen cloths could also be worn. Linen clothing was generally bleached white, the Baltic Slavs still wearing white clothes as late as the 13th century. However, during the earlier part of this period clothing tended to be rather greyish.

Arms consisted of spear and 2 or 3 javelins or darts and a heavy circular or rectangular shield. Short one-edged knives were also carried, while the Moravians and Croats adopted the axe as a standard weapon.

Hair was reddish-blonde. Slavs under Turkish influence or domination often cropped or shaved their heads.

For standards the Slavs, like the earlier Celts, used animal images mounted on poles during the early part of this period, though from the 10th century onwards ordinary banners were adopted. However, the Pagan Lutitians are recorded carrying an idol on a 'portable altar' into action as late as the 11th century.

76

76. SLAV ARCHER

This figure is based on a 9th century Moravian plaque. He wears a cloth, fur or felt cap, linen tunic and baggy trousers taped at the ankles. Bows were another of the Slavs' principal weapons. The Byzantine Strategicon claims that their arrows were poisoned, though this seems rather unlikely. Archers were a particularly important element in Polish armies.

77. 10TH CENTURY SLAV CHIEFTAIN

This represents either a chieftain or one of the upper-class warriors who constituted his Druzhina. Armour was to be found only amongst such upper-class types and even then was only commonplace after the 10th

77

century. It was usually of mail or sometimes lamellar. This man also wears a copper or iron grivna or torque, these still being worn until at least the 11th century, and his Persian-style helmet is decorated with gold inlay. Arms consist of spear, javelins and sword, the sword being an insignia of his social status.

Spurs are of bronze or iron and could be gilt. Stirrups were introduced by the Avars during the 6th or 7th century. Under Avar influence sabres, decorated belts and composite bows had also been temporarily adopted and Avar-style armour worn.

78 & 79. 11TH CENTURY SLAV INFANTRYMEN

Due to her eastward ambitions, particularly in Poland, the states along the Eastern frontier of the German Ottonian Empire soon became westward in their outlook.

78 is a Pole of the mid-century. He carries a circular shield, sword suspended from a baldric, and spear. As noted earlier, the Poles also made considerable use of archers, to the discomfiture of German cavalry!

79 is a Hungarian of 1086. He wears baggy linen trousers and a tunic with contrasting bands at cuffs and collar and a vertical panel down the chest. His kite-shield is shorter, broader and more convex than those shown in most Western sources, this kind being prevalent in Eastern Europe where they are usually referred to as almond-shields rather than kite-shields.

Their costume is otherwise no different to that current in Western Europe, the Slavs being greatly influenced by foreign fashions of dress. Cloaks could be worn by either, while furs and sheepskin would be commonly worn in winter.

Southern Slavs were more influenced by Byzantine styles of clothing and armour.

80. 11TH CENTURY SLAV CAVALRYMAN

This man is also a Pole. His armour is no different from that worn throughout Europe at this time, except that his helmet appears to have an aventail, and there are recorded instances of 11th century Slav cavalry being mistaken for Germans.

The metal framework of his shield is practically the same as that of 55.

81, 82, 83 & 84. ASIATIC LIGHT CAVALRYMEN

For this period information on the Central Asian nomad hordes has to be gleaned from those contemporary 'outsiders' – Germans, Scandinavians, Russians, Byzantines, Armenians, Arabs and Chinese – with whom they came into contact. Fortunately styles of costume and armour were almost universal across the steppes and changed little through the centuries.

Therefore although 81 is an Avar his general appearance is characteristic of nearly all the steppe peoples. His dirty black hair is shaved high on the scalp, with one long lock plaited with coloured ribbons and held by gold clasps. One source claims that their long hair earnt the Avars their name – probably in much the same way that it has been suggested, albeit inaccurately, that the name Khazar may have derived from Russian 'kosa', meaning pigtail. 2 tresses, one at each ear, were sometimes worn in addition (see 73a). The shaved head was especially characteristic of most of the Turkish peoples of Central Asia, amongst whom it was also customary to shave off the beard (what little most of them could grow). The Magyars at least often had scarred faces like the earlier Huns, as did some Slavs.

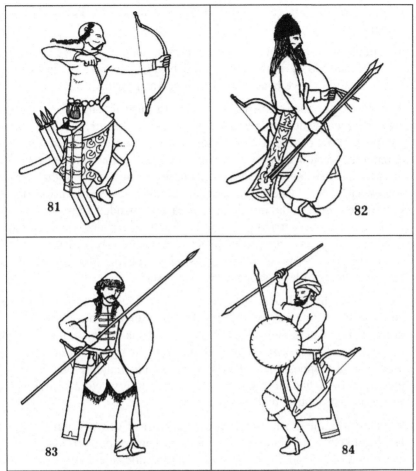

Basic costume consisted of a long, loose under-tunic split at front and back, a kaftan, a short over-tunic, trousers, boots and occasionally a cloak. Clothing materials included silk brocade, dyed leather (scarlet, red and purple leather often being supplied by the Byzantines as payment to mercenaries), furs (sable, ermine, fox, stoat, grey squirrel, wolf, bear, and sometimes more exotic furs such as leopard and monkey) and wool. Boots were felt and/or leather, with soft soles so that when squeezed through the stirrup the foot could maintain a tight grip.

82 is from a late-9th century Byzantine ms. His costume appears to be somewhat different, but the apparent baggy shirt and wide, flowing trousers are probably no more than a long Arab-style topcoat split for riding. His long hair is unusual and marks him as a Pecheneg or Patzinak, who in addition sported impressive beards and moustaches. Their clothes were of gabardine, except for nobles who wore silk.

Pointed fur or felt caps were characteristic of the Pechenegs and usually black.

Several sources also record the Khazars as having long flowing hair; this is described as both reddish and black. One part of the Khazar nation is said to have been as dark-skinned as Indians.

81 and 82 are each armed with sabre (a curved, one-edged cutting sword which generally replaced the straight sword c. 700) and a composite bow of which 2 or sometimes 3 were often carried. Quivers apparently contained up to 60 arrows but more commonly held 24–30, usually carried point uppermost. These arrows were light, which somewhat limited their penetration. Both carry in addition light, hollow javelins, 81 having them in a case suspended from the saddle. Lassoes were also carried to entangle enemy riders and horses in close combat. Magyars and Pechenegs at least are recorded to have sometimes carried axes, and most Asiatics probably also carried small circular shields of leather or interwoven osiers.

83 is a Danube Bulgar of c. 1017 from the Menologium of Basil II. Another Byzantine source records that the Bulgars had adopted Avar dress, while Liudprand of Cremona records a 10th century Bulgar nobleman with a bronze chain belt and Magyar-style haircut (like 81). However, the appearance of this figure would indicate that many of these practices had died out by the 11th century. Note also that he carries a sword rather than a sabre.

84 is a Burta, the most important of a number of similar Finnish tribes. His headwear is a Persian kulah with a turban wrapped round it. He is armed with bow and 2 javelins and carries a hide shield but, despite the fact that only their upper-classes fought on horseback, he owns no body armour. Note the ear-ring; only one would be worn, as is still the case among many modern Central Asian nomads. Clothing consisted largely of reindeer and stoat, worn hairy side out, though Marvazi records the Yuras, another Finnish tribe, wearing sable and other furs. Since the reindeer jerkins mentioned under 68 were of Finnish origin it would seem that some of their outer coats at least served as a form of armour. The Baskirs were practically identical and Volga Bulgars were also similar, though they shaved their heads and wore boots and were apparently virtually indistinguishable from Arabs in their basic dress, wearing trousers, long topcoats and turbans.

Some Turks continued to tattoo themselves Scythian-fashion until at least the 10th century, Psellus recording 'Scyths' (probably Pechenegs) 'painting' themselves even in the mid-11th century.

85, 86, 87 & 88. ASIATIC HEAVY CAVALRYMEN

85 is probably an Avar. He wears a lamellar corselet and a typical plumed helmet with cheek-guards, nasal and eyebrows. He is armed with lance, bow and sabre, and a thumb-ring for drawing the bow hangs from his right hand (see 107). The long lance of 10–12 feet held in both hands, originally adopted from the Sarmatians and Alans by the Asiatic peoples, was adopted in turn from the Avars by the Byzantines; the Strategicon actually records that much Byzantine cavalry equipment of the late-6th century was based on that of the Avars.

85

Note the decorated belts, which were worn by all steppe peoples. The quality of such belts indicated social status – gold for royalty, followed by silver and then bronze or brass, with the number of ornaments on each belt and the number of belts themselves, 2 or sometimes 3 being

86

worn, as a further indication of seniority. Other symbols of rank were gold and silver decorated scabbards, bowcases, quivers, sabres, saddles, horse trappings, and probably armour.

86 dates to the 8th–10th centuries. He wears a long, open-necked lamellar corselet with shoulder-pieces, fabric or leather coif and segmented helmet of splint construction topped by a plume tube. Forearms and shins are protected by leather vambraces and greaves. 86a shows an alternative helmet.

87 is based on an 8th century Persian source but possibly represents one of the Khazar Arsiyah horse-archers, whose armour is described as helmet, mail and breastplate, probably lamellar. Arsiyah lancers were dressed and armed like Arabs and carried shields. The Khazars themselves wore tunic, trousers and long Arab topcoat, and their principal weapons were the spear, sabre and shield. They also carried a bow but relied more on their lances.

88 is from a gold vessel that is usually described as Magyar c. 860, though one expert claims Pecheneg origin c. 900–920 and others claim Bulgar origin. He wears splint-armour greaves and vambraces and long mail corselet with coif. His splint-armour may be of iron but wood is more probable, wooden foot-armour also being recorded amongst some Asiatic peoples during this period. Shields are mentioned in several sources as being carried by Magyars and were clearly not small. They were probably of wicker or hide and were apparently dyed in bright colours. Some at least must have been wood since the shields of 2 Magyar chieftains captured at Lechfield in 955 had silver cruciform shield-bosses; these same chieftains wore gold collars, probably grivnas. The feathers in his helmet are characteristic of later Hungarians, who however contained a large Pecheneg element.

All the above are basically interchangeable.

89. ASIATIC STANDARDS

Each Asiatic tribal chieftain carried his own standard.

89a is the Khazar royal standard, described as a highly-polished metal disc constructed like a tambourint which reflected light and could thus be distinguished in battle.

89b is a horse-tail banner. These and yak-tails appear to have been the principal standards of the Asiatic hordes, and even the relatively civilised Danube Bulgars were still using them in the 10th and 11th centuries. Many were probably dyed but others were left their natural colour; such were the 'pigeon-blue' standard of the Pechenegs from the tail of a grey horse, and the black standard of the later Mongols, from the tails of bay stallions. Turcomans similarly used black or white horse-tail standards.

89c is an embroidered or painted silk standard taken from a 9th–10th century Caucasian source.

Animal images were also in use in the early part of this period. Turk standards represented wolves' heads, that of the Khagan being of gold.

90. ALAN LIGHT CAVALRYMAN

The Alans were a Sarmatian people, whose name their own had displaced. The largest body of Alans surviving in this period were those settled in the Caucasus; they were at various times subject to the Avars, Bulgars, Khazars and Georgians.

This figure is based mainly on a 5th century source, but archaeological finds indicate that their dress and equipment changed little throughout this period. Dress still closely follows the Iranian-Scythian tradition, consisting of fur-trimmed cap, short jacket, trousers and short, soft boots. Jacket and trousers were brightly coloured, usually embroidered and often with small gold, silver or bronze plaques sewn on. He carries spear, bow, wicker shield and Khazar sabre. Hair was mainly blonde.

Heavy cavalry, many of whom would have ridden armoured horses, probably

resembled the Asiatic types described above.

At the end of this period some Alans fought as infantry, armed with axes.

91. ARMENIAN CAVALRYMAN

The Armenians were a warlike race who were pushed around throughout this period by Sassanids, Byzantines, Arabs and Khazars and ultimately overrun by the Seljuks.

This figure dates to c. 920. He wears helmet with neck-guard, mail cape and lamellar corselet, and is armed with sword and spear. Some may have also carried a bow and arrows since at Yarmuk in 636 the accuracy of the Armenian archers is specifically attested; however, these were probably infantry. Clothing was of wool, silk and brocade, red and crimson being the most popular colours.

The military strength of Armenia always lay in her cavalry, supplied chiefly by the azats (the lesser nobility). Some of the lower-classes also sometimes fought as cavalry, but always in units distinct from the azats. Until about the 5th century, and possibly even into the Dark Age period, the senior nobility (the nakharars) could each muster as many as 100 to 10,000 cavalry.

92. ARMENIAN INFANTRYMAN

This figure is based on a 10th century Armenian casket and betrays considerable Byzantine influence – hardly surprising since up until the Battle of Manzikert in 1071 large numbers of Byzantine soldiers were recruited in Armenia, particularly as infantry; one source records how 'in the wars of the Byzantines the foot soldiers of the Armenians marched, and they aided them greatly.' As early as the mid-6th century Procopius records as many as 17

Armenian generals in the Byzantine army (including Narses, the victor of Taginae in 552 and Casilinum in 553), and most of the Empire's military aristocracy could claim Armenian ancestry. By the 9th–10th century Armenians formed as much as 25 per cent or more of the Empire's total armed forces.

His corselet appears to be either quilted or leather and has broad pteruges at shoulder and waist. The shield is convex and relatively small, only about 24 inches in diameter. The helmet appears to have a leather aventail.

93. LATE SASSANID CLIBANARIUS

The clibanarii were the backbone of the Sassanid army, being supplied by warrior-nobles, their retainers, and professional soldiers. The term clibanarius itself probably derived from the Persian grivpanvar, 'neck-guard wearer', in the same way as the later European term hauberk derived from halsberge, 'neck protection'.

This figure is based on existing rock reliefs and a list of regulation equipment of the reign of Chosroes I (531–579), recorded by the later Arab author Tabari.

The list requires each man to appear on parade with mail, breastplate, helmet, greaves, lance, shield, sword, mace, axe, quiver with 30 arrows, bowcase with 2 bows and 2 spare bowstrings, and horse-armour. An alternative rendering by the Persian author Balami gives vambraces instead of greaves so probably both were worn; certainly both appear in the reliefs, as does foot-armour. However, it seems unlikely that many clibanarii appeared with their full quota of equipment, and quite possibly in practice they were not expected to. It is more probable that the list only applies to regular elite regiments such as the Pushtighban (the Imperial Bodyguard, 6,000 strong under Chosroes II, 591–628), the Immortals (10,000 strong) and the Gyanavspar (literally 'Sacrificers of their lives').

Bows were fired with a curious 3-finger draw with the arrow to the left of the stave, as opposed to the usual oriental thumb-draw described under 107. The lance, which was up to 12 feet in length, was used overarm held in either one or both hands.

The breastplate was worn either over the mail corselet as here, or underneath it, as is presumably the case with the outstanding equestrian relief of Chosroes II at Taqi Bustan. The straps, which cross at the back, are held by a clasp on the chest. This is the normal Sassanid method of securing the breastplate.

The shield here, from the Chosroes II relief, carries a device representing the rays of the sun (the Sassanids being Zoroastrians). The laminated greaves (vambraces would be the same) are based on a variety of other sources. Lamellar armour was also in common use.

The clibanarii rode partly (sometimes fully) armoured horses as described in *The Armies and Enemies of Imperial Rome*. Light cavalry are described in the same book, though others would be similar to the Sogdian described under 95 here. Some Asiatic auxiliaries were also used for this arm, notably White Huns in the early-6th century and Turks in the late-6th and early-7th centuries.

94. LATE SASSANID LEVY INFANTRYMAN

Peasant warriors of this type were present in large numbers in the last battles fought by the Sassanids, an indication of the extent of the Empire's military exhaustion following the wars against the Byzantines which ended in 628. They were unpaid and unreliable and all too often decided that the battle was over shortly after it had begun. This justifies the decision of the Sassanid commander to chain them together at the Battle of Nihawand in 642!

This figure is based on a 9th century copy of an earlier Byzantine ms. He wears typical Sassanid dress with the characteristic felt or leather cap, here dyed with a simple pattern. His arms consist of a thrusting spear and a dagger, with the large leather-covered cane shield as his only defence. The latter is decorated with a single solid block of colour, perhaps intended as a unit recognition device.

Better-quality infantry were supplied by sling and bow-armed mercenaries and by Kurds, Daylamis, Armenians and other Caspian mountaineers, usually armed with javelins. There were at least some heavy infantry.

95. SOGDIAN HORSE-ARCHER

The Sogdians, with their capital at Samarkand, were to all intents and

purposes a Sassanid successor state. They continued to dress, arm and fight exactly like the Sassanids down to 737, when they were in turn subjugated by the Arabs. Their principal difference was the adoption of the stirrup under Asiatic influence. Likewise some substituted the sabre for the straight sword in the early-8th century.

They also employed large numbers of Turk auxiliary horse-archers.

It was 'Arabs' settled in Sogdia and the old Iranian state of Khwarizm (conquered c. 712) who were generally known to contemporaries as Khwarizmians. These feature as a major element in Khazar armies of the 8th–10th centuries. Since the main part of their strength lay in horse-archers they can be assumed to have adopted much in the way of military practices from the defeated Iranians and Sogdians.

96. ARAB INFANTRYMAN

At the beginning of their period of expansion the Arabs clearly relied on infantry rather than cavalry, though reckoning a cavalryman worth twice as much in pay.

This man is a Bedouin (i.e. a nomad, as distinct from the settled Arabs), described as 'the raw material of Islam', and he wears the traditional Bedouin costume. The long topcoat and the under-tunic would have been woven from camel-wool. On his arms are tiraz, bands woven in coloured silk bearing embroidered inscriptions, often from the Koran. Clothing colours were bright, such as scarlet, red, blue, yellow, green and white, and were sometimes striped. Chieftains wore the brightest clothing, decorated with gold and coloured embroidery. Turbans were most commonly white but were sometimes coloured. All Arabs wore beards.

An early-9th century source mentions uniforms, and as early as 737 an entire army on campaign against the Khazars had been issued with white uniforms, white being the colour of the ruling Umayyad dynasty. Likewise some Abbasid troops appear to have worn black.

Principal weapons were saif and spear, the former being a straight steel or iron sword traditionally suspended from a baldric. The wearing of the sword at the waist-belt was officially introduced in the mid-9th century. The javelin or harbah was also used and had been a favourite weapon of pre-Islamic Quraish mercenaries. Shields were called either turs (large and round, of wood and leather) or daraqa (smaller and entirely of leather).

Some infantry wore armour, these forming the front ranks when available.

97. ARAB ARCHER

The Arabs were using composite and self bows of up to 5 feet in length long before the advent of Islam and the bow had become one of their national weapons. Unusually, they carried it on the right shoulder. Legend records that Mohammed often used to lean on a bow while preaching, and the Koran says 'the hand of man has not wielded a weapon which the bow cannot excel.' Quivers normally contained 30 arrows.

Fatimid armies recruited their archers from the Sudanese (see note 104). Earlier sources call them Nubians and the accuracy of their archery is recorded as early as 643, when they blinded so many Arabs by their showers of arrows that they were nicknamed 'the archers of the eyes'.

98 & 99. ARAB CAVALRYMEN

Iron stirrups were probably introduced from Eastern Persia in the late-7th century, probably in 694. Prior to this date (though for exactly how long is uncertain – perhaps 30 years or more) the Arabs appear to have used wooden stirrups.

98 is based on a 10th century drawing. He carries a sword and a lance called a rumh, often with a bamboo shaft. Usually a dagger was carried as well. Some others at least were bow-armed, though mounted Arab archers are not encountered very often in the sources and seem to have disappeared entirely after the 9th century.

Shields were small, circular and slightly convex, with a binding round the edge. Later sources describe them as wood, metal, leather, or sometimes of various types of wood sewn together with cotton. They were usually brightly painted.

99 is similar to 96 except that over his tunic he wears leather or quilted felt body-armour with short puffed sleeves, probably a bambakion as described under note 3. Constantine Porphyrogenitus is probably

referring to armour of this type when he speaks of the Fatimids wearing 'pink-coloured jerkins' instead of mail.

Spurs do not appear to have been worn at this date.

100 & 101. ARAB HEAVY CAVALRYMEN

100 dates to the early-8th century. He wears a long scale corselet, leather coif and a helmet with a solid neckguard, a type that was called a mighfar. It should be noted that at this date heavy cavalry were pretty rare – of the 4,000 Arabs present at the Battle of Ohud (625) only 800 had armour and at least 600 of these were infantry. On average probably a third of their cavalry at the very most would have been heavies.

101 dates to the 9th or 10th century, by which time armoured cavalry were far more commonplace. He wears a long mail zardfaa (the Byzantine zaba), tall Persian helmet with mail aventail, and wooden or metal greaves and vambraces of Byzantine design, though tubular vambraces of Persian design were also in circulation.

Other types of body-armour included leather and felt corselets as described under 99, plus lamellar and breastplates, probably of Sassanid type. Some armour even had pteruges attached Byzantine-fashion, so it is no surprise that Leo VI says of Arab equipment that it was like that of 'the Romans'.

Both are armed with sword and lance, 101 adding a mace, carried particularly by ghulams, usually on the right side tucked beneath the knee and stirrup strap. Some Arabs also carried an axe suspensed from the saddle.

Only elite cavalrymen such as chieftains or ghulams wore armour, as did standard-bearers, musicians and officers, who may have been distinguished by small bells on their armour.

The Scylitzes ms. shows Arabs wearing similar helmets to that worn by 101 but with a turban wrapped round the lower part, some with scale or lamellar aventails and others with a small, fluttering plume.

102. ARAB STANDARDS

Arab standards were initially no more than strips of cloth wrapped round the ends of lances. Umayyad standards were white, adopted from the tribal standards of the pre-Islamic Quraish Arabs; those of the Abbasids were black,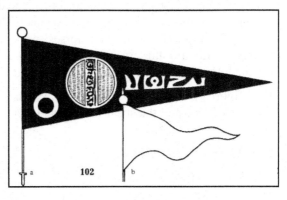
Khawarij red, and Spanish Umayyads, Alids and Fatimids green. Green standards as well as yellow and black are also recorded during the very earliest part of the Moslem era. Mohammed's personal standard was called 'Eagle' and may therefore have depicted an eagle device; it was still carried by Khaled ibn al-Walid at Aznaidan in 634. Chroniclers variously claim this standard to have been white or black.

The two standards shown here are both from painted bowls, 102a an infantry standard of the 10th century and 102b a cavalry standard of the 9th century. Interestingly both have short staffs, though those of 2 black Abbasid standards (aptly named 'Shadow' and 'Night') recorded in the mid-8th century were possibly as much as 13–14 feet in length.

It should also be noted that most Arab armies were accompanied by musicians by the 10th century at the very latest, their bands including drums, trumpets, pipes and other instruments.

103. SUDANESE TRIBESMAN

The Sudanese were armed mainly with short thrusting spears, javelins or bows, which they appear to have fired from the kneeling position. They wore absolutely no armour and generally fought naked; the Hudud al-'Alam records as late as 982 that they still went about largely naked, despite undergoing a considerable amount of Arab influence by that date.

Some fought mounted on camels, but even such mounted Sudani warriors were usually completely naked, even though they must have represented the wealthier upper classes. Those defeated by the Arabs at Dongola in 854 were not only naked but were armed with nothing more than shields and short spears. (The Arabs defeated them by tying camel-bells round their horses' necks and charging at the last moment with a loud cry of 'Allahu Akbar', the din thus created stampeding the Sudani camels, which threw their riders in the process.)

This figure is from 6th–9th century sources. The shallow circular shield is of hide and the spear has a broad, leaf-shaped blade.

104. SUDANESE GHULAM

In addition to fighting the Sudanese, the Moslems also employed them in their own armies in large numbers, principally as archers but also as swordsmen and spearmen and often in guard roles.

Khumarawayh, son of Ahmad ibn Tulun (who had as many as 45,000 black ghulams in his employ at his death in 884 – almost twice as many as he had white ghulams), maintained a unit of 1,000 Sudanese guardsmen who must have made a rather awesome spectacle; an 11th century historian says that they wore 'black coats and black turbans so that the onlooker could fancy them to be a black sea spreading over the face of the earth, because of the blackness of their skin and of their clothes. With the glitter of their shields, of the chasing on their swords, and of the helmets under their turbans, they made a really splendid sight.' The drawing depicts one such guardsman.

As archers the Sudanese were held in high regard, and the Fatimids recruited most of their archers from amongst them. Leo describes these as lightly armed and unarmoured. Others still were employed as cavalry, but this was mainly in North Africa.

105. BERBER TRIBESMAN

105

The Berbers were North African tribesmen. They were generally treated as second-class by the Arabs but bore the brunt of military duties in the early North African campaigns and Spain.

They were at first mostly infantry, with a few light cavalry who were much the same as the earlier Moors (still employed by the Byzantines throughout the 6th and into the early-7th century). Later they became primarily cavalry and much more Arabised in both dress and weapons, though many continued to resemble Moors or dressed as here, with the simple addition in both cases of a turban.

At the time of the conquest of Spain in 711 the Berbers fought either naked or in a loincloth, armed primarily with javelins, spears, bows and slings.

106. DAYLAMI TRIBESMAN

The Daylamis were a rough mountain people of the Caspian region. During this period they served as mercenaries with the Sassanids, Samanids, Buyids (themselves a Daylami dynasty), Fatimids, Saffarids and Ghaznavids, and later with the Seljuks until the end of the 12th century.

They fought mainly as infantry though they used mules or camels for transport and the wealthiest rode

106

horses. Their cavalry were supplied chiefly by Turkish mercenaries and ghulams.

Their standard arms consisted of sword, brightly painted shield and zupin, the latter a short javelin used for thrusting or throwing.

Contemporary descriptions of the zupin are usually translated as '2-bladed" or '2-pronged', but the impracticalities of such a weapon make this seem unlikely; more probably '2-edged' is intended. In addition Daylamis often used axes, and bows are recorded as well as a crossbow called a nawak, mentioned in 9th–11th century sources.

107. KHORASANIAN HORSE-ARCHER

The 'Khorasanian' peoples, with their largely Persian ancestry and frequent infusions of Turks, continued to utilise horse-archers. The Arabs, Khawarij and Bedouins also used some horse-archers, but it is not clear from the sources just how many.

This figure is based on an 8th century fresco. Note the oriental thumb-draw with the arrow held to the right (the outside) of the bow. A ring was worn on the right-hand thumb to assist the draw (see 85). This draw was used by most Asiatic peoples.

107

He wears a Sassanid-style decorated head fillet and a ribbon tied round his waist with 3 bells attached to each end. Persian styles of dress, armour and weapons predominated in the eastern Moslem provinces throughout this period (see next note), and many Turks in the service of the later Saffarids, Samanids, Ghaznavids and Buyids would have dressed almost identically.

Many 'Khorasanian' units serving the Abbasid Caliphs were simply Arabs who had settled in that region.

108. PERSIAN CAVALRYMAN

This figure from a 10th century fresco is included to show that Sassanid-style armour persisted in the East, and in fact equipment of this kind can even be found as far west as Fatimid Egypt so was probably widespread throughout the greater part of the Moslem world. Turkish mercenaries were probably largely responsible for its distribution. He may be an Abbasid but could equally well be a Samanid, or Buyid warrior; either way he is fairly certainly an amir or palace guard.

Note the slight curve of the sword, the tubular vambraces and the small shield slung from the saddle-bow. The original does not show a bow but undoubtedly one was normally carried. The decorated belt is typical.

109. GHAZNAVID INFANTRYMAN

The Ghaznavids were Turkish mercenaries who had overthrown their Samanid employers in 999. Their multi-racial armies included Turks, Indians, Tajiks, Daylamis, Arabs (called Divsuvaran, 'Dare-devil riders'), Kurds, Afghan mountain peoples and ghazi irregulars. Ghuzz were employed from 1025, and later Seljuks.

Infantry were principally Indians but included Daylamis, Tajiks and others. They were armed with bow, spear, mace or short sword, leather-covered or metal shield, helmet and mail corselet, all official issue. Lamellar would often be substituted for mail.

Cavalry carried bow, lance, mace, axe, sabre or qalachur (a 2-edged, curved sword) and lasso and according to their rank were accompanied by a number of spare horses. Many still bore a close resemblance to late Sassanid clibanarii and probably looked like 108.

Ghaznavid standards were black and carried a moon and phoenix device, those of their ghulams substituting lions – a common motif on eastern standards both during and subsequent to this era. The chatr or royal umbrella, which was black and at the end of this period surmounted by a jewel-covered falcon, was probably also used as a type of standard.

110. GHAZNAVID GHULAM

110

This is based on murals discovered in 1949 in the Ghaznavid palace of Lashkari Bazar in Afghanistan, the only known pictorial representations of ghulams in ceremonial dress. They date to the 11th century, but ghulams would have been similarly equipped throughout this period. No uniformity of dress is apparent.

In the written sources ceremonial dress was of embroidered silk and brocade, while equipment was heavily ornamented; shields were decorated with silver and gold and were sometimes bejewelled, while weapons too had gold and silver mountings – some maces even appear to have been solid gold! Ornamental belts were also worn, indicative of the original composition of the ghulam slave soldiers (see 85); those of palace ghulams were usually gold, often decorated with precious stones. As well as the mace a sword, short spear and bow were normally carried.

A late-11th century author, ostensibly describing the training of ghulams in the service of the Samanids, records that they underwent a 7-year course. They only received the characteristic mace, together with richly embroidered clothing, in their fifth year, a full-dress ceremonial uniform in the sixth year, and became junior officers in the seventh and eligible to wear a black felt hat decorated with silver lace.

The long topcoats often worn by Asiatic peoples were much the same as that shown here.

111 & 112. 7TH–9TH CENTURY ANGLO-SAXON CHIEFTAINS

Both these men wear mail byrnies and helmets, considerable rarities among the early Saxons though, like swords, they became more common as time went on.

111 is taken from the late-7th or early-8th century Franks Casket. His helmet is similar to the later nasal types except that it has a leather or fabric coif which is laced round the throat. 111a shows a similar type which is clearly of fabric or leather.

112 has a longer mail corselet split to facilitate riding, and a boar-crested helmet. Such helmets are mentioned in many literary sources though to date only one has been found, at Benty Grange in 1848. It consisted of plates of horn reinforced by an iron framework, while the boar itself is silver-plated bronze. The helmet may have originally had a mail aventail.

112a and b show alternative types of crest as depicted in manuscript sources. 112c shows the Sutton Hoo helmet, with face, cheek and neck guards. Although much decorated with bronze and gilt it was originally a late Roman cavalry helmet.

113 & 114. 7TH–10TH CENTURY ANGLO-SAXON WARRIORS

Saxon dress consisted of a woollen or linen tunic with sleeves tightly puckered on the forearm, over breeches which could be cross-gartered or bound puttee-fashion. Upper classes could wear silk. Cloaks were held by a brooch at the right shoulder or sometimes at the throat. Clothing colours included scarlet, red, brown, dark green, purple, indigo, deep blue and white. Tunics could also be of unbleached wool or linen with embroidered borders, particularly amongst the lower classes.

113 wears a hip-length leather jerkin and a cloth or leather Phrygian cap. 113a shows an alternative cap, while 113b and c show metal-reinforced leather helmets. He is armed with spear and sword, the scabbard hanging from a baldric. Identical figures appear in various sources up to the close of this period.

114 is lower-class, armed with the traditional shield and 6–7 foot gar, the ash war-spear, which was so typical of Anglo-Saxon equipment that poets often referred to warriors as 'ash-bearers'. Secondary armament is a scramaseax, a one-edged knife reputed to have given the Saxons their name. These averaged 18 inches though some were up to 2½ feet in length and used as swords. 114a shows the traditional shape of the Saxon scramaseax, based on excavated examples, while 114b shows a scramaseax as depicted in use by a Saxon warrior in a 10th century ms.

Shields were of leather-covered lime-wood – the 'yellow linden' of written sources – held by a grip behind the boss and often with an additional arm-brace. The leather was cow-hide, a 10th-century law making it a fineable offence to use sheepskin on a shield! Diameter averaged around 30 inches though some were larger and some as small as 12 inches. Bosses were of iron and the orb was bound in iron or more commonly leather, though the Sutton Hoo shield had a gilt bronze rim. The patterns shown on the shields of 113, 116 and 119 are typical. Carolingian-type patterns are also to be found in later Saxon mss.

115. ANGLO-SAXON ARCHER

Although the bow is often mentioned in their poetry as a weapon of war it never seems to have been widely adopted by the Saxons or, if it was, it would seem to have been singularly ineffective. One version of the Anglo-Saxon Chronicle even insists that the bow was 'held of

115

little account against an armed man', while Henry of Huntingdon records William the Conqueror describing the Saxons as a people who 'knew not the use of the bow.'

However Roger Ascham, the 16th century toxopholite, records a story told to him by Sir Thomas Elyot that when the Saxons had first entered England as mercenaries of Vortigern they had been bow-armed, and the weapon was apparently new to Britain. Elyot is said to have found this story in an ancient chronicle.

The bow averaged between 4 and 5 feet in length and many were of yew. The quiver was usually suspended at the right hip from a strap across the left shoulder but could sometimes be found slung at the back.

116 & 117. SAXON SELECT FYRDMEN

The 'Select Fyrd' consisted of lesser nobility and others due for service under the 5 hide system. Being a selective militia their equipment was much better than that of the general Fyrd. By Cnut's time thanes were expected to serve with sword, spear, shield, byrnie, helmet and horse. The sword was often gold-hilted.

116 is characteristic of the 9th–11th centuries. His short corselet is a mail version of the leather jerkin worn by 113.

117 dates to c. 1035. He wears a knee-length byrnie unusually split at the sides, with sword-belt worn underneath, and an iron-strengthened Phrygian cap. The panel on his chest probably represents a mail reinforce; these panels occur in only a few sources, largely 11th

century, including the Bayeux Tapestry where it is exclusive to the Normans. Since it appears here, where no coif is worn, it was obviously nothing to do with securing a frontal opening.

Leather armour also continued to be worn on occasion, as in 1063 when, fighting the lightly-armed Welsh, Earl Harold persuaded his men to substitute boiled-leather armour for their mail and to carry lighter weapons – presumably javelins rather than axes and thrusting spears.

118 & 119. LATE SAXON FYRDMEN

118 is from the Bayeux Tapestry. He differs from 114 principally in the substitution of a kite-shield, which was in use in England from c.1000. Most Saxons in the Tapestry have moustache or beard.

Other Fyrdmen shown in the Tapestry have no shields and are armed only with wooden or metal-headed clubs (see 123). According to William of Poitiers many were armed with javelins, stones tied to wooden handles, and 'missiles of all sorts.' He also records axes used as missiles, a practice likewise current in Cnut's reign and probably throughout this period. Such weapons were probably similar to franciscas. The Tapestry also shows Danish axes in use by some Fyrdmen.

119 is from a mid-11th century ms. He is obviously a wealthier man, wears a nasal helmet and an embroidered tunic, and is armed with

spear, shield and sword suspended from a baldric. Other 11th century mss. continue to show figures like 113 and 114.

120. LATE-SAXON OR ANGLO-DANISH HUSCARL

This figure is from the Tapestry. A description in Florence of Worcester of the equipment of warriors given with a ship to Edward the Confessor by Earl Godwin in 1040 matches the Tapestry depictions almost perfectly, and these were fairly certainly Huscarls too (Godwin's most probably) since a mercenary was the only such well-equipped warrior that could realistically be 'given away'.

120

Being Danish in origin the Huscarl's principal weapon was the double-handed axe with a shaft between 4 and 5 feet long. Wace records this weapon to have been capable of felling a horse and rider with one blow and speaks of one such weapon with a blade a foot broad (Laxdaela Saga mentions a Danish axe measuring 18 inches along its curved edge). In all but one instance the Tapestry shows it swung from the left shoulder, presumably to catch the opponent on his unshielded side. Its one disadvantage was that the shield had to be slung behind the back since both hands were needed, leaving the man defenceless against missiles, a fact noted by contemporary Norman chroniclers. When not in use the axe could be hung from the left shoulder or held behind the shield.

He wears a knee-length byrnie with coif of mail or leather and three-quarter length sleeves. The coif may be separate. Helmets were beaten from one piece of iron, constructed from several pieces with a framework of strengtheners, or were even of leather. The Tapestry shows them with vari-coloured panels, which may indicate the leather was dyed. Wace even records a wooden helmet with a string chin-strap.

Other weapons were sword, and javelins of a type called aetgar. Sword-belts were worn either over the byrnie, or under it with a special slit for the hilt. Helmet, sword-hilt, shield and axe could all be partly gilded, and gold-decorated axes and hilts were part of the regulation equipment of Cnut's huscarls.

121. MOUNTED SAXON WARRIOR

Whether or not the Saxons had cavalry is an academic debate which has raged almost incessantly for more than a century. The problem is that there is no conclusive proof (if there were there would be no debate), though incidental evidence in support of the motion that they did is fairly commonplace, for which see the section on Saxon tactics. As I have concluded there, Saxons certainly fought mounted when in pursuit of routed or mounted enemies, and probably by the 11th century small bodies even occasionally fought mounted on the battlefield or at least knew how to – King Harold, while still Earl of Wessex, even served as a horseman in a Norman cavalry force during his enforced sojourn in Normandy in 1064.

121

If one were to accept Snorri's account of Stamford Bridge then the debate would be over and done with for good, for he mentions both cavalry and infantry in the Saxon army and provides a detailed account of their tactics, but there are currently valid reasons for treating his account with a degree of suspicion.

Nevertheless, there are enough (indeed, innumerable) references to Saxon horsemen in the sources to justify the inclusion of one in this section, who can be looked upon as a mounted infantryman or a cavalryman according to your convictions. This particular figure is based on several 11th century Saxon ms. illuminations, some of which show armoured horsemen and some unarmoured.

122. SAXON STANDARDS

122a and b are dragon standards, evolved once again from late Roman originals via the sub-Roman Britons. The most famous was Alfred the Great's Golden Wyvern, the standard of Wessex. We know that Edmund Ironside carried a dragon standard during his campaigns against Cnut, and 2 such standards appear in the Bayeux Tapestry. The

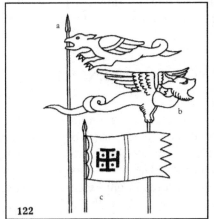

Mercian Saxons too seem to have used a golden dragon standard, King Aethelbald having one at Burford in 752, though it may have been an embroidered banner rather than a windsock. The Old Saxons too used dragon standards, such as that of the rebel leader Widukind in the late-8th century, a banner with a dragon on one side and a lion on the other.

122a is one of the 2 dragon standards shown in the Tapestry, one red and the other ochre (possibly representing gold). Harold's personal standard at Hastings appears to have been the figure of an armed warrior embroidered in pure gold and decorated with precious stones. Other Saxon banners in the Tapestry are of the type described under 126, similar standards to which can be found in 10th century mss.

122b is from an early-14th century Arthurian romance but was almost certainly copied from an earlier Saxon original.

122c shows a religious standard, such as were often used when fighting the pagan Vikings. This one is from an 11th century ms.

123. PEASANT INFANTRYMAN

Infantrymen armed with everyday tools or makeshift weapons probably appeared in most armies involving general levies, although Charlemagne at least forbade those armed only with staves to appear in his.

The Saxons recorded at Hastings as armed with stakes, 'iron forks', maces and stones tied on sticks, or shown in the Tapestry armed only with clubs as here, were probably such, as were the infantry recorded in various sagas and chronicles as armed with staves, clubs, pointed sticks and stones. Stakes and pointed sticks could apparently be of

considerable length – Heimskringla records 'stakes' 5 ells (over 8 feet) long.

Undoubtedly others would have carried knives, slings, scythes, bills, flails, pitchforks, etc., as in later mediaeval times. Unfortunately contemporary artists do not appear to have considered such subjects worth recording.

124 & 125. 11TH CENTURY NORMAN, FRENCH OR BRETON HEAVY CAVALRYMEN

Arms consisted of a sword and an ash spear a maximum of 8–9 feet long. The spear was either couched as a lance, used overarm as a thrusting spear, or hurled as a javelin, especially by Bretons, in which case more than one may have been carried. The sword was preferred in close combat. Sometimes 2 or even 3 swords might be carried, spares being suspended from the saddle.

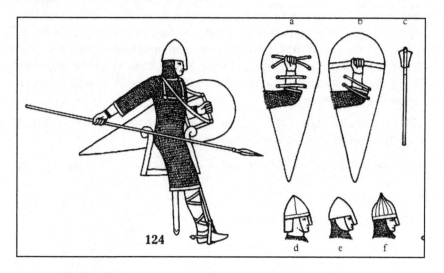

The odd 'trouser' effect used by the artist of the Bayeux Tapestry for the mail hauberks of both Normans and Saxon Huscarls *may* be explained by the skirt being tied close around the leg with tapes on the inside. Whatever the explanation, the hauberk was certainly not 'trousered' as is sometimes suggested, since several figures are shown pulling hauberks off over the head. Anna Comnena remarks of the Norman hauberk that it was fully capable of resisting arrows and made the wearer 'almost if not completely invulnerable'; however, she is probably referring to the light arrows of the Turks. 125, from a French ms. of c. 1050, wears a shorter hauberk with long sleeves.

The kite-shield, with a bronze or iron boss, was hung round the neck and against the left shoulder by a strap. 124 and 127 show 2 methods of holding it by a further arrangement of straps, while 124a and b show other alternatives from the Tapestry. Other sources show shields held by the Byzantine-style grip of figure 22. In the Tapestry these shields appear to be flat, though other 11th century sources certainly speak of kite-shields as convex or slightly curved. They were of wood, but could apparently be pierced by a strong lance thrust. Anna describes the face as 'smooth and shining' and says that it could repel any arrow fired against it, a description which suggests that by the late-11th century at least some may have been faced with a thin sheet of metal.

125

Both figures wear nasal helmets. 124d shows an alternative with nape-guard from the Tapestry, here worn with a fabric or leather coif. 124e and f are other helmet types in use at about this date.

124c is a type of flanged mace shown held by Duke William in the Tapestry. The mace may have been a symbol of rank for officers, as in Byzantium. It hung at the right side when not in use, probably from the saddle.

126. 11TH CENTURY NORMAN, FRENCH OR BRETON STANDARDS

This figure, from the Tapestry, portrays Eustace of Boulogne. Note the addition of mail protection for forearms and lower leg, which appear on only a few figures, one of whom appears to wear a mail sleeve on

126

his right arm only (see note 55). It was probably this more complete armour which prompted Anna Comnena to call Norman knights kataphraktoi.

The standard is probably the Sacred Banner granted to William by the Pope, though there is evidence to suggest that it might represent Eustace's personal

193

banner. Central cross, edging of main field, spots on the vertical panel, and the central tail are all ochre, probably representing gold; upper and lower tails and spots quartering the cross are dark green; the central field, vertical panel and tail extremities are white.

126a–h are representative of the lance pennons, called at this time gonfanons, carried by many of the knights in the Tapestry. They may be purely decorative or for recognition purposes; Wace, though writing in the third quarter of the 12th century, definitely implies the latter. They were probably carried only by the officer nobility.

127. 11TH CENTURY NORMAN, FRENCH OR BRETON MEDIUM CAVALRYMAN

127

This is one of 4 generally ignored figures in the Tapestry, these being shown in action at Dol in the campaign against the Bretons.

Only one wears a helmet and coif, while all carry shield and lance/javelin. Later-11th century mss. show identical figures, usually with helmets and also swords. The Tapestry figures probably also carry swords, but their left sides are away from us.

They are probably retainers of the better-armoured knights, comparable to such earlier types as are described under 54. By the end of the 11th century they were commonly called servientes, or sergeants, and a French document of 1133 still specifies their equipment as lance, shield and sword; there is no mention of armour, though it is safe to assume that quilted or mail body-armour was worn when available.

'Off-duty' knights shown in the Tapestry are identical except that they are bare-headed. They carry lance and shield everywhere when mounted.

128 & 129. NORMAN ARCHERS

128 shows the famous Norman haircut, shaved high at the back and sides and giving a beret effect. It was this hair style which prompted the rumour that William had brought an army of priests to England! Most were clean shaven but some wore moustache or beard.

His trousered garment may represent a tunic split for riding, except that in the Tapestry, where it is almost exclusive to the Normans, many of the figures dressed thus are clearly infantry. Others wear normal tunics, sometimes with the skirt pulled up at the sides and tucked through the belt. Most would be bareheaded, though 128a shows a brightly coloured cloth or leather cap that could be worn. In the Tapestry both Normans and Saxons wear tunics and leggings in all 8 original colours in which it was embroidered, these being red, ochre, yellow, 2 shades of blue, turquoise, and 2 greens.

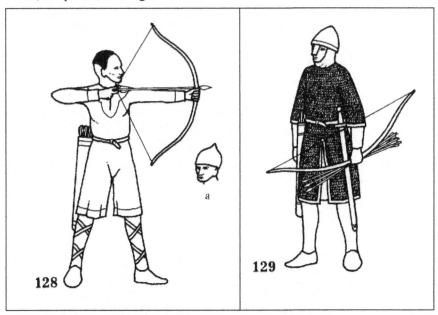

Quivers are shown hanging either from the waist-belt, or from a strap across the right shoulder or round the neck. Secondary armament consisted of a sword.

129 is the only armoured archer shown in the Tapestry, perhaps an officer or mercenary, or even a dismounted knight. He carries several arrows ready in his left hand, probably as an aid to rapid firing. Similar heavy-armed archers appear in a few other sources. Wace records Norman archers wearing leather and quilted armour, which seems generally more likely.

Modern tests indicate that during this period an arrow could penetrate mail at 50 yards range. It should be noted in passing that the tactic of shooting arrows into the air to fall on the Saxons' heads ascribed to the Normans at Hastings is in fact only recorded in 3 non-contemporary sources, written over the middle 50 years of the 12th century.

130. FRENCH CROSSBOWMAN

The first written record of the crossbow in post-Roman Europe is in the 10th century chronicler Richer's 'History of France'. He records it in use at the siege of Senlis in 949 and at Verdun in 985. This figure from a French ms. dates to c. 1000 though he may be late-10th century. Crossbowmen also appear in 2 Spanish mss. of c. 1050 and c. 1060; see also figure 36.

Early crossbows were loaded by putting both feet on the inside curves of the bow and pulling back the string until it locked on a catch. The short, thick arrow, called

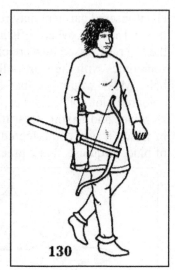

130

a bolt or later a quarrel (fiom its 4-sided head), was placed in a groove on the stock. It was fired with the stock against the shoulder by a lever-operated metal trigger mechanism and easily outranged self or composite bows. The bolts, discharged with tremendous force, could pass through shield, armour and body without being stopped; Anna Comnena relates how a crossbow bolt passed clean through a bronze statue, or could disappear out of sight into a city wall!

Although crossbows are not shown in the Tapestry William of Poitiers records their use at Hastings.

131. 11TH CENTURY FRENCH INFANTRYMAN

131

He is typical of the Arriere-Ban and except for the substitution of a kite-shield is little different to his Carolingian counterpart described under 46. Circular shields also continued to be used though they were less common.

The ms. from which he is taken shows tunics mainly red, deep crimson, blue and a neutral colour probably intended as unbleached wool or linen, and trousers red or natural wool. Other sources show yellow, scarlet, green, brown and grey tunics and trousers. Clothing colours were generally much brighter than those of today. The 3-dot pattern of his cloak remained popular well beyond the end of this period.

132 & 133. 11TH CENTURY EUROPEAN HEAVY INFANTRYMEN

Chroniclers record heavy infantry to have fought at Hastings though none (other than the archer described in 129) are shown in the Tapestry. Their equipment was identical to that of the knights, and indeed some at least may have been dismounted knights. However, contemporary sources, though conceivably exaggerating, record how helpless European knights generally were when dismounted so these were probably mercenaries who favoured foot-combat, perhaps Swabians, Old Saxons or other North Germans. Certainly if any were dismounted knights they would have been Normans or Frenchmen rather than Bretons, who seem to have depended so exclusively on cavalry that they probably were useless as infantry – there are certainly no records during this period or that immediately after of Bretons fighting on foot; a source of c. 1120 even records Bretons as being 7 times better fighting on horse than on foot.

These figures are based on French sources. 133 dates to 1110 but practically identical warriors appear in ms. illustrations from the early-11th century to the early-13th. His hauberk is coloured green in the original and probably represents horn scales. His shield is extremely large, almost the same length as his body.

Swabian mercenaries at the Battle of Civitate in 1053 fought mainly with double-handed swords, but the armoured infantry at Hastings were armed with javelins and spears.

134. ITALO-NORMAN HEAVY CAVALRYMAN

This figure is based on 11th century South Italian chess-pieces. His corselet is of lamellar, betraying Byzantine influence, the Normans first encountering the Byzantines in Italy while fighting as mercenaries for Apulian rebels from c. 1015.

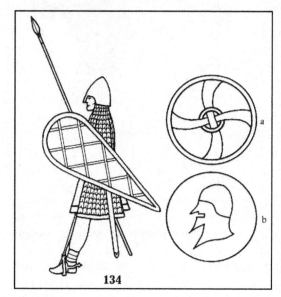

134

The helmet is classical in style and the pattern on his shield probably represents strengthening bands. Other figures show longer tunics, boots, leather and fabric coifs, and round shields. A ms. of c. 1028 shows Italian cavalrymen practically identical to 124, most in helmets with no nasal and some wearing no coif; their red shields are unclear but appear to be circular.

The bulk of Italian troops were citizen militiamen, of whom the best-equipped would have resembled the figures described under 132, 133 and 137. Others would have been crossbowmen, archers or spearmen similar to contemporary French and German types.

The shields depicted in 134a and b are from the ms. of c. 1028 mentioned above and are probably typical of the simple designs that militiamen would have carried.

135 & 136. SPANISH HEAVY CAVALRYMEN

The heavy European knight never attained considerable popularity in Spain, where cavalry were largely non-noble. They rode mostly with a low saddle and short stirrups, both better suited to the hilly Spanish kingdoms. 10th century sources indicate that equipment basically comprised helmet, mail or scale corselet, wood or leather shield, lance and sword.

Spears were generally used overarm, and despite the introduction of the kite-shield in the late-10th or early-11th century the round shield remained popular until the late-12th. The shield carried by 135 is one of the leather ones mentioned, with tassels adopted from the Moslems of Andalusia; his helmet too appears to be of Andalusian design. Helmets were often decorated in gold and silver, as were sword-hilts and shields.

136, dating to c. 1050, wears a shorter corselet and an alternative helmet with the back extended into a neckguard. The ms. from which he comes shows horsemen all using kite-shields. Note the chest-panel as described under note 117. Other cavalrymen in this source are equipped like 127 except that they have no coifs.

137. SPANISH HEAVY INFANTRYMAN

The Spanish kingdoms attached considerable importance to infantry because of the mountainous nature of their lands. They were often issued with

strong, lightweight leather shoes or sandals since they marched to battle on foot, any wealthy enough to own horses being automatically expected to serve as cavalrymen.

This man, dating to the early-11th century, wears a short mail corselet and Phrygian-style helmet. Others wore armour identical to that described under 120, 132 and 133, or were unarmoured.

138. ANDALUSIAN CAVALRYMAN

138

Christian Spanish cavalry were favoured by the Andalusians and in high demand as mercenaries. Likewise Spanish contingents were often supplemented by Andalusian auxiliaries.

This figure is from an ivory casket of 1005, 10th century sources showing identical dress. The bare head and 'page-boy' haircut appear to be fairly characteristic. He is armed with lance, sword and small light shield (probably a daraqa), the typical equipment of Andalusian and North African Moslem light cavalrymen. Ibn Hawqal tells us that until at least the 10th century Andalusians often rode with their feet dangling free of the stirrups, or even rode without stirrups altogether, and his statement is vindicated in this source. However, note that spurs are nevertheless worn, contrary to the custom of the Eastern Moslems who, as we have seen, did not use them. This is probably evidence of Spanish influence.

In addition to light cavalry there were armoured horsemen like 101. These wore long or short mail corselets, or scale corselets of unspecified length which could apparently be worn over the mail. Vambraces and greaves are also recorded. Helmets were usually called baida (meaning 'egg') because of their shape, and one type unique to Spanish Moslems at this date was the zahiqa, which had a mail hood like that of figure, 93 leaving only the eyes uncovered.

Each cavalry unit had a different standard, chiefly bearing lion, leopard, eagle or dragon devices.

Some mss. show bows in use by horsemen, though it is not known how many were thus equipped. Descriptions of army reviews held in the reign of al-Hakam II (961–976) record mounted black archers wearing white capes. (Black cavalry, in fact, were not uncommon in Spain and North Africa.)

139 & 140. ANDALUSIAN INFANTRYMEN

139 is a black soldier, fairly typical of those who fought for the North African and Spanish Moslem states from the late-8th century. He wears only light clothes, in this case a white cotton skirt and coloured waistband, and carries typical arms consisting of javelin, sword and a light, brightly decorated shield probably of hippopotamus hide. Some substituted a long dagger for the sword and many carried bows. Chieftains would have undoubtedy resembled Arabs more closely and some at least wore armour.

140 shows an eleventh century infantryman in more characteristically Arab dress, though the baggy knee-breeches are unusual. His shield is decorated with several bosses and is probably a turs.

Other Andalusian infantry of this era would have been little different from the Arabs described under 96 and 97, though even many Berbers would have been dressed similarly to 139.

141. KITE-SHIELD PATTERNS

141a–h are all from the Bayeux Tapestry. 141a–c are typical of the zoomorphic designs used on kite-shields; in the Tapestry they are

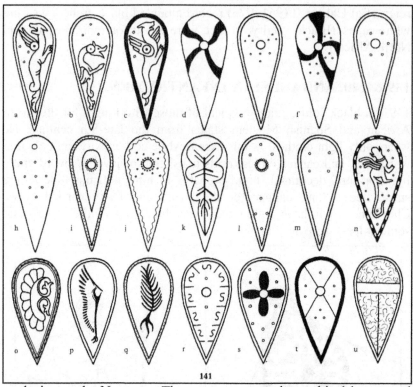

141

exclusive to the Normans. They represent purely mythical beasts and are in no way heraldic.

141 d–h are characteristic of the simpler designs used by both Normans and Saxons, h being held by King Harold in one scene.

141i–k are from a mid-11th century French ms. Principal colours are red, mauve, blue and white.

141l and m are Spanish, where principal shield colours appear to have been red and a bright blue. The 4 dots on m are the heads of rivets holding the strap arrangement on the inner face described under 124 and 125. Contemporary sources record other shields of the type described under a–c.

141n–u are Byzantine designs. 141n is very similar to the Norman designs shown in a–c and is fairly certainly the shield of a Western mercenary in Byzantine employ. 141p–u are from the Scylitzes ms. and are typical of the large number of simple designs it depicts. 141p appears to be a claw and wing device such as became popular in later Ottoman heraldry, and 141q may be a variant of the same pattern. 141s and t again show similarities to Bayeux Tapestry types. Several variants of 141u are fairly common in Scylitzes, where they are invariably shown in the hands of Rus or Bulgars. The horizontal band appears to be some form of strengthener.

142. GREEK FIRE

Although incendiary mixtures had been used in warfare at least as early as the 5th century BC, the particular mixture commonly referred to as Greek Fire is usually taken to have been invented c. 673 by Kallinikos, a Syrian architect in Byzantine service. Its first use was against the Arab fleet besieging Constantinople in 674–676, and throughout its history it was used almost exclusively in naval and siege warfare.

Its actual chemical make-up is uncertain and probably the original 7th century mixture was adapted and developed as time went on. Contemporary sources such as the Liber Ignium, a 12th or 13th century compilation of earlier material, record a large number of mixtures of which the main ingredients include naptha, pitch, resins, sulphur, quicklime, bitumen, oil, charcoal, turpentine and even saltpetre.

Several of these elements have distinct merits. Those containing quicklime would ignite on contact with water and obviously could not have been extinguished easily. This produced the variant names Wet Fire, Wild Fire and Sea Fire (Pyr Thalassion), the latter being the name by which it was known to the Byzantines, 'Greek Fire' being a later appellation applied indiscriminately by Europeans to any kind of Eastern incendiary. Mixtures containing saltpetre, which are unlikely during this period (though not impossible), would have been at least semi-explosive, while those with sulphur would produce poisonous gasses. However, the principal characteristic of Greek Fire was that it was liquid, implying a large naptha content. Other names included Prepared or Artificial Fire, Median Fire, and Volatile or Molten Fire.

The list of ingredients was traditionally a closely-guarded secret, being restricted to Kallinikos' descendants, the Lampros family, but the Arabs were using a liquid incendiary at least as early as 835 in the Tyrrhene Sea or 844 when the Amir of Cordoba equipped his newly-built fleet with mangonels and naptha. According to one source Caliph Mu'awiya (660–680) already had ships fitted with fire-spouting engines, perhaps siphons (see below), while another says a variety of Greek Fire was in use by the Moslems as early as c. 600!

The best-known method of use is shown in 142a, from the Scylitzes ms. of c. 1200. The Fire is sprayed from twin tubes or siphons in the prow of the ship, undoubtedly by hydraulic pumps; a Scandinavian source, Yngvars Saga Vidforla, says that the Fire was projected by means of bellows, while an Arab source of c. 1013 records siphons operated by a piston as in a syringe, and the Byzantine word for siphon (klysteros) could also mean syringe. The siphons themselves were of ('covered with') copper, bronze or iron. Leo's description indicates that they were fixed to a higher false deck so as to be above the prow-level of any attacking vessel, and swivel-mounted to enable them to fire in any direction. Alexius I mounted gilt lion-heads on the prows of his ships so that the Fire issued from their mouths. We are told that it was best if the sea was becalmed when Greek Fire was in use.

As early as c. 560 one source mentions fire propelled by siphons (klysteroi), and Theophanes too records that siphon-fitted ships predated Kallinikos' Greek Fire, which suggests that they were possibly used to discharge the earlier mixtures such as that of sulphur, naptha and bitumen used by the Sassanids at the siege of Petra in 551, and the similar mixture invented by the Athenian Proclus during the reign of Anastasius I (491–518).

Alternatively petraries, mangonels and other engines could be used to hurl earthenware pots of incendiaries, sealed and with fuses set in place. Other pots contained already burning mixtures. A 13th century source records the pots themselves to be glass, paper, metal and leather as well as earthenware. Small pots were often thrown by hand by the Arabs, as at the siege of Salonika in 904, while later Western mss. sometimes show small jars being thrown by staff-slings. However, the incendiaries used in this way were not the same as the liquid Fire used by the Byzantine navy.

Leo mentions 'hand-tubes' for Fire that were invented during his reign (886–912), to be fired from behind iron shields. 142b shows what is apparently such a hand-siphon, from an 11th century ms. There was also some kind of portable small calibre siphon, mentioned in use at the siege of Dvin in 928. This may have been a strepton, a term used by both Leo and Constantine Porphyrogenitus meaning 'flexible device' – probably a pump and hose.

Anyone interested in further details on Greek Fire and other incendiaries can do no better than read 'A History of Greek Fire and Gunpowder' by J. R. Partington, republished in 1998.

143. BYZANTINE CAVALRY HORSE

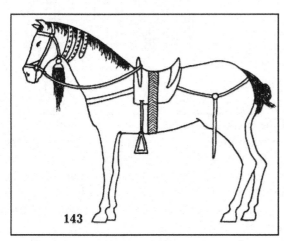

143

This shows typical Byzantine harness as would have been used by trapezitae, most Thematic troops, and probably some auxiliaries. The saddle is high front and back, with girth, breast and rump straps. It is positioned on a hide or sheepskin blanket which could be folded to various thicknesses to suit the horse's condition. There is a snaffle bit, harness and bridle of yellowish leather (often dyed red), and iron stirrups that are worn long. The knotting of the tail is characteristically Eastern and was probably the result of Persian or Asiatic influence.

Plumes at throat, forehead and suspended from breast and rump straps are recorded in some sources but are not often shown in contemporary illustrations.

Byzantine horses were bred and trained at special stud-farms and supplied to the government as and when needed, although at the very beginning of this period the Strategicon records that cavalrymen had to supply their own mounts; such was also true of Thematic cavalry. Other horses were compulsorily donated by the church and nobility, or supplied as a form of exemption from service – in the mid-10th century the Peloponnesos Thema certainly excused itself from an Italian campaign by a payment of gold and 1,000 fully equipped cavalry horses.

144. BYZANTINE FULLY ARMOURED HORSE

Armoured horses were ridden by all klibanophoroi, by front rank Thematic kataphraktoi and all Tagmatic lancers, and probably officers in general.

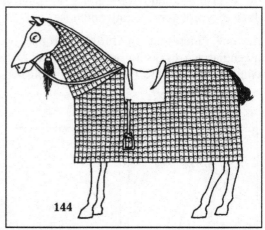

144

The armour consisted of 3 pieces, one covering the head except for the eyes and nostrils, one covering the neck, and a body-piece like a large blanket draped across the back with a hole left for the saddle. The bodypiece reached to the horse's knees and was split to the chest at the front. Others might substitute a sort of apron for the third piece, covering only the horse's chest and front legs. One early source records in addition iron shoes to protect the hooves against caltrops.

According to most of the manuals armour consisted of 2 or 3 layers of quilted felt glued together, or ox-hide, horn or iron lamellae, probably on a cloth backing to prevent chafing. The Sylloge, however, mentions horse-armour of mail lorikia, and Psellus, describing an army of 1047, speaks of 'horses clad in mail at all points.'

It is probable that a small percentage of Asiatic nomads, perhaps only the nobility, rode similar horses, armoured principally in felt. In addition Procopius records that when the Goths marched on Rome in 537 many of their cavalry were mounted on armoured horses, while the fact that some Bretons were riding armoured horses until at least the mid-9th century makes it feasible that a minority of Franks and Visigoths may have done likewise. A very small number of Arabs may have also employed horse-armour of some description.

145. ASIATIC HORSE

Asiatic horses were of many types, ranging from Mongol ponies, through others not dissimilar from the modern Przewalsky horses, to those of the Khazars, described as bigger than Arab steeds. However, contemporaries usually describe them as small, shaggy, generally lean, with large heads and strong necks. Tails were normally knotted.

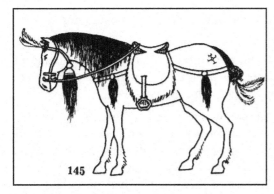

Vegetius' description of Hun ponies as hardy, accustomed to frost and cold, and bearing wounds well, is equally applicable to these later horses, which were scrupulously trained and had a tremendous staying power. In addition to suffering climatic hardships the horses were often bled and the mares milked when no other food was available.

Each warrior was usually accompanied by a number of spare mounts, on campaign riding them in rotation so that a fresh mount was always to hand, changing from one to another without dismounting. The later Cumans are recorded as accompanied by 10–12 horses, the Mongols variously by 2–7. The norm was probably 3–5, and the majority were geldings.

Saddles were of wood, often decorated, and stirrups were also of wood or less commonly iron. Spurs were not worn, the horse instead being controlled by a whip.

The mark shown on the rump is a tamga, an identification brandmark. These were used even by the Russians, who bought all their horses from their Asiatic neighbours, particularly the Pechenegs.

It is possible that within a horde there may have been a degree of uniformity in horse-colour from tribe to tribe.

146. 7TH–10TH CENTURY CAVALRY HORSE

This shows typical harness of the period. Based on 9th and 10th century Carolingian examples it comprises girth, breast and rump straps, which seem to have been standard. The hanging bells and ornaments, often suspended from the saddle as well, are characteristic of

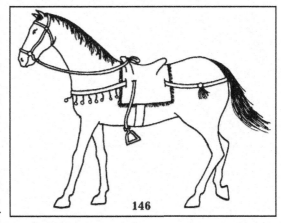

Visigoths, Franks, Saxons, Scandinavians and Slavs. Arab horses were often similarly ornamented.

The stirrup, worn short, would have been absent at the beginning of this period, being only generally adopted in Europe in the late-8th century and by the Arabs in the late-7th century.

The wood and leather saddle is low, but already beginning to develop before and behind into the type described under 147. However, even as early as the 9th century some sources occasionally show saddles which appear to have definite arcons of almost mediaeval type. Saddle-cloths appear to have been the same size or even smaller than the saddle since they are rarely visible in contemporary sources.

In Europe at least the best war-horses were stallions, though mares were often ridden for the simple reason that they were cheaper.

147. 11TH CENTURY CAVALRY HORSE

Taken from the Bayeux Tapestry, this harness is little different to that of 146 except that the stirrup is now worn long. The saddle, with its high arcons at front and rear, is specifically designed for the new form of shock combat which was beginning to evolve towards the end of this period, preventing the rider from being pushed from his saddle by the shock of impact. These arcons could, however, be dangerous to the rider; William of Normandy himself died of internal injuries inflicted by being thrown forward onto the front arcon of his saddle, and it

seems reasonable to assume that this accident was in no way unique.

The Tapestry clearly depicts most horses as stallions. These appear to have been formidable war-horses whose hooves could kill in close combat.

Dark, solid horse colours appear to have been favoured at this time.

147

148. ASIATIC WAGON

This is based chiefly on miniatures in the 15th century Radziwill ms., copied from a 13th century original. Considerably earlier eastern sources show that there was little or no real change throughout this period.

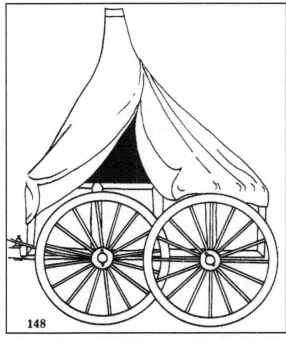

Such wagons were either light and 2-wheeled or heavier with 4 wheels, and were normally drawn by 2–4 oxen, horses or even camels. They were high-sided with tall, many-spoked wheels, and were reinforced with iron. A Bulgar wagon of the 10th century is described as having sharp scythes on the wheels.

The erection of a tent in the back was standard practice. These tents were removable and usually of felt or hide, though the tent of a Khazar Khagan's command wagon recorded in the mid-8th century was of silk brocade surmounted by a pomegranate of gold and the wagon itself was spread with rich carpets.

The Pechenegs' 'large wagons in which were large loop-holes for shooting through', recorded in their laager at the Battle of Eski Zagra in 1122, may possibly indicate that the gaps between the wagons were filled with pavisses mounted on wheels or rollers as are known to have been used by the later Hussites and Cossacks.

In Radziwill the driver rides one of the draught horses, driving with rein and whip; a raised seat at the front of the wagon was probably more common.

SELECT BIBLIOGRAPHY

Abels, Richard P., and Bachrach, Bernard S. (eds.). *The Normans and their Adversaries at War*, 2001.

Abun-Nasr, J.M. *History of the Maghrib*, 1971.

Aitchison, Nick. *The Picts and Scots at War*, 2003.

Alcock, Leslie. *Arthur's Britain: History and Archaeology AD 367–634*, 1971.

Anderson, Alan Orr. *Early Sources of Scottish History AD500 to 1286*, vol.2, 1922.

Bachrach, Bernard S. 'Procopius, Agathias and the Frankish Military' *Speculum* XLV, 1970.

— 'Charles Martel, Mounted Shock Combat, the Stirrup and Feudalism' *Studies in Medieval and Renaissance History* VII, 1970.

— *Merovingian Military Organization, 481–751*, 1972.

— *A History of the Alans in the West*, 1973.

— *Armies and Politics in the Early Medieval West*, 1993.

— 'On Roman Ramparts, 300–1300' in Geoffrey Parker (ed.) *The Cambridge Illustrated History of Warfare: The Triumph of the West*, 1995.

— 'Magyar-Ottonian Warfare: à propos a New Minimalist Interpretation' *Francia* 27, 2000.

— *Early Carolingian Warfare: Prelude to Empire*, 2001.

— *Religion and the Conduct of War, c.300–1215*, 2003.

— *Charlemagne's Early Campaigns (768–777)*, 2013.

— *Warfare in Tenth-Century Germany*, 2014.

Balbi, Marco. *L'Esercito Longobardo 568/774*, 1987.

Barclay, C.N. *Battle 1066*, 1966.

Bartlett, Thomas, and Jeffrey, Keith (eds.). *A Military History of Ireland*, 1996.

Beeler, John H. *Warfare in Feudal Europe 730–1200*, 1971.

Belezos, D. *Byzantine Armies 325 AD–1453 AD*, 2009.

Benedikz, B.S. 'The Evolution of the Varangian Regiment in the Byzantine Army' *Byzantinische Zeitschrift* LXII, 1969.

Bennett, Matthew; DeVries, Kelly; and Dickie, Ian. *Fighting Techniques of the Medieval World: Equipment, Combat Skills and Tactics*, 2005.

Bivar, A.D.H. 'Cavalry Equipment and Tactics on the Euphrates Frontier' *Dumbarton Oaks Papers* XXVI, 1972.

Blöndal, Sigfus. 'The Last Exploits of Harald Sigurdsson in Greek Service: A Chapter from the History of the Varangians' *Classica et Mediaevalia* II, 1939.

— revised and rewritten by Benedikz, B.S. *The Varangians of Byzantium*, 1978.

Blum, Jerome. *Lord and Peasant in Russia from the Ninth to the Nineteenth Century*, 1961.

Boba, I. *Nomads, Northmen and Slavs: Eastern Europe in the Ninth Century*, 1967.

Bonner, Michael (ed.). *Arab-Byzantine Relations in Early Islamic Times*, 2004.

Boswell, A. Bruce. 'The Kipchak Turks' *The Slavonic Review* VI, 1927.

Bosworth, C.E. 'Ghaznevid Military Organisation' *Der Islam* XXXVI, 1960.

— *The Ghaznavids, their Empire in Afghanistan and Eastern Iran*, 1963.

— 'Military Organisation under the Buyids of Persia and Iraq' *Oriens* XVIII–XIX, 1965–66.

— 'The Armies of the Saffarids' *Bulletin of the School of Oriental and African Studies* XXXI, 1968.

Bowlus, Charles R. *The Battle of Lechfeld and its Aftermath, August 955: The End of the Age of Migrations in the Latin West*, 2006.

Bradbury, Jim. *The Battle of Hastings*, 2000.

Brondsted, Johannes. *The Vikings*, 1965.

Brooks, E.W. 'Arabic Lists of the Byzantine Themes' *Journal of Hellenic Studies* XXI, 1901.

Brooks, F.W. 'The Battle of Stamford Bridge' *East Yorkshire Local History Series* VI, 1956.

Brooks, Nicholas. *Communities and Warfare 700–1400*, 2000.

Brown, R. Allen. *The Normans and the Norman Conquest*, 1985.

Browning, Robert. *Byzantium and Bulgaria*, 1975.

Bruce-Mitford, Rupert, et al. *The Sutton Hoo Ship Burial vol.2: Arms, Armour and Regalia*, 1978.

Burne, A.H. 'The Battle of Badon – A Military Commentary' *History* XXX, 1945.

Bury, J.B. 'The Imperial Administrative System in the Ninth Century' *Proceedings of the British Academy, Supplementary Papers* I, 1911.

— *A History of the Eastern Roman Empire from the Fall of Irene to the Accession of Basil I (802–867)*, 1912.

— *A History of the Later Roman Empire from Arcadius to Irene (395–800)* (2 vols), 1923.

Butt, John J. *Daily Life in the Age of Charlemagne*, 2002.

Caldwell, David. 'The Use and Effect of Weapons: The Scottish Experience' *Review of Scottish Culture* 4, 1988.

The Cambridge Medieval History 2nd edition vol.IV, 1967.

Campbell, Alistair. *The Battle of Brunanburh*, 1938.
Carey, Brian Todd. *Warfare in the Medieval World*, 2006.
— *Road to Manzikert: Byzantine and Islamic Warfare 527–1071*, 2012.
Carstens, Friedrich Ludwig. *The Origins of Prussia*, 1954.
Chandler, David. *Battlefields of Europe*, 1965.
Christie, Neil. *The Lombards*, 2002.
Clapham, J.H. 'The Horsing of the Danes' *English Historical Review* XXV, 1910.
Coss, Peter. *The Knight in Medieval England 1000–1400*, 1996.
Coupland, Simon. 'Carolingian Arms and Armor in the Ninth Century' *Viator: Medieval and Renaissance Studies* 21, 1990
Crosby, Everett U. *Medieval Warfare: A Bibliographical Guide*, 2000.
Cummins, Antony. *The Illustrated Guide to Viking Martial Arts*, 2012.
Curta, Florin (ed.). *The Other Europe in the Middle Ages: Avars, Bulgars, Khazars and Cumans*, 2008.
Dabrowa, Edward (ed.). *The Roman and Byzantine Army in the East*, 1994.
D'Amato, Raffaele. *The Varangian Guard 988–1453*, 2010.
— *Byzantine Imperial Guardsmen 925–1025*, 2012.
Davies, Sean. *Welsh Military Institutions 633–1283*, 2004.
— *War and Society in Medieval Wales 633–1283*, 2014.
Davidson, H.R. Ellis. *The Sword in Anglo-Saxon England: Its Archaeology and Literature*, 1962.
— 'The Secret Weapon of Byzantium' *Byzantinische Zeitschrift* LXVI, 1973.
— *The Viking Road to Byzantium*, 1976.
Dawkins, R.M. 'The Later History of the Varangian Guard: Some Notes' *Journal of Roman Studies* XXXVII, 1947.
Dawson, Timothy. *Byzantine Infantryman: Eastern Roman Empire c.900–1204*, 2007.
— *Byzantine Cavalryman c.900–1204*, 2009.
— *Armour Never Wearies: Scale and Lamellar Armour in the West, from the Bronze Age to the 19th Century*, 2013.
Decker, Michael. *The Byzantine Art of War*, 2012.
Dennis, George T. *Maurice's Strategikon: Handbook of Byzantine Military Strategy*, 2001.
— *Three Byzantine Military Treatises*, 2009.
DeVries, Kelly. *The Norwegian Invasion of England in 1066*, 2003.
— *A Cumulative Bibliography of Medieval Military History and Technology*, 2008.
— and Smith, Robert Douglas. *Medieval Weapons: An Illustrated History of their Impact*, 2007.
— and Smith, Robert Douglas. *Medieval Military Technology*, 2012.

Dickinson, William Croft. *Scotland from the Earliest Times to 1603*, 1961.

Dolley, R.H. 'The Warships of the Later Roman Empire' *Journal of Roman Studies* XXXVIII, 1948.

Dougherty, Martin J. *Weapons and Fighting Techniques of the Medieval Warrior 1000–1500 AD*, 2008.

Douglas, D.C. *William the Conqueror: The Norman Impact upon England*, 1964.

— *The Norman Achievement*, 1969.

Duncan, Archibald A.M. *Scotland: The Making of the Kingdom*, 1975.

Duczko, Wladyslaw. *Viking Rus: Studies on the Presence of Scandinavians in Eastern Europe*, 2013.

Dunlop, D.M. *A History of the Jewish Khazars*, 1954.

Durham, Keith. *Viking Longship*, 2002.

Encyclopaedia of Islam, first edition 1913–38; second edition 1960–2005; third edition in progress 2007–.

Ensslin, W. 'The Byzantine Army' *Cambridge Medieval History* vol.IV, 1967.

Estopanan, Sebastian Cirac. *Skyllitzes Matritensis Tomo I Reproduciones y Miniaturas*, 1965.

Evans, Stephen S. *The Lords of Battle: Image and Reality of the Comitatus in Dark Age Britain*, 2000.

Ewing, Thor. *Viking Clothing*, 2006.

Farrokh, Kaveh. *Sassanian Elite Cavalry AD 224–642*, 2012.

Fine, John V.A. *The Early Medieval Balkans: A Critical Survey from the Sixth to the Late Twelfth Century*, 1991.

Ffoulkes, Charles. *Armour and Weapons*, 1909.

Forbes, R.J. *Studies in Ancient Technology vol.I: Bitumen and Petroleum in Antiquity*, 1964.

France, John. 'The Composition and Raising of the Armies of Charlemagne' *Journal of Medieval Military History* 1, 2002.

— and DeVries, Kelly. *Warfare in the Dark Ages*, 2008.

Furneaux, Rupert. *Conquest 1066*, 1966.

Ganshof, François Louis. *Frankish Institutions under Charlemagne*, 1968.

Garipzanov, I.H. et al (eds.). *Franks, Northmen and Slavs: Identities and State Formation in Early Medieval Europe*, 2008.

Gibbs-Smith, Charles H. *The Bayeux Tapestry*, 1973.

Gilbert, John M. 'Crossbows on Pictish Stones' *Proceedings of the Society of the Antiquaries of Scotland* CVII, 1976.

Glover, Richard. 'English Warfare in 1066' *English Historical Review* LXVII, 1976.

Golden, Peter B. *Nomads and their Neighbours in the Russian Steppe: Turks, Khazars and Qipchaqs*, 2003.

— Ben-Shammai, Haggai; and Róna-Tas, András (eds.). *The World of the Khazars: New Perspectives*, 2007.

Gorelik, Mikhael V. *Warriors of Eurasia from the VIII Century BC to the XVII Century AD*, 1995.

Grabar, A. *Bulgarian Mediaeval Wall Paintings*, 1961.

Gravett, Christopher. *Norman Knight AD 950–1204*, 1993.

Grotowski, Piotr L. *Arms and Armour of the Warrior Saints: Tradition in Byzantine Iconography (843–1261)*, 2009.

Grousset, René. *The Empire of the Steppes: A History of Central Asia*, 1970.

Hackett, Martin. *Lost Battlefields of Wales*, 2014.

Haidar, Mansura. *Medieval Central Asia: Polity, Economy and Military Organization*, 2004.

Haldon, John. 'Solenarion: The Byzantine Crossbow?' *University of Birmingham Historical Journal* XII, 1971.

— 'Some Aspects of Byzantine Military Technology from the Sixth to the Tenth Centuries' *Byzantine and Modern Greek Studies* I, 1975.

— *Recruitment and Conscription in the Byzantine Army c.550–950*, 1979.

— *State, Army and Society in Byzantium: Approaches to Military, Social and Administrative History, 6th–12th Centuries*, 1995.

— *Warfare, State and Society in the Byzantine World 565–1204*, 1999.

— *Byzantium at War AD 600–1453*, 2002.

— *The Byzantine Wars*, 2008.

— *The Palgrave Atlas of Byzantine History*, 2010.

— *A Critical Commentary on 'The Taktika of Leo VI'*, 2014.

Halsall, Guy (ed.). *Violence and Society in the Early Medieval West*, 1998.

— *Barbarian Migrations and the Roman West, 376–568*, 2007.

— *Warfare and Society in the Barbarian West 450–900*, 2008.

Harden, Jill. *The Picts*, 2010.

Harrison, Mark. *Viking Hersir, 793–1066 AD*, 1993.

— *Anglo-Saxon Thegn AD 449–1066*, 1993.

Hawkes, Sonia Chadwick. *Weapons and Warfare in Anglo-Saxon England*, 1989.

Hayes-McCoy, G.A. *Irish Battles: A Military History of Ireland*, 1988.

Haywood, John. *Dark Age Naval Power: A Reassessment of Frankish and Anglo-Saxon Seafaring Activity*, 2006.

Heath, E.G. *The Grey Goose Wing*, 1973.

Heath, Ian. *Byzantine Armies 886–1118*, 1979.

— *The Vikings*, 1985.

Hewitt, John. *Ancient Armour and Weapons in Europe* (3 vols), 1855–60.

Hildinger, Erik. *Warriors of the Steppe: A Military History of Central Asia 500 BC to 1700 AD*, 1997.

Hill, Paul. *The Anglo-Saxons at War 800–1066*, 2012.

Hodgkin, Thomas. *Italy and her Invaders, 363–813* (8 vols), 1892.

Hoffmeyer, Ada Bruhn de. 'Arms and Armour in Spain: A Short Survey, vol.1' *Gladius, Tomo Especial*, 1971.

Hole, Edwyn. *Spain under the Muslims*, 1958.

Hollister, C.W. *Anglo-Saxon Military Institutions on the Eve of the Norman Conquest*, 1962.

Hooper, Nicholas, and Bennett, Matthew (eds.). *The Cambridge Illustrated Atlas of Warfare: The Middle Ages 768–1487*, 2003.

Howorth, H.H. 'The Avars' *Journal of the Royal Asiatic Society* XXI, 1889.

Hudson, Benjamin. *The Picts*, 2014.

Hyland, Ann. *The Medieval Warhorse: From Byzantium to the Crusades*, 1995.

Jankovich, Miklos. *They Rode into Europe: The Fruitful Exchange in the Arts of Horsemanship between East and West*, 1971.

Jenkins, Romilly. *Byzantium, the Imperial Centuries: AD 610–1071*, 1966.

Jones, Gwyn. 'Egil Skallagrimsson in England' *Proceedings of the British Academy* XXXVIII, 1952.

— *A History of the Vikings*, 1968.

Kaegi, Walter E. *Byzantium and the Early Islamic Conquests*, 1995.

— *Muslim Expansion and Byzantine Collapse in North Africa*, 2010.

Karasulas, Antony. *Mounted Archers of the Steppe 600 BC–AD 1300*, 2004.

Keen, Maurice (ed.). *Medieval Warfare: A History*, 1999.

Kennedy, Hugh. *The Armies of the Caliphs: Military and Society in the Early Islamic State*, 2001.

Koestler, Arthur. *The Thirteenth Tribe*, 1976.

Konstam, Angus. *Strongholds of the Picts: the Fortifications of Dark Age Scotland*, 2013.

— *Byzantine Warship vs Arab Warship 630–1000 AD*, 2015.

Laing, Jennifer. *Warriors of the Dark Ages*, 1999.

Laking, G.F. *A Record of European Armour and Arms through Seven Centuries* (5 vols), 1920–22.

Lang, David Marshall. *The Bulgarians, from Pagan Times to the Ottoman Conquest*, 1976.

Larson, Laurence Marcellus. *The King's Household in England Before the Norman Conquest*, 1904.

— *The Earliest Norwegian Laws: Being the Gulathing Law and the Frostathing Law*, 1935.

Lavelle, Ryan. *Alfred's Wars: Sources and Interpretations of Anglo-Saxon Warfare in the Viking Age*, 2010.

Leask, Anthony. *Sword of Scotland*, 2006.

Lepage, Jean-Denis G.G. *Medieval Armies and Weapons in Western Europe: An Illustrated History*, 2005.

Lev, Yaacov. *State and Society in Fatimid Egypt*, 1991.

— (ed.). *War & Society in the Eastern Mediterranean, 7th–15th Centuries*, 1997.

Levy, Reuben. *The Social Structure of Islam*, 1957.

Leyser, Karl. 'The Battle of the Lech: A Study in Tenth Century Warfare' *History* L, 1965.

— 'Henry I and the Beginnings of the Saxon Empire' *English Historical Review* LXXXIII, 1968.

— *Medieval Germany and its Neighbours 900–1250*, 1982.

— *Communications and Power in Medieval Europe: The Carolingian and Ottonian Centuries*, 1994.

Lourie, Elena. 'A Society Organised for War: Medieval Spain' *Past and Present* XXXV, 1966.

Luttwak, Edward. *The Grand Strategy of the Byzantine Empire*, 2009.

Macartney, C.A. 'The Petchenegs' *The Slavonic Review* VIII, 1929–30.

— *The Magyars in the Ninth Century*, 1930.

Macdowall, Simon. *Germanic Warrior 236–568 AD*, 1996.

Mansouri, M. Tahar. 'Byzantium and the Arabs from the VIIth to XIth Century' *Mediterranean World* 20, 2010.

McClintock, H.F. *Old Irish and Highland Dress*, 1950.

McCotter, Stephen. *The Strategy and Tactics of Siege Warfare in the Early Byzantine Period: From Constantine to Heraclius*, 1995.

McEvedy, Colin. *The Penguin Atlas of Medieval History*, 1961.

Maenchen-Helfen, Otto. *The World of the Huns*, 1973.

Mann, J.G. 'Notes on the Armour worn in Spain from the Tenth to the Fifteenth Century' *Archaeologia* LXXXIII, 1933.

— *An Outline of Arms and Armour in England*, 1969.

Marren, Peter. *Battles of the Dark Ages: British Battlefields AD 410 to 1065*, 2006.

Martin, Paul. *Armour and Weapons*, 1968.

Marwick, Hugh. 'Naval Defence in Norse Scotland' *Scottish Historical Review* XXVIII, 1949.

McGeer, Eric. *Sowing the Dragon's Teeth: Byzantine Warfare in the Tenth Century*, 2012.

Megaw, B.R.S., and McClintock, H.F. 'The Costume of the Gaelic Peoples' *Journal of the Manx Museum* V, 1941–46.

Metcalfe, Alex. *The Muslims of Medieval Italy*, 2009.

Moravcsik, Gyula. *Byzantium and the Magyars*, 1970.

Morris, John. *The Age of Arthur*, 1973.

Mortimer, Paul. *Woden's Warriors: Warfare, Beliefs, Arms and Armour in Northern Europe during the 6th–7th Centuries*, 2011.

Mould, Quita; Carlisle, Ian; and Cameron, Esther. *Leather and Leatherworking in Anglo-Scandinavian and Medieval York*, 2003.

Munz, Peter. *Life in the Age of Charlemagne*, 1969.

Nagy, Katalin. 'Notes on the Arms of the Avar Heavy Cavalry' *Acta Orientalia Academiae Scientiarum Hungaricae* 58, 2004.

Nelson, J.L. *The Frankish World 750–900*, 1995.

— *Opposition to Charlemagne*, 2007.

The New Cambridge Medieval History vols.1–4, 1994–2005.

Nicholson, Helen. *Medieval Warfare: Theory and Practice of War in Europe, 300–1500*, 2003.

Nickerson, Hoffman. *Warfare in the Roman Empire and the Middle Ages*, 2003.

Nicolle, David. 'Early Medieval Islamic Arms and Armour' *Gladius, Tomo Especial*, 1976.

— *The Age of Charlemagne*, 1984.

— *Arthur and the Anglo-Saxon Wars*, 1984.

— *Attila and the Nomad Hordes*, 1990.

— *Romano-Byzantine Armies 4th–9th Centuries*, 1992.

— *Medieval Warfare Source Book* (2 vols), 1996.

— *Armies of the Caliphates 862–1098*, 1998.

— *Armies of Medieval Russia 750–1250*, 1999.

— (ed.). *A Companion to Medieval Arms and Armour*, 2002.

— *Medieval Siege Engines (1): Western Europe AD 585–1385*, 2002.

— *Medieval Siege Engines (2): Byzantium, the Islamic World & India AD 476–1526*, 2003.

— *Carolingian Cavalryman AD 768–987*, 2005.

— *Medieval Polish Armies 966–1500*, 2008.

— *The Moors: The Islamic West 7th–15th Centuries AD*, 2011.

— *European Medieval Tactics (1): The Fall and Rise of Cavalry 450–1260*, 2011.

— *The Conquest of Saxony AD 782–785: Charlemagne's Defeat of Widukind of Westphalia*, 2014.

Noble, Thomas F.X. *From Roman Provinces to Medieval Kingdoms*, 2006.

Norman, Vesey. *Arms and Armour*, 1964.

— *The Medieval Soldier*, 1971.

— and Pottinger, Don. *English Weapons & Warfare 449–1660*, 1979.

Oakeshott, R. Ewart. *The Archaeology of Weapons*, 1960.

— *Dark Age Warrior*, 1974.

Obolensky, Dimitri. *Byzantium and the Slavs: Collected Studies*, 1971.

— *The Byzantine Commonwealth – Eastern Europe 500–1453*, 1971.

O'Callaghan, Joseph F. *A History of Medieval Spain*, 1975.

Odegaard, C.E. *Vassi and Fideles in the Carolingian Empire*, 1945.

Oman, C.W.C. *A History of the Art of War in the Middle Ages* (2 vols), 1924.

Ostrogorsky, G. *History of the Byzantine State*, 1952.

Owen-Crocker, Gale R. *Dress in Anglo-Saxon England*, 1986.

Partington, J.R. *A History of Greek Fire and Gunpowder*, 1960.

Payne-Gallwey, Ralph W. *The Projectile Throwing Weapons of the Ancients*, 1907.

Peirce, Ian G.; Oakeshott, Ewart; and Jones, Lee A. *Swords of the Viking Age*, 2002.

Pollington, Stephen. *The English Warrior from Earliest Times till 1066*, 1996.

Powers, James F. 'The Origins and Development of Municipal Military Service in the Leonese and Castilian Reconquest, 800–1250' *Traditio* XXVI, 1970.

— 'Townsmen and Soldiers: The Interaction of Urban and Military Organisation in the Militias of Mediaeval Castile' *Speculum* XLVI, 1971.

Pryor, John H., and Jeffreys, Elizabeth M. *The Age of the ΔΡΟΜΩΝ: The Byzantine Navy ca.500–1204*, 2006.

Purton, Peter F. *A History of the Early Medieval Siege, c.450–1220*, 2009.

Radaelli, Matteo. *I Longobardi, II a.C.–VIII Secolo*, 2012.

Rautman, Marcus Louis. *Daily Life in the Byzantine Empire*, 2006.

Reuter, T. *Germany in the Early Middle Ages c.800–1056*, 1991.

— 'Carolingian and Ottonian Warfare' in Maurice Keen (ed.) *Medieval Warfare: A History*, 1999.

Rice, David Talbot (ed.). *The Dark Ages: The Making of European Civilization*, 1965.

Riché, P. *Daily Life in the World of Charlemagne*, 1978.

Robinson, H. Russell. *Oriental Armour*, 1967.

Rodgers, W.L. *Naval Warfare under Oars*, 1967.

Rogers, Penelope Walton. *Cloth and Clothing in Early Anglo-Saxon England AD 459–700*, 2007.

Rollason, David. *Early Medieval Europe 300–1050*, 2012.

Runciman, Steven. *A History of the First Bulgarian Empire*, 1930.

— *The Emperor Romanus Lecapenus and his Reign: A Study of Tenth Century Byzantium*, 1963.

Ryan, John. 'The Battle of Clontarf' *Journal of the Royal Society of the Antiquaries of Ireland* LXVIII, 1938.

Rynne, Etienne. 'The Impact of the Vikings on Irish Weapons' *Atti del VI Congresso Internazionale delle Scienze Preistoriche e Protoistoriche* III, 1966.

Saks, Edgar. *The Estonian Vikings*, 1981.

Santosuosso, Antonio. *Barbarians, Marauders, and Infidels: The Ways of Medieval Warfare*, 2004.

Sawyer, P.H. *The Age of the Vikings*, 1971.

Shadrake, Dan and Susanna. *Barbarian Warriors: Saxons, Vikings, Normans*, 1997.

Shahid, Irfan. *Byzantium and the Arabs in the Sixth Century*, 2010.

Short, William R. *Viking Weapons and Combat Techniques*, 2014.

Shpakovsky, Viacheslav, and Nicolle, David. *Armies of the Volga Bulgars & Khanate of Kazan*, 2013.

Siddorn, J.K. *Viking Weapons and Warfare*, 2000.

Simpson, Jacqueline. *Everyday Life in the Viking Age*, 1967.

Smyth, Alfred P. *Warlords and Holy Men: Scotland AD 80–1000*, 1984.

Sophoulis, Panos. *Byzantium and Bulgaria, 775–831*, 2012.

Spinei, Victor. *The Romanians and the Turkic Nomads North of the Danube Delta from the Tenth to the Mid-Thirteenth Century*, 2009.

Stenton, Frank M. *The Bayeux Tapestry: A Comprehensive Survey*, 1957.

— *Anglo-Saxon England*, 1971.

Stephenson, I.P. *The Anglo-Saxon Shield*, 2002.

— *The Late Anglo-Saxon Army*, 2007.

Stillman, Yedida Kalfon. *Arab Dress from the Dawn of Islam to Modern Times*, 2003.

Stone, George Cameron. *A Glossary of the Construction, Decoration and Use of Arms and Armor in all Countries and in all Times*, 1934.

Story, J. (ed.). *Charlemagne, Empire and Society*, 2005.

Strickland, Matthew. *Anglo-Norman Warfare: Studies in Late Anglo-Saxon and Anglo-Norman Military Organization and Warfare*, 1992.

Sullivan, Denis. *Siegecraft: Two Tenth-Century Instructional Manuals by Heron of Byzantium*, 2000.

Talbot, Alice-Mary, and Sullivan, Denis F. (intro., trans. & annotations). *The History of Leo the Deacon: Byzantine Military Expansion in the Tenth Century*, 2005.

Thompson, E.A. *The Goths in Spain*, 1969.

Thordeman, Bengt. 'The Asiatic Splint Armour in Europe' *Acta Archaeologia* IV, 1933.

Toynbee, Arnold. *Constantine Porphyrogenitus and his World*, 1973.

Treadgold, Warren T. *The Byzantine Revival, 780–842*, 1991.

— *Byzantium and its Army, 284–1081*, 1996.

Vana, Zdenek. *The World of the Ancient Slavs*, 1983.

Vasiliev, A.A. *The Goths in the Crimea*, 1936.

— *The Russian Attack on Constantinople in 860*, 1946.

— *History of the Byzantine Empire*, 1971.

Verbruggen, J.F. *The Art of Warfare in Western Europe during the Middle Ages*, 1977.

— 'L'art Militaire dans l'Empire Carolingien (714–1000)' *Revue Belge d'Histoire Militaire* 23, 1979–80.

Vinogradoff, P. *English Society in the 11th Century*, 1908.

Wagner, Paul. *Pictish Warrior AD 297–841*, 2012.

Watt, W. Montgomery. *The Majesty that was Islam: The Islamic World 661–1100*, 1974.

Weitzmann, Kurt. *The Joshua Roll*, 1948.

Whitby, Michael. *Rome at War AD 293–696*, 2002.

White, Lynn. *Medieval Technology and Social Change*, 1962.

Whitting, Philip (ed.). *Byzantium: An Introduction*, 1971.

Wilson, D.M. *The Anglo-Saxons*, 1971.

— *The Bayeux Tapestry: The Complete Tapestry in Colour*, 1985.

— and Foote, P.G. *The Viking Achievement*, 1970.

Wilson, Eunice. *A History of Shoe Fashions*, 1974.

Wortley, John (trans.). *John Skylitzes: A Synopsis of Byzantine History, 811–1057*, 2010.

Wyatt, David R. *Slaves and Warriors in Medieval Britain and Ireland: 800–1200*, 2009.

CPSIA information can be obtained
at www.ICGtesting.com
Printed in the USA
BVOW06*1953040218
507198BV00005B/11/P